Implementing housing policy

Edited by
PETER MALPASS
AND ROBIN MEANS

OPEN UNIVERSITY PRESS
Buckingham · Philadelphia

Open University Press
Celtic Court
22 Ballmoor
Buckingham
MK18 1XW

and
1900 Frost Road, Suite 101
Bristol, PA 19007, USA

First Published 1993

A catalogue record of this book is available from the British Library

Library of Congress Cataloging-in-Publication Data

Implementing housing policy / edited by Peter Malpass, Robin Means.
    p.   cm.
    Includes bibliographical references and index.
    ISBN 0–335–15751–3   ISBN 0–335–15750–5 (pbk.)
    1. Housing policy—Great Britain.   2. Housing—Law and
legislation—Great Britain.   I. Malpass, Peter.   II. Means, Robin.
HD7333.A3I458   1993
363.5′8′0941—dc20
    92–23835
    CIP

Typeset by BP Integraphics Ltd, Bath, Avon
Printed in Great Britain by St Edmundsbury Press Ltd,
Bury St Edmunds, Suffolk

To the memory of Ruth Sekyi

Contents

The contributors

Glen Bramley, Senior Lecturer, School for Advanced Urban Studies, University of Bristol

Ian Cole, Head of Housing Division, Sheffield Hallam University

Valerie Karn, Professor of Environmental Health and Housing, University of Salford

Peter Kemp, Joseph Rowntree Professor of Housing Policy, University of York

Philip Leather, Senior Research Fellow, School for Advanced Urban Studies, University of Bristol

Sheila Mackintosh, Research Fellow, School for Advanced Urban Studies, University of Bristol

Peter Malpass, Professor of Housing Policy, University of the West of England, Bristol

Robin Means, Lecturer, School for Advanced Urban Studies, University of Bristol

David Mullins, Lecturer, Centre for Urban and Regional Studies, University of Birmingham

Pat Niner, Senior Lecturer, Centre for Urban and Regional Studies, University of Birmingham

Bill Randolph, Principal Research Officer, National Federation of Housing Associations

Moyra Riseborough, Lecturer, Centre for Urban and Regional Studies, University of Birmingham

Matthew Warburton, Under Secretary for Housing and Public Works, Association of Metropolitan Authorities

Acknowledgements

As editors, we would like to start by acknowledging the major efforts made by all the contributors to meet tight deadlines, under what were often very difficult and hard pressed circumstances. Even with their best efforts, the pulling together of the final manuscript was a major exercise required in a very short time, and was only made possible by the marvellous efforts of Jenny Capstick at Bristol University's School for Advanced Urban Studies.

The production of a book like this places pressure upon editors, but equally upon partners, sons and daughters. We would like to thank both our families for their support and encouragement.

Finally, we would like to thank our housing students for their continued enthusiasm for debating housing policy and their role in its implementation, which in turn became a major stimulus to producing a book on implementing housing policies.

CHAPTER 1

Introduction: focus and outline

PETER MALPASS
AND ROBIN MEANS

In the late 1980s there was a major review of housing policy within government, resulting in two new Acts designed to effect fundamental changes in the structures and processes of housing provision in Britain in the 1990s. The Housing Act 1988 was mainly concerned with the 'independent' rented tenures, introducing deregulation of commercial private renting, and a new market-orientated financial regime for housing associations. The Act also proposed 'tenants' choice', a device to enable local authority tenants to opt for a new landlord, and Housing Action Trusts as a new way of tackling the most pressing problems in the local authority sector. The Local Government and Housing Act 1989 continued the reshaping of housing policy by introducing a new financial regime for local authority housing, and a new approach to the renovation and improvement of older properties.

This book is about the implementation of these policy initiatives. It brings together in one volume contributions from leading researchers who are studying the impact of the 1988 and 1989 Acts. Indeed, it is possible to describe the late 1980s and early 1990s as an implementation phase for these Acts. It is, therefore, a very appropriate point to focus on issues of what has happened, and is happening, to put the new policies into effect, or to frustrate the legislators' intentions. Certainly, it is a common perception that several of the various radical policy measures have had much less impact than appeared likely as the Bills passed through Parliament. Tenants' choice and Housing Action Trusts are seen as having almost completely misfired and the revival of private renting appears to have been minimal. In other areas, other unintended outcomes have occurred: the new era for housing associations got off to a very shaky start as the Housing Corporation became involved in a major short-term funding crisis, and the new financial regime for local authority housing produced a pattern of outcomes in 1990/91 which was out of line with official guidelines.

Implementing Housing Policy tackles such implementation issues. What has happened on the ground, how close is this to the aspirations of central government and how can any implementation gap be explained? As such, the emphasis is markedly different to much of the established housing policy literature, which is much stronger on policy formation and policy outcomes than it is on implementation issues. For example, the recent work of Hills and Mullings (1990) provides a marvellously clear description of housing goals and policies since 1974 and goes on to juxtapose this against policy outcomes in terms of whether decent and affordable homes have or have not been generated for the vast majority of the population. But they have very little to say about the implementation battles and dilemmas which have emerged in this period and how these may have influenced both policy objectives and policy outcomes. *Implementing Housing Policy* draws on broad policy studies literature and thus seeks to develop an approach to housing studies in which an understanding of implementation issues plays a central role. As a result, this book is much more than just a collection of essays on topical issues in housing.

Chapter 2 by Robin Means looks at perspectives on implementation, providing a theoretical underpinning for the book as a whole, and setting out a broad frame of reference within which later chapters can be located. The starting point is the emergence of concern in the 1960s and 1970s at the persistent failure of government policies to achieve their objectives. The 'top-down' and 'bottom-up' approaches to explaining this implementation gap are discussed. The chapter then goes on to explore such key issues in policy implementation as central–local government relations, new ideas about public sector management, the politics of collaboration, street level bureaucrats and professional power. This policy implementation focus is complemented in Chapter 3 by Peter Malpass, who takes an overview of housing policy and the housing system from the election of the Conservative Government in 1979 through to the General Election of 1992. This chapter sets out the broader housing policy context for the subsequent chapters with their more detailed focus. It offers an overview of recent trends and developments and illustrates how housing policy since 1979 has been a complex blend of continuity and change.

Bill Randolph, in Chapter 4, takes a detailed look at the impact on housing associations of the pricing and subsidy systems introduced by the Housing Act 1988. He looks at whether or not this sparked off a development boom in housing associations. He then addresses the key issues of rents and affordability, the implications of the greatly increased financial risks introduced by the new system, and the costs and availability of private funding. In Chapter 5, Peter Kemp looks at the attempt of the Conservative Government to rebuild private renting. This chapter draws on research on the Business Expansion Scheme and other evidence to assess the reactions of market-based actors and institutions to the deregulation of private renting. Valerie Karn, in Chapter 6, focuses upon Housing Action Trusts (HATs). The Government proposed six HATs in the first wave of a rolling programme originally conceived as a way of renovating and privatizing the most problematic parts of the public sector. Karn considers why all six were subsequently abandoned and discusses whether this is an indication of permanent, or only temporary, policy failure.

Chapter 7 moves on to a consideration of the new financial regime for local authority housing which was introduced by the 1989 Act. Peter Malpass and Matthew Warburton outline and then discuss explanations of the wide variation in local responses and outcomes in terms of rent increases and management and maintenance expenditure. Another important feature of the 1989 Act was the changes made to the system of home improvement grants for owner occupiers, which included the introduction of a strong means-tested element as well as a new minor works grant. In Chapter 8, Philip Leather and Sheila Mackintosh consider urban renewal in an era of mass home ownership. They explore how well the new grant system is working and also outline the complexity involved in mobilizing the multiplicity of actors and agencies involved in area-based improvement. In Chapter 9, Glen Bramley looks at the enabling role of the local housing authorities, with particular reference to the provision of new or additional social housing. After outlining what the Conservative Government means by 'enabling', Bramley goes on to ask if the policy is genuine or symbolic and whether it is necessary, sufficient and fair.

The next two chapters are less grounded in the provisions of the 1988 and 1989 Acts; instead, they look at policy initiatives which have been pioneered and developed at the local level. In Chapter 10, Ian Cole looks at the various approaches to the decentralization of housing services being adopted by local authorities. Reference is made to the cost implications of decentralization and to other implementation issues such as the achievement of new working practices and staff training. David Mullins, Pat Niner and Moyra Riseborough, in Chapter 11, look at the large-scale voluntary transfers of local authority housing stocks to new or existing housing associations. Implementation issues are drawn out by looking at both successful and unsuccessful transfer initiatives.

The final chapter by the editors is on the politics of implementation. It draws together the key points from Chapters 3 to 11 and links them back to Chapter 2, in order to develop a deeper understanding of implementation issues and the implications for policymaking in housing. In doing so, the chapter addresses a number of key questions. These include: what are the lessons of the 1980s which can be applied to policy action in the 1990s? Did the centre consider sufficiently the need for clear implementation strategies? How far have local housing agencies been able to adapt the housing policies of central government to meet their own priorities? What is the appropriate level of discretion in policymaking at the local level?

This book was written during the long run-up to the April 1992 General Election. Chapter 12 concludes by reflecting upon the policy implementation challenges to be faced by the new incoming Conservative Government. Will these be similar to, or markedly different from, those of the 1980s? And what can be learnt from this book about some of the pitfalls to be avoided?

Reference

Hills, J. and Mullings, B. (1990) 'Housing: A decent home for all at a price within their means?', in J. Hills (ed.) *The State of Welfare*, pp. 135–205, Oxford, Clarendon.

CHAPTER 2

Perspectives on implementation

ROBIN MEANS

Introduction

Given that this book is called *Implementing Housing Policy*, the reader might well expect us to begin with clear and unambiguous definitions of the noun 'policy' and the verb 'to implement'. One possibility is to characterize 'policy' as 'a plan of action adopted by government' and 'to implement' as 'the process of turning that plan into reality through an administrative process'. Indeed, one interpretation of the title could be that its chapters should have no concern with policy choice and formulation, but rather be concerned solely with the administrative challenge of turning such policy, once agreed, into practical activities on the ground.

Such a perspective would be hopelessly narrow and very misleading. This chapter draws on key debates on implementation in the wider policy studies literature to illustrate how developing implementation strategies need to be part of the policymaking process and how policies become shaped, amended or blocked through the implementation process. Nevertheless, a focus on implementation implies a concern with issues of policy in action – what actually happens in practice (in terms of process as well as outcomes) and how this can be explained. Do those responsible for policy implementation have a clear picture of what they are expected to do, and do they have the tools to enable them to do the job? This suggests further questions about whose policy it is and who else has interests at stake in the pattern of policy action.

The emergence of implementation theory

It is widely agreed that policy implementation received little interest from political and social scientists prior to the mid-1970s. A great deal of energy was expended on studying the process of policy formation and an equally impressive energy was directed to measuring policy outcomes. However, concern was increasing throughout the 1960s and early 1970s about the disappointing results from various policy initiatives, one of the most dramatic and high profile of which was the American War on Poverty. Marris and Rein (1967), for example, looked at several school and youth projects, based on the development of community action agencies and all designed to tackle local problems of delinquency, poor school performance, poverty and unemployment. The researchers uncovered much admirable energy and commitment, but overall achievements were limited, as the clear objectives of the funders (the Ford Foundation and federal government) became diffused by the competing agendas and aspirations of all the local agencies and interest groups which subsequently became involved. As a result, 'a vision of opening opportunities for millions of maltreated youngsters might end with a dozen children in a makeshift nursery school, or a class of seamstresses learning a poorly-paid trade for which they were already in demand' (Marris and Rein 1967: 236).

This gap was subsequently described as an implementation deficit by Pressman and Wildavsky (1973) in their seminal study of the failure of a federal job-creation scheme to provide employment for black people in Oakland. They argued such schemes could only be successful if numerous organizations linked up to create a successful implementation chain. Relatively small failures of co-operation between the different organizations can easily multiply to create a major implementation deficit as in the Oakland scheme. It was this study more than any other which encouraged the emergence of a distinctive literature on implementation studies, based not only on a belief in the frequency of policy failure (the gap between objectives and outcomes) but also from the observation that the explanation for this policy failure is commonly to be found in the politics of policy implementation.

The development of this literature was not restricted to the USA: Britain saw the emergence of numerous books and articles on implementation theory from the late 1970s onwards (Dunsire 1978; Gunn 1978; Barrett and Fudge 1981; Rhodes 1981). Several factors contributed to the emergence of this interest. First, as in the USA, there was growing concern about policy 'failure', although, in this instance, in terms of early concerns about the effectiveness of the welfare state in abolishing poverty, tackling educational disadvantage, and so on. The oil crisis of the mid-1970s was bringing to an end the rather cosy view that further welfare gains could only be achieved by investing more resources into the welfare state rather than directing attention to the efficiency and effectiveness with which existing money was being spent. This in turn sharpened tensions between central government and local government in the British political system.

Ham and Hill (1992: chapter 6) provide an excellent summary of implementation theory and the differing perspectives which have emerged. The two main approaches are usually referred to as the *top-down perspective* and the *bottom-up perspective* (see also Younis and Davidson 1990). Ham and Hill argue that the top-down perspective, as epitomized by such authors as Hogwood and Gunn (1984), is concerned with the generation of advice to those at the top (the policymakers) on how to minimize implementation deficit as a result of the subsequent behaviour of the implementors. Ham and Hill (1992: 79) summarize the message of such studies in the following way:

- the nature of policy – see that it is unambiguous
- the implementation structure – keep links in the chain to a minimum
- the prevention of outside interference
- control over implementing actors.

The top-down perspective is, therefore, prescriptive, perceives the definition of both policy and implementation as non-problematic and sees the control of implementing agencies as feasible and desirable. All of these assumptions have been challenged by implementation theorists operating from bottom-up perspectives. One key challenge concerns the feasibility of establishing clear policies with clear objectives. The early American studies concerned themselves with discrete programmes, which had unambiguous objectives and earmarked budgets. However, even in this type of 'clear cut' programme, the policies and especially the objectives start to shift over time (Room 1986). But most 'policies' are even more ambiguous than this. Legislative change in housing, education and community care will be only tenuously linked to earmarked resources and the required reforms will normally leave implementing agencies with considerable discretion in terms of meshing in the new programme or approach with previous practice and with other responsibilities. Finally, as Ham and Hill point out, 'the executive dominates the governmental system and legislates in a multiplicity of ways, only some of which are made manifest in specific Acts of Parliament, and thus practises legislative fine tuning continuously in subtle and often ambiguous ways' (1992: 81). Such fine tuning will often not formally indicate whether this represents a fresh attempt to meet old objectives or a refinement of those objectives.

Above all, the bottom-up perspective stresses that nearly all policies are the product of negotiation and compromise. As Barrett and Hill (1984: 222) argue:

- many policies represent compromises between conflicting values
- many policies involve compromises with key interests within the implementation structure
- many policies involve compromises with key interests upon whom implementation will have an impact
- many policies are framed without attention being given to the way in which underlying forces (particularly economic ones) will undermine them.

Such tensions mean that some decisions on goals and objectives are left to what is normally seen as the implementation stage. Top-down theorists tend to see this as regrettable and undesirable. Bottom-up theorists see this as inevitable and some would perceive it as desirable on the grounds that field-level implementors are in the best position to assess the local situation and set appropriate objectives (see Ingram and Schneider 1990: 79–80; Hjern and Hull 1982). Even where the discretion to make policy is not formally given by the 'policymaker', lower-level implementors will still perceive themselves as important 'stakeholders' with the right to pursue their own agendas. Smith and Cantley (1985) in their study of a psychiatric day hospital illustrated how this complicates assessment of 'success' or 'failure' for any given policy initiative. The key stakeholders (administrators, doctors, nurses, relatives and patients) may all try to influence the policy and its implementation, and all will have differing views about what represents success and failure. At the very least, stakeholders may have the power to block or disrupt policy innovation as the literature on street-level bureaucrats indicates (Lipsky 1980), a point discussed in more detail later in this chapter. Again, the emphasis of the bottom-up perspective is upon an ongoing process of bargaining and compromise. In other words, implementation should be seen as part of 'a policy/action continuum in which an interactive and negotiative process is taking place over time between those seeking to put policy into effect and those upon whom action depends' (Barrett and Fudge 1981: 25).

The major criticism of the bottom-up approach is that it is excellent at describing complexity, but incapable of providing prescriptive help to 'policy-makers' on how to make things better. Elmore (1978) is a leading proponent of the bottom-up approach yet admits the strength of the rationalist critique that this approach 'elevates confusion and mindless drift to the level of principle, that it provides an easy excuse ... for acquiescing in results that satisfy no one, and that it provides no basis for improving the implementation process'. There are two responses to this. First, the insights of the bottom-up approach can be used by the centre to ensure that implementation plans develop a level of strategic 'nous' previously lacking. Second, the top-down approach assumes that the 'top' is a reflection of representative democracy, that the implementors are unelected officials, and that the policies pursued are relatively unambiguously in the public good. The poll tax and council house sales provide two recent examples of where such assumptions could be challenged. Not all stakeholder resistance to change can be dismissed as bureaucratic obstinacy and narrow-mindedness, and perhaps the best examples of this can be found in the arena of British central–local government relations.

Central–local government relations

As already indicated, tensions between central government and local government are an important factor in the emergence of British interest in and contribution to the implementation literature from the late 1970s onwards. Initially, this was largely driven by the increasing demands of local government upon public expenditure. Local expenditure constituted only 4 per cent of Gross National Product in 1885 but this had risen to 18 per cent by 1975. The Layfield Enquiry into local government finance estimated that in the mid-1970s, local authorities were spending £15 000 million a year, were serving a capital debt of £25 000 million and were employing 3 million people (quoted in Loughlin 1986: 10). For central government, this was seen as requiring far greater control over local authorities because of its implications for broader economic management (Stoker 1988). But others were expressing concern at how central government was squeezing the autonomy of local authorities who were moving from being the partners of central government to that of being mere agents (for a further discussion see Rhodes 1981: chapter 2). Two strands of argument were used to back up this concern. First, a growing proportion of local government income was coming from central government rate support grants rather than from local government rates, and hence there was an increased capacity to 'interfere' through the annual public expenditure decisions of the Cabinet and Treasury. Second, British local government had little protection from interference through this or other mechanisms since local government has no special constitutional status in the United Kingdom; Parliament is sovereign, so that 'the structure, functions, finance and even the very existence of local government can be altered by a simple majority at Westminster' (Butcher *et al.* 1990: 18). Local authorities can only act within the legal framework set down by central government and they have no general capacity to ignore this legal framework on the grounds that it conflicts with the interests of their local communities.

The conclusion in the late 1970s from academics influenced by implementation theory was that the conventional wisdom of a drift from partnership to agent in central–local relations represented a massive and misleading simplification. Instead, it was argued that relations between central and local government were based on a system of structural bargaining and compromise within complex policy networks in which officials rather than politicians increasingly held the power and influence. Such an emphasis upon a mutual power-dependence relationship suggested the need to take a bottom-up perspective on central–local government relations (Rhodes 1981: 110):

> ... many discussions of central–local relations adopt a 'top-down' model of policy-making – that is, goals are set up by a central department and implemented by a local authority. The above discussion suggests that it is equally important to explore the reverse situation – that is, the redefinition of a policy/goal in the process of implementation – if we are to perceive the full scope or limits of local discretion.

But Rhodes was developing his analysis just before and just after the 1979 General Election victory of the Conservatives, which brought to power a government with rather less enthusiasm for compromise and bargaining than most of its predecessors. Subsequent conflict in the recent years of Conservative central government has involved both the content and the cost of local government activity. Since 1979, these governments have wished to control and then reduce overall levels of public expenditure in general, and local government expenditure in particular, on a permanent basis rather than as a response to a short-term crisis. The Treasury, however, has found this extremely difficult to achieve and Thain and Wright (1990) have estimated that total public expenditure has grown in real terms (cash adjusted for inflation) by between 1.3 and 2 per cent per year in the period 1977/78 to 1989/90. Both Stoker (1988) and Loughlin (1986) provide detailed accounts of the early 1980s' conflicts between central government and local authorities over finance, while Bramley (1990) has outlined how these struggles were a factor in the subsequent decision to replace the rates with the community charge or poll tax.

In general, central government has found it easier to control capital rather than revenue expenditure. For example, total capital expenditure for all government programmes was £12 billion in 1974 but was only £4.8 billion in 1987. In terms of local government, housing capital expenditure was reduced from 1.8 per cent of Gross National Product in 1975 to only 0.3 per cent in 1987 (Butcher *et al*. 1990: 64). In reviewing local finance in the 1980s, Butcher *et al*. (1990: 75) conclude that there has been

> little evidence to show a willingness to compromise by the government, instead experience shows a single-minded commitment to alter the dynamics of local government finance, whether by cutting central government grants, using competitive tendering to reduce labour costs, or introducing the community charge to remove local government financial autonomy.

Local authorities have varied in their response to this hostile climate, but few, if any, have acted as if they are the simple agents of central government. Amongst Conservative controlled local authorities, some have protested at the abandonment of one nation Conservatism with its commitment to municipal government while others have propounded with passion and commitment the vision of the enabling authority (Brooke 1989), which has a minimal role in service provision. Labour controlled authorities used a variety of defence strategies to combat the assault of central government on local spending and these included increasing the rates, creative accounting, anti-rate capping campaigns and anti-poll tax campaigns (Stoker 1988; Butcher *et al*. 1990).

But resistance and conflict between many local authorities and central government was about the content as well as the cost of their activities. Central government has been keen to privatize services as well as to reduce public subsidy costs. This was part of a New Right ideology which Flynn (1989) claims contained the following four elements:

1 Market mechanisms should be used wherever possible, even if there cannot be a fully free market for the services.
2 Competition should be established between providers, and consumers should be allowed to opt out of state provision to sharpen competition, with the private and voluntary sectors where possible, but also between different public providers. Competition is seen as a spur to efficiency and customer-orientation.
3 Individualism and individual choice take precedence over collective choices and planned provision.
4 State provision should be kept to a minimum, to encourage those who can afford it to supplement state provision or opt out. If possible, individuals should manage without help from institutions of any sort, except their own families.

Central government has wished to bring this New Right ideology to local government services. However, socialists perceived local government as a possible base from which to undermine the recent ascendency of the right. At the very least, there was a need to defend public services against cutbacks, but for some the task was also 'to explore the socialist potential of local government and local political space' (Boddy and Fudge 1984: 2). Such islands of successful socialism could be used to wean the general population away from its apparent growing scepticism about large-scale state intervention. These more radical Labour authorities were developing a range of new initiatives in such areas as employment, women, race and the decentralization of services.

A feature of the early defence campaigns of local government services was that service users, especially council-house residents, seemed remarkably reluctant to identify with councillors and activists in this struggle and this suggested to many the need to reconsider the relationship of service consumers to service providers. The culprit was centralized public service provision which was generating growing dissatisfaction (Hambleton and Hoggett 1984: 4):

> This dissatisfaction rolls together concern about the remoteness of centralized decision making structures, irritation with the insensitivity and lack of accountability of officers employed by the state, and discontent with the sectional and blinkered approach to problem solving and service provision often associated with departmental (or functional) organizational structures.

One response to such dissatisfaction was to decentralize services into neighbourhood offices in which rigid departmental boundaries could be broken down. Such initiatives usually involved at least the aspiration to more fully involve local residents in the running of services. Initiatives developed in authorities such as Walsall, Hackney, Islington and Birmingham (see Hoggett and Hambleton 1987).

This critique of central bureaucracies had much in common with aspects of the argument put forward by the New Right. However, the proposed solution differed in that the concern was not to turn away from state provision but rather to change the way in which public services are provided: 'it involves shifting attention from the quantity of service provision to questions of quality and seeks to change the relationship between public servants and the public they serve' (Hambleton and Hoggett 1984: 5). The aim was not only to improve the distribution, accountability and quality of public services, but also to raise political awareness. This was to be achieved primarily via the empowerment of the consumers and local residents through giving them more direct control over local services.

The term 'local socialism' is now out of vogue and to a considerable extent this can be seen as a victory of central over local government, a victory achieved through the successful implementation of the Conservative policy agenda of privatization, cost cutting and de-politicization for local authorities. However, care needs to be taken in making such judgements. Many local authorities continue to support a wide range of equality, local employment and decentralization initiatives, many of which have spread well beyond a limited number of authorities associated with the radical Left. For example, the most adventurous and far-reaching experiment in decentralization has taken place in Tower Hamlets when under the control of the Liberal Democrats. Research by Lowndes and Stoker (1992a,b) suggests these policies have had a broadly beneficial impact upon local residents. As such, this provides support for the bottom-up perspective views of Elmore (1978) and Hjern and Hull (1982) with their emphasis that policymakers and funders should maximize the discretion of field-level staff because they are in the best position to respond to local needs. Indeed, the truth of this is often stressed in recent Government reforms; the Local Management Scheme for schools, GP budgets and Hospital Trusts are all based on a belief in local management responding to local needs, rather than centralized bureaucratic prescription from the top, although the emphasis of these reforms is, also, upon the discipline of competition and clear, finite local budgets.

Public sector organizations in the 1990s

The 1980s was a period of great turbulence in the public sector in Britain and this is often explained by reference to the impact of a single, strong-willed individual with a vision of an enterprise culture, in which the majority pay little in taxation but rather make their own choices through the market about how to meet their education, housing, health care and pension needs. There could be a post-Thatcher gradual return made to the type of public-sector organizations which dominated in the twentieth century up to the late 1970s. This is unlikely, irrespective of the policy agenda which may eventually come to be known as 'Majorism'. To begin with, dissatisfaction has long existed in the writings of the Left and Centre as well as the Right with what Hadley and Hatch (1981) called 'the Failure of the State' which they saw as a failure of large-scale bureaucracies with monopoly or near monopoly powers to deliver flexible and appropriate services. And similar debates have emerged in nearly all other countries with developed economies (Mishra 1984). More specifically, Hoggett (1990) argued that the public sector reflects the private sector in its dominant forms of organization. In the 1950s and 1960s, industry was dominated by the large-scale production of standard commodities (sometimes called 'Fordism'). The growth of the large-scale bureaucracies in the public sector during this same period seemed to mimic large-scale factory production. However, as Hoggett (1990: 11) points out:

> The replacement of mass production technologies by flexible automation technologies and information technologies which grew apace throughout the 1970s, undermined the technological base of bureaucracy within the private sector ... The emerging market conditions of the late 1970s and 1980s heralded a shift towards a much greater degree of market segmentation built around more highly differentiated products with a much shorter lifespan.

In terms of private-sector management, this saw the development of 'tight/loose' systems of organization (Peters and Waterman 1982) in which the centre loosens its grip over many aspects of production so that it can more effectively control the essentials of values, culture and strategy. Contracting out, decentralized production units and localized cost centres have been made possible by the emergence of computerized management and financial management systems.

It is this core–periphery model that has now come to the British public sector. But this does not mean that there are no alternatives to present Conservative policies in areas such as housing, education and community care (Hoggett 1990: 15):

> ... whilst contemporary processes of modernisation may be technologically driven, they are not technologically determined. A variety of social choices are possible within the frame provided by a given techno-managerial paradigm. It follows that a variety of different forms of the post-bureaucratic welfare state will be constructed in different nations – even within the UK today the ultimate form that the welfare state will assume is by no means a closed book.

Indeed, Hoggett believes that the opportunities created by the new paradigm could be used to develop internal decentralization within local authorities, backed up by a strong commitment to democratic accountability and community involvement. However, what cannot happen is a return to the old systems of delivering inflexible services through organizations such as conventional, bureaucratic housing departments, social services departments and health authorities (Hoggett 1991).

At one level, the move away from the bureaucratic organizational form can be seen as a sign of agreement that it is always likely to generate high levels of implementation deficit. But the newer emerging systems generate their own implementation challenges. It is very easy for public-sector organizations to decide on devolved budgets for decentralized offices, but it is difficult to back this up with the sustained capital investment and revenue expenditure on computer-based information and budgetary systems upon which the successful introduction of such changes has to be based. Yet a failure to do this can lead to massive overspending or service deterioration during the introduction of the reforms (Hoyes *et al.* 1992). Second, market-led systems are often based on multiple service providers and this raises major problems for financial and quality regulation. It is one thing to frame a contract for a service provider but another to monitor that contract in such a way as to minimize implementation deficit. Third, an emphasis upon markets and devolved budgets does not reduce the need for collaboration. Indeed, the move away from large-scale bureaucracies may intensify the number of collaborative organizational relationships at work. And yet making such collaboration work is highly problematic.

The politics of collaboration

As already discussed, the seminal work of Pressman and Wildavsky (1973) stressed that a major factor in implementation deficit was the failure of different organizations to collaborate effectively. The move to market-led systems of service delivery, or to other kinds of post-bureaucratic organizational forms, does not reduce reliance upon different agencies and different professionals working together. This may involve collaboration between different parts of the same organization (housing management section and development section; head office and area office) or between different professions (architects, planners, housing officials and social workers). Indeed, the very essence of the enabling housing authority is its capacity to pull together the myriad resources of public-sector, voluntary-sector and private-sector organizations to meet local housing needs (see Chapter 9). The full implications of this are illustrated by Fraser's (1990) guide to local authorities and housing associations on *Working Together in the 1990s*. Figure 2.1 is taken from his chapter on 'Special Needs' housing and illustrates the complex liaison structure which has been set up in West Suffolk to generate appropriate housing for a wide variety of different groups.

Yet the history of collaboration and co-ordination is that it usually fails to emerge. Webb (1991: 229) has recently pointed out that 'exhortations to organisations, professionals and other producer interests to work together more closely and effectively litter the policy landscape', yet the reality throughout much of British social policy remains 'all too often a jumble of services fractionalised by professional, cultural and organisational boundaries and by tiers of governance'.

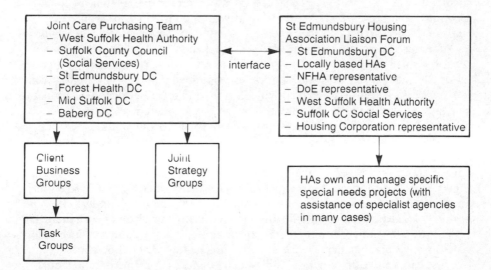

Figure 2.1   West Suffolk 'Special Needs' liaison structure
Source: Fraser (1990) *Working Together in the 1990s*, Institute of Housing

This section will attempt to identify some of the blockages to effective collaboration as well as some strategies that might be available for overcoming those blockages.

The crux of the problem has been well identified by Hudson (1987). Collaborative working seems such a worthy and obviously necessary activity that few stop to think about the costs and dilemmas imposed upon the actors and agencies who are expected to work together. But, as Hudson points out (1987: 175):

> From an agency's viewpoint, collaborative activity raises two main difficulties. First, it loses some of its freedom to act independently, when it would prefer to maintain control over its domain and affairs. Second, it must invest scarce resources and energy in developing and maintaining relationships with other organisations, when the potential returns on this investment are often unclear or intangible.

This suggests that mere exhortations about client welfare are not enough and that many agencies will seek to avoid extensive collaborative activity unless forced to do so. Despite this pessimistic starting point, Hudson goes on to outline four factors which might predispose agencies to work together. These are inter-organizational homogeneity (do the agencies have functional and structural similarity?), domain consensus (is there agreement on roles and responsibilities?), network awareness, organizational exchange (will all parties gain from working together?) and the absence of alternative resource avenues. The subsequent work of Webb (1991) has stressed the importance of trust. Most agencies have a previous history of contact and limited attempts to co-operate and work together. This can generate trust or it can generate conflict and suspicion. The lower the levels of trust, the more important it is that the focus of any new collaborative structure is relatively modest, low risk and easy to achieve. Early success can then be used to build up better relationships which mean larger-scale projects and initiatives can then be tackled. However, organizations which are hostile and suspicious of each other are frequently asked to work together on major issues, a good example being joint planning for community care services between health authorities and social services departments. The subsequent inability to make this work has generated yet further distrust between health care professionals and social services professionals.

Hudson, drawing on the work of Benson (1975), identifies three strategies for encouraging collaboration. These are co-operative strategies (based on mutual agreements), incentive strategies (based on 'bribes' to encourage working together) and authoritative strategies (agencies are instructed to work together). With regard to housing departments, central government has undermined the ability of local authorities to build and manage its own stock and hence there has been little alternative but to foster an enabling role built upon developing collaborative arrangements with a wide range of agencies. But conflicts and distrust can still easily emerge. Will social services departments and housing departments prove able to agree on the provision and funding of services for young homeless people under the Children Act 1989? When social services departments approach housing associations about a joint scheme for people with learning difficulties, do they do this from an appreciation of, or deep ignorance about, their organization and decision-making profile, their present financial concerns and the new system of funding 'special needs' schemes being developed through the Housing Corporation? Are they seen as a source of money or a genuine collaborative partner?

This last point underlines the scope at the local level for individuals to foster or block collaborative efforts. Agency personnel can seek knowledge of, and information about, a potential partner or be 'happy' to remain in ignorance. The policy studies' literature suggests that some individuals are especially adept at spanning different policy networks and encouraging collaborative activity at the local level. This literature often refers to them as reticulist (Friend *et al.* 1974), while the Audit Commission (1986) referred to such individuals as 'champions of change'. They are skilled at mapping policy networks and identifying the key resource holders and fellow enthusiasts from their own and from other agencies. They are often happy to operate above their hierarchical position, and they are willing to operate in a way not bounded by narrow organizational self-interest.

However, such individuals may be the exception rather than the rule; professionals and other staff in implementing agencies are often perceived as a source of implementation deficit because of their narrow and obstructive approach to their work.

Bureaucrats and professionals

In recent debates about the crisis of the Welfare State, considerable attention has been paid by commentators of the Right, Left and Centre to the importance and power of those who are employed by the state to produce its goods and services (Mishra 1984). It is frequently argued that the Welfare State operates in the interests of producer groups rather than consumer groups. It is therefore not surprising that the behaviour and attitudes of the staff of implementing agencies have often been a focus of attention by implementation theorists as a major explanation of implementation deficit.

Numerous studies have illustrated the power and influence of staff with low or only limited hierarchical or professional status within their organizations on the actual services received by consumers. Several studies have been carried out upon the impact of reception staff upon potential or ongoing service users (Hall 1974). This author was involved in a study of the local implementation of the national rent rebate scheme which preceded the present housing benefit system (Means and Hill 1981). The rent rebate scheme was meant to be based upon clear rules and regulations which were to be nationally applied and there was only limited formal scope for officers involved in assessment to use discretionary powers. Yet the five local authorities studied were found to vary either in their formal procedures or in their informal day-to-day practices over their assessment of the income of the self-employed, the reclaiming of overpayment, the backdating of arrears, their definition of 'registered handicapped' and their general approach to rebate review.

Equally, there is an extensive literature on professional power (see, for example, Johnson 1972; Wilding 1982; Laffin and Young 1990) in which the emphasis is upon the misuse of their claims to exclusive competences. Professional power can be used to justify ignoring the rights and needs of consumers and it can be used to undermine the authority and the policies of their senior managers and councillors. Professionalization can thus become a mechanism for avoiding control from the centre or accountability to the consumer. Social workers are one group frequently cited (Cohen 1985) but planners, architects and housing managers received harsh criticism from a number of studies for their role in the redevelopment and mass housing policies of the 1960s (Dennis 1970, 1972; Gower Davies 1972; English *et al.* 1976; Malpass 1975). Much of this literature concerns how large-scale property demolition and the use of factory building methods to replace these dwellings with tower blocks and other high density developments were partly driven by professional self-interest which coincided more with private-sector builders than local residents.

One of the most interesting critiques of the behaviour of professionals and other staff during policy implementation is the literature on street-level bureaucrats, which focuses specifically upon field-level staff from public services. This largely American body of work argues that (Lipsky 1980):

> ... the decisions of street level bureaucrats, the routines they establish, and the devices they invent to cope with uncertainties and work pressures, effectively become the public policies they carry out.

The argument of Lipsky and others (Prottas 1978) is that most people enter public employment with at least some commitment to service. Yet large classes, huge caseloads or extensive demands for council housing combine with inadequate resources to defeat their aspirations as service workers. Hence the need for 'people slotting' behaviour by which the attributes of the applicant are routinized in such a way as to mesh with the resources available for allocation. Hill (1982) has applied this type of analysis to social workers in Britain while its insights can also be used to understand much behaviour within council-house allocation systems where there is often a major gap between need and demand (Means 1990).

The street-level literature emerged from the bottom-up policy implementation perspective. It argues that much welfare work is based on judgement and this cannot be easily regulated, which opens up the scope for large-scale discretion at lower levels in public-sector organizations. Street-level bureaucrats are policymakers as well as policy implementors. The message for those at the top with formal policymaking responsibilities is that implementation strategies need to bear this in mind. The development of more subtle forms of surveillance and regulation is one possibility and New Right theorists stress the discipline of provider competition and service contracts. But others argue for mechanisms which seek to reach out to street-level staff, communicate the importance of what they do and so re-establish their sense of service mission. A good example of this approach is the attempt of local authorities to back up specific policies with an emphasis on and training for a more general public orientation which stresses the need for customer care (Clarke and Stewart 1987).

However, many street-level staff feel such criticisms and campaigns are always directed at them when the crucial implementation tensions emerge when politicians and senior managers collude to generate policy objectives which are not underpinned by appropriate resources (Dalley 1991). It has already been seen that some bottom-up theorists perceive street-level staff as defenders of the public against faceless managers, and such attitudes were found by Gaster (1990) in her study of referral staff in the decentralized neighbourhood offices of Birmingham. One mechanism for attempting to justify a refusal to follow policies from the top is by referring to the right and obligation of professionals to make discretionary decisions based on competences exclusive to their profession. From this point of view, people slotting comes from central government and the top of hierarchies rather than from field-level professionals who have direct access to the pain of consumers.

Better policies or better policy design?

An increasing response to the implementation dilemmas created by tensions in central–local relations, the politics of collaboration and street-level bureaucrat behaviour is to argue that the crunch issue is not to carry on studying the implementation deficit but rather to focus on improved policy design in which a heavy emphasis is placed upon including a consideration of the policy instruments most likely to overcome implementation challenges (May 1991).

As such, it is a part of what Ingram and Schneider (1990) call 'smarter statutes'. Their starting point is to argue that it has long been recognized that weak statutes or laws are the source of many implementation problems and policy failures, yet policy analysts have made little progress in providing clear advice on how they can be improved. They then go on to argue the centrality of policy content as crucial to the understanding of the relationship between statutes and/or laws, policy implementation and policy consequences. In other words, statutes need to vary in the assumptions they make about policy implementation issues according to the context specific to that statute. This makes policy design crucial, especially in terms of the policy tools and policy instruments to be employed within any given statute. This is because (Ingram and Schneider 1990: 71):

> Tools or instruments are intended to motivate implementing agencies and target populations to make decisions and take actions consistent with policy objectives ... Theories or assumptions explain why the tools and rules are expected to produce the intended behaviour and how the behaviour is linked to desired objectives.

Ingram and Schneider are particularly interested in the extent to which the policy design maximizes or minimizes the discretion of the implementing agencies, and they argue that advice from policy analysts is contradictory in terms of the best way forward. There are four main strands of thought:

1 *Strong statute approach* – discretion over design elements held by the statutory designers and implementors are expected to reproduce faithfully the statutory design.
2 *Wilsonian perspective* – 'the statute retains complete control over policy goals and purposes while agencies are left to add the details related to providing the means for attaining goals' (Ingram and Schneider 1990: 77).
3 *Grassroots approach* – 'discretion over all the elements of policy logic, rather than being worked through in the statute, should be allocated to the lowest level implementor or to target populations themselves' (Ingram and Schneider 1990: 79).
4 *Support building approach* – this approach stresses 'how statutes influence values and participation patterns and how various groups reconcile their interests' so that 'there is considerably less emphasis on achievement of instrumental goals' (Ingram and Schneider 1990: 81).

The message of Ingram and Schneider is that statutory design should be matched to the policy context so that each of these four perspectives/approaches are appropriate in different policy contexts. For them, the crucial issues are the levels of support for the policy, levels of information about the policy area and the capacity or motivation of the implementors. Where information levels are poor, Ingram and Schneider argue that strong statute advice is inappropriate because information is not available through which to specify the detailed policy logic for the implementors. Where there is agreement about goals and knowledge but weakness in the motivation and capacity of the implementors, then strong statute advice is the best approach and environmental policies are cited as a good example of this. More controversially, they argue that statutory designs which provide discretion are needed where support levels are low and that 'strong statutes in situations of broad value conflict will usually fail' (Ingram and Schneider 1990: 83). This is not advice which seems to have been followed by Conservative governments in Britain since 1979.

Ingram and Schneider may draw on the insights of the bottom-up perspective but their concerns are about the offering of strategic advice to the centre. One danger of this approach is that it risks failing to address the desirability of the policies of the centre, particularly in terms of their impact upon consumers and the general public. Is the responsibility of the policy analyst and evaluator to inform government of the rate at which council housing is being transferred into private ownership, and to back this up with some insightful comments on tactical possibilities for speeding up sales even in reluctant local authorities? Or are their responsibilities to explore the longer-term implications and impact of such policies upon homelessness rates, labour mobility, house disrepair and so on?

The question becomes smarter statutes for whom? One way out of this dilemma is to attempt an assessment of the broader aims of specific policies. If the restructuring of the British Welfare State has been designed to improve efficiency, maximize choice yet protect equity (Le Grand 1990), then it should be possible, theoretically at least, to see whether the market-driven reforms of recent years have delivered in those terms. But numerous problems exist. First, the development of policy-outcome measures relating to efficiency, equity and choice are problematic (Hoyes *et al.* 1992). Second, it is difficult to know how long a new policy or package of policies should be given before attempting an assessment of impact since in the short-term, there is likely to be dislocation and service deterioration during the disruption of initial implementation (Sabatier 1986). Third, governments may choose not to fund, or at least to marginalize, research which is generating information that their policy initiatives are not generative of equity, choice and efficiency. This may be true of governments of all political hues (Wenger 1987).

Conclusion

This chapter started by looking at the emergence of implementation theory in the late 1970s and has gone on to explore a variety of approaches towards explaining the gap between objectives and outcomes. The early policy literature tended to assume that policymaking was inherently conservative or incremental (Lindblom 1959: 1963). But subsequent chapters of this book are the story of a central government determined, in its housing and other policies, to make a dramatic break with past practice. However, Gregory (1989) warns that all governments, however clear cut and rational their objectives, are engaged in a political process with a wide range of interest groups, stakeholders and implementing agencies, and as such all are involved in the science of muddling through. The following chapters explore how this has worked out in British housing policy since 1979.

References

Audit Commission (1986) *Making a Reality of Community Care*, London, HMSO.
Barrett, S. and Fudge, C. (eds) (1981) *Policy and Action*, London, Methuen.
Barrett, S. and Hill, M. (1984) 'Policy, bargaining and structure in implementation theory: towards an integrated perspective', *Policy and Politics*, Vol. 12, No. 3: 219–40.
Benson, K. (1975) 'The interorganisational network as a political economy', *Administrative Science Quarterly*, Vol. 20, June.
Boddy, M. and Fudge, C. (eds) (1984) *Local Socialism*, London, Macmillan.
Bramley, G. (1990) 'Explaining the puzzles in policy change: local finance reform in Britain', *Journal of Public Policy*, Vol. 10, No. 1: 45–65.
Brooke, R. (1989) *Managing the Enabling Authority*, London, Longman.
Butcher, H., Law, I., Leach, R. and Mullard, M. (1990) *Local Government and Thatcherism*, London, Routledge.

Clarke, M. and Stewart, J. (1987) 'The public service orientation–developing the approach', *Public Administration*, Vol. 65, No. 2.

Cohen, S. (1985) *Visions of Social Control*, Cambridge, Polity Press.

Dalley, G. (1991) 'Beliefs and behaviour: professionals and the policy process', *Journal of Ageing Studies*, Vol. 5, No. 2: 163–80.

Dennis, N. (1970) *People and Planning*, London, Faber and Faber.

Dennis, N. (1972) *Public Participation and Planners' Blight*, London, Faber and Faber.

Dunleavy, P. (1981) *The Politics of Mass Housing in Britain 1945–1975*, Oxford, Clarendon Press.

Dunsire, A. (1978) *Implementation in a Bureaucracy*, Oxford, Martin Robertson.

Elmore, R. (1978) 'Organisational models of social program implementation', *Public Policy*, Vol. 26, No. 2.

English, J., Madigan, R. and Norman, P. (1976) *Slum Clearance*, London, Croom Helm.

Flynn, N. (1989) 'The New Right and social policy', *Policy and Politics*, Vol. 17, No. 2: 97–110.

Fraser, R. (1990) *Working Together in the 1990s*, Coventry, Institute of Housing.

Friend, J., Power, M. and Yewlett, C. (1974) *Public Planning: The Intercorporate Dimension*, London, Tavistock.

Gaster, L. (1990) *Quality at the Front Line*, DRIC Paper No. 2, School for Advanced Urban Studies, University of Bristol.

Gower Davies, J. (1972) *The Evangelistic Bureaucrat*, London, Tavistock.

Gregory, R.C. (1989) 'Political rationality or 'incrementalism'?', *Policy and Politics*, Vol. 17, No. 2: 139–54.

Gunn, L. (1978) 'Why is implementation so difficult?', *Management Services in Government*, November.

Hadley, R. and Hatch, S. (1981) *Social Welfare and the Failure of the State*, London, Allen and Unwin.

Hall, A. (1974) *The Point of Entry*, London, Allen and Unwin.

Ham, C. and Hill, M. (1992) *The Policy Process in the Modern Capitalist State*, Brighton, Wheatsheaf.

Hambleton, R. and Hoggett, P. (eds) (1984) *The Politics of Decentralisation*, Working Paper No. 46, School for Advanced Urban Studies, University of Bristol.

Hill, M. (1982) 'Street level bureaucracy in social work and social services departments', in J. Lishman, (ed.) *Social Work Departments as Organisations*, Research Highlights No. 4, University of Aberdeen.

Hjern, B. and Hull, C. (eds) (1982) 'Implementation research as empirical constitutionalism', *European Journal of Political Research*, Vol. 10, No. 2.

Hoggett, P. (1990) *Modernisation, Political Strategy and the Welfare State: An Organisational Perspective*, DQM No. 2, School for Advanced Urban Studies, University of Bristol.

Hoggett, P. (1991) 'A new management in the public sector?', *Policy and Politics*, Vol. 19, No. 4: 243–56.

Hoggett, P. and Hambleton, R. (eds) (1987) *Decentralisation and Democracy: Localising Public Services*, Occasional Paper No. 26, School for Advanced Urban Studies, University of Bristol.

Hogwood, B. and Gunn, L. (1984) *Policy Analysis for the Real World*, Oxford, Oxford University Press.

Hoyes, L., Means, R. and Le Grand, J. (1992) *Made to Measure? Performance Measurement, Performance Indicators and the Reform of Community Care*, School for Advanced Urban Studies, University of Bristol.

Hudson, B. (1987) 'Collaboration in social welfare: a framework for analysis', *Policy and Politics*, Vol. 15, No. 3: 175–82.

Ingram, H. and Schneider, A. (1990) 'Improving implementation through framing smarter statutes', *Journal of Public Policy*, Vol. 10, No. 1: 67–88.

Johnson, T. (1972) *Professions and Power*, London, Macmillan.

Laffin, M. and Young, K. (1990) *Professionalism in Local Government*, London, Longman.

Le Grand, J. (1990) *Quasi-Markets and Social Policy*, DQM No. 1, School for Advanced Urban Studies, University of Bristol.

Lindblom, C. (1959) 'The science of muddling through', *Public Administration Review*, Vol. 19, No. 2: 79–88.

Lindblom, C. (1965) *The Intelligence of Democracy: Decision Making Through Mutual Adjustment*, New York, Free Press.

Lipsky, M. (1980) *Street Level Bureaucracy*, New York, Russell Sage.

Loughlin, M. (1986) *Local Government in the Modern State*, London, Sweet and Maxwell.

Lowndes, V. and Stoker, G. (1992a) 'An evaluation of neighbourhood decentralisation, Part 1: customer and citizen perspectives', *Policy and Politics*, Vol. 20, No. 1: 47–62.

Lowndes, V. and Stoker, G. (1992b) 'An evaluation of neighbourhood decentralisation, Part 2: councillor and staff perspectives', *Policy and Politics*, Vol. 20, No. 2: 143–52.

Malpass, P. (1975) 'Professionalism and the role of architects in local authority housing', *RIBA Journal*, June: 6–29.

Marris, P. and Rein, M. (1967) *Dilemmas of Social Reforms*, London, Routledge.

May, P. (1991) 'Reconsidering policy design: policies and publics', *Journal of Public Policy*, Vol. 11, No. 2: 187–206.

Means, R. (1990) 'Allocating council housing to older people', *Social Policy and Administration*, Vol. 24, No. 1: 52–64.

Means, R. and Hill, M. (1981) 'The administration of rent rebates', *Journal of Social Welfare Law*, July: 193-208.

Mishra, R. (1984) *The Welfare State in Crisis*, London, Wheatsheaf.

Peters, T. and Waterman, R. (1982) *In Search of Excellence*, New York, Harper and Row.

Pressman, J. and Wildavsky, A. (1973) *Implementation*, Berkeley, University of California Press.

Prottas, J. (1978) 'The power of the street-level bureaucrat in public service bureaucracies', *Urban Affairs Quarterly*, Vol. 13, No. 3.

Rhodes, R. (1981) *Control and power in central–local government relations*, Aldershot, Gower.

Room, G. (1986) *Cross-national Innovation in Social Policy: European Perspectives in the Evaluation of Social Research*, London, Macmillan.

Sabatier, P. (1986) 'Top down and bottom up approaches to implementation research: a critical analysis and suggested synthesis', *Journal of Public Policy*, Vol. 6, No. 2: 21–48.

Smith, G. and Cantley, C. (1985) *Assessing Health Care: A Study in Organisational Understanding*, Milton Keynes, Open University Press.

Stoker, G. (1988) *The Politics of Local Government*, London, Macmillan.

Thain, C. and Wright, M. (1990) 'Coping with difficulty: the Treasury and public expenditure 1976–89', *Policy and Politics*, Vol. 18, No. 1: 1–16.

Webb, A. (1991) 'Co-ordination: a problem in public sector management', *Policy and Politics*, Vol. 19, No. 4: 229–42.

Wenger, G. (ed.) (1987) *The Research Relationship*, London, Allen and Unwin.

Whitting, G., Burton, P., Means, R. and Stewart, M. (1986) *Urban Programme and the Young Unemployed*, London, HMSO.
Wilding, P. (1982) *Professional Power and Social Welfare*, London, Routledge.
Younis, T. and Davidson, I. (1990) 'The study of implementation', in T. Younis (ed.) *Implementation in Public Policy*, pp. 3–15, Aldershot, Dartmouth.

CHAPTER 3

Housing policy and the housing system since 1979

PETER MALPASS

Introduction

Subsequent chapters will focus on specific aspects of housing policy action in the late 1980s and early 1990s. This chapter is therefore designed to set out the broader policy context, and to provide an overview of recent trends and developments, putting forward a perspective on the overall shape of policy since 1979. The election of the first Thatcher Government represents a convenient starting point for this discussion in view of the important policy changes that were then initiated, although the significance of 1979 as a break point in policy development should not be overstated; indeed, a theme to be pursued in this chapter is the blend of change and continuity during the period. Other key themes to be discussed are the emergence of privatization and deregulation, and the problems of implementing policies which rely on the actions of private sector agencies. The apparent disengagement of the Government in certain areas of housing policy requires to be balanced by reference to the continued erosion of local authority autonomy in relation to housing and other policy areas. Throughout the period under review housing remained close to the top of the political agenda, in the sense that there was frequent legislation on the subject. Given that subsequent chapters concentrate on initiatives arising from a major review of housing policy in the late 1980s it is appropriate to ask why such a review was considered to be necessary by a government which had been in office for eight years: was it because of the failure of previous policies, or was it that as a result of the successful implementation of those earlier policies it was possible to move on?

The political and economic context

Housing policy cannot be understood in isolation from the wider political and economic context. British housing policy since 1979 has to be located in relation to the fluctuating fortunes of the economy and the political project pursued by three successive Conservative governments under the leadership of Margaret Thatcher and, more recently, John Major. This is not the place to attempt a detailed analysis of 'Thatcherism' (see Hall and Jacques 1983; Kavanagh 1987; Gamble 1988; Wilson 1992), but it is important to refer to the extent to which the formulation of housing-policy goals and their translation into action have been influenced by the particular ideological stance adopted by successive Conservative governments during the period. In addition the housing system has been much affected by the ups and downs of the economy, while housing policy has been used as a tool of economic management and subordinated to the primacy of economic policy.

Under the Thatcher leadership, from 1975 to 1990, the Conservatives were committed to a social revolution which involved an attempt to reverse the tide of history since the Second World War in the sense that the Party rejected the social democratic values associated with collectivism and the interventionist role of the state. Egalitarianism and consensus were also dismissed as ideas which had held the country back for too long. Instead Thatcherite values gave priority to the idea of 'rolling back the state', in order to create opportunities for enterprising individuals and businesses operating in the marketplace. Local government was seen as being at the heart of the problem, partly because it was responsible for delivering a large proportion of state services, and partly because it provided an opportunity for the articulation of an alternative political perspective (Boddy and Fudge 1984; Newton and Karran 1985; Blunkett and Jackson 1987; Stoker 1988; Lansley *et al.* 1989; Butcher *et al.* 1990. Faith in the market mechanism was accompanied by commitment to reductions in public expenditure and, most obviously during 1979–82, adherence to a belief in monetarism as the best available approach to economic management. An early White Paper identified public expenditure as being at the heart of Britain's economic difficulties (HMSO 1979: 1), and throughout the period the Government tried (not altogether successfully) to cut, or at least restrain, public expenditure.

Four aspects of the wider political and economic context can be identified as having a big impact on housing in the period since 1979. First, the tight public spending regime; second, the government's deep hostility to local government, coupled with the belief that many public services associated with the post-War Welfare State can be better provided by the private sector; third, the Government's attempts to manage the economy as a whole; and, fourth, the Government's belief that the expansion of home ownership meant an increase in electoral support for the Conservative Party and a corresponding decline in support for Labour.

In marked contrast to the housing-policy concerns of earlier decades, the new Conservative administration publicly abandoned belief in the value of estimates of housing need, relying instead on what the market would provide and 'what the country can afford' (House of Commons 1980). This was interpreted by some critics as showing that housing policy was essentially Treasury led. Housing was soon singled out as a programme area in which expenditure savings could be concentrated. At least 75 per cent of all public expenditure savings in the period 1980/81 to 1983/84 were to come from the housing programme, and the programme itself was to be cut by 48 per cent (House of Commons 1980: v). In practice, the housing cuts were over-achieved: between 1979/80 and 1983/84, housing expenditure fell by 58 per cent in real terms (HMSO 1984: 25). However, public expenditure as a whole did not fall in the same way, as a result of factors such as the Government's commitment to increased spending in some areas, notably defence and law and order, and the recession which drove up unemployment and social security spending. As a proportion of Gross Domestic Product (GDP), total public expenditure actually rose during the early 1980s, and it was not until 1987/88 that expenditure, as a proportion of GDP, fell below its 1979/80 level (Newton 1991: 103).

It is important to add here that the official measure of public spending on housing gives a partial and misleading picture, omitting mortgage interest relief, and housing benefit (until 1990/91). When these expenditures are taken into account, it becomes clear that there has been a major redistribution of spending on housing (Malpass and Murie 1990: 106):

> What has occurred has been a major transfer of resources from those programmes conventionally defined as public expenditure on housing (mainly subsidies to public sector housing and new capital investment) towards other expenditure (Housing Benefit and support to owner occupiers), rather than a simple cut in spending. In the government's own terms this must count as a major failure in public expenditure policy. However the nature of the transfer, from the public sector to the support of owner occupation, from investment to subsidy, and from the subsidisation of the production of public housing to the subsidisation of individual consumption reflects other priorities which have tended to override expenditure considerations.

These 'other priorities' included the commitment to a broad programme of privatization involving the sale of a wide range of publicly owned enterprises and assets. Council housing was the part of the welfare state most easily attacked by a government committed to privatization, because housing provision has never been seen as a comprehensive public service comparable with health and education. Most people have continued to be housed in the private sector, and home ownership was widely seen as a popular option.

However, the vicissitudes of the economy during the 1980s and early 1990s and the Government's approach to economic management have had adverse effects on the private sector in housing. Whereas previous post-War governments had approached economic management with a commitment to maintaining full employment, the monetarist approach of the first Thatcher Government insisted that the control of the money supply was the single most important objective, and to achieve this unemployment was allowed to rise to very high levels; unemployment virtually doubled between 1979 and 1981, and continued to rise to a peak of over 3 million in 1986 (Newton 1991: 98). Unemployment officially exceeded 10 per cent of the workforce during a five-year period,

1983–87, and, together with the threat of unemployment must have had an effect on the demand for owner occupation.

Throughout the 1980s the Government used control of interest rates to regulate demand in the economy and at times to maintain the value of sterling. In the recession of the early 1980s, interest rates rose to very high levels, deepening the recession by adding to the costs of borrowing by businesses, but also driving up the mortgage rate to a record 15 per cent in 1980 and 1981. The effect was that house prices fell in real terms in 1981 and 1982 (Ball 1990: 152), and in 1981 output in the private housebuilding industry in the United Kingdom fell to a twenty-five year low of just 118 500 dwellings. The market later recovered and as interest rates fell below 10 per cent for a while in 1988 activity in the housing market became frenetic, fuelled by the Chancellor's budget announcement that 'double' mortgage interest relief (available to non-married couples where each partner could claim relief on up to £30 000) would be stopped from August 1988. This was followed by five hikes in mortgage interest rates over the next 18 months, taking the normal rate from just under 10 per cent in July 1988 to 15. 4 per cent by February 1990.

This episode illustrates how the Government has used the housing market to regulate the economy, because it was a clear strategy of the Chancellor to deflate an overheated economy by reducing consumer demand by raising the cost of mortgages. However, the effect on the housing market was severe, bringing activity to a virtual standstill. The combined effect of high mortgages, taken out in the boom period, high interest rates and rising unemployment was to create a situation where prices fell in real and nominal terms (Newton 1991: 36), and where unprecedented numbers of people found themselves unable to maintain their repayments and unable to sell their homes for as much as they owed to the mortgage lender. The result was a rapid increase in mortgage arrears and repossessions during 1990 and 1991 (*Housing Finance*, November 1991: 26; Ford 1991).

A final point to be made in this section concerns the way that the private-sector institutions which are so important on the supply side of the housing system, have been engaged in restructuring activity in recent years. The Government's decision to deregulate the banking system in 1980 meant that the clearing banks became much more active in the mortgage market, increasing the competition on the building societies. The societies responded by abandoning their interest-rate cartel and moving to a system of market-based interest rates from 1983 (Boddy 1989; Ball 1990). The effect of this was to make mortgages more readily available, but also rather more expensive. The building societies also lobbied the Government for a change in the legal framework governing their activities, securing much of what they wanted in the Building Societies Act 1986. This enabled the societies to broaden the range of financial services offered to the public, making them more like banks; and one large society, the Abbey National, actually turned itself into a bank in 1988. Another notable development of the 1980s was the takeover of large numbers of estate agency businesses by banks, building societies and insurance companies. This was more to do with the selling of financial services than housing, and was not altogether successful (Ball 1990: 54–5).

The shape of housing policy

Housing is an area in which Conservative administrations in Britain since 1979 have been very actively engaged; to take just one indicator of policy activity, in this period there have been ten Acts of Parliament dealing with housing or closely related areas (Malpass and Murie 1990: 96). Rather than attempting to summarize the details of these developments, the purpose of this section is to sketch in the overall shape of policy since 1979 (see also Balchin 1989; Clapham 1989; Coleman 1989; Malpass 1990a,b; Malpass and Murie 1990: chapter 5). In one sense it is possible to see housing policy conforming to conventional rational models of the policy process. The Conservative Party in opposition in the late 1970s worked out a position on housing which involved a fairly coherent set of specific proposals; once in power after May 1979 they set about putting those proposals into effect, by means of legislation and other measures; there was then a period of consolidation as the policies took effect, to a greater or lesser extent. In 1986/87 there was a 'fundamental and much needed review of housing policy' (Young 1991), and a further bout of legislative and other activity designed to move policy forward again.

The overall approach of Conservative administrations since 1979 has been based on an entrenched belief in the superiority of the market, which in terms of housing policy has been reflected in measures to reduce the scale of the public sector and to encourage private-sector investment. Since 1979 they have continued to be committed to exploration of the limits to the growth of owner occupation, and have been willing to subordinate other traditional housing-policy concerns to that project. They have also been ready to introduce a range of new policy instruments designed specifically to achieve tenure restructuring, and to reduce local authority autonomy in the process. Much of what has been done in housing policy can be understood in terms of the overwhelming commitment to owner occupation as the solution to virtually all housing problems. This has led some observers to argue that the Government is pursuing a tenure policy rather than a housing policy (Donnison and Maclennan 1985). The assault on council housing can be directly related to the preference for home ownership, and important parts of policy directed at local authority housing have been about increasing both the demand for and supply of owner occupied housing. As a result, owner occupation in Great Britain has grown from 55.3 per cent in 1979 to 67.6 per cent in 1990, while council housing has declined from 31.5 per cent to 22.4 per cent over the same period (HMSO 1991).

The first phase of post-1979 housing policy consisted of a series of measures to promote home ownership, either directly or indirectly. The most prominent of the Government's early promises concerned the introduction of a statutory right for council tenants to buy their homes at a substantial discount. It was claimed by the Prime Minister, Mrs Thatcher, that the promise of the right to buy was sufficient to persuade thousands of people to vote Conservative for the first time (House of Commons Debates 1979). A full statement of the Government's housing policy objectives was set out by the Secretary of State for the Environment in an address to the Institute of Housing conference in June 1979. Four key objectives were identified:

1 To increase individual freedom of choice and sense of personal opportunity. This referred to the expansion of home ownership but also included a commitment to providing choice between renting from public or private landlords.
2 A continuing improvement in the quality of housing. 'This means enough new housebuilding to meet the demand for home-ownership, and to meet essential needs in the public sector. It also means more rehabilitation.'
3 Greater value for money; this included the removal of 'unnecessary, time-consuming and costly controls on the house-building industry.'
4 Better use of resources by concentrating them where housing needs are most acute.

(*Housing*, September 1979)

These objectives were translated into legislation in the Housing Act 1980 which introduced, among other measures, the right to buy and a new subsidy system designed to make council renting less attractive to those who could afford to buy. This was, then, the period when privatization emerged as a powerful theme in housing policy (sales of council houses rose to a peak of almost 215 000 dwellings in 1982, and amounted to over 1.5 million in the period 1979–90 (Forrest and Murie 1990)). The pursuit of privatization was accompanied by debate about the extent to which the sale of council houses led to a residualization of the public sector (English 1982; Clapham and Maclennan 1983; Forrest and Murie 1983; Malpass 1983).

Notably absent from policy at this time were any estimates of house building targets, and the refusal to adopt planning totals became a feature of ministerial speeches as meeting demand in the market place took over from need as a basic tenet of housing policy. In evidence to the Select Committee on the Environment in 1980 the Secretary of State (House of Commons 1980: 15) made his position clear:

One relies on the creation of a climate in which the private sector finds the opportunities to expand, and that, as I see it, is the central contribution which this government has to make. There is no question of the capacity of the builders to expand. There is no question of the capacity to build houses. What they want is a climate.

After the radicalism of the early period, the second Thatcher Government, from 1983 to 1987, was characterized by continued active involvement in housing-policy legislation, but it was of a different order of importance. There were Acts to respond to problems which had arisen for some people who had bought defective council houses, and to extend the discounts available to council tenants under the right to buy, but overall this period can be seen as one of consolidation or drift, depending on one's point of view.

It was in the approach to the General Election of 1987 that ministers seemed to gird themselves for another round of reforming legislation, and by then the emphasis had shifted to new ground. The concern for the continued growth of home ownership remained intact but to it was now added renewed interest in the provision of rented housing. It was as if the Government had realized that there was a limit to the growth of home ownership and that a significant proportion of the population would continue to need to rent. Whereas the right to buy had been concerned with getting the better-off council tenants into owner occupation, the new approach aimed at transferring much of what remained of the council stock to new 'independent' landlords, either private landlords or housing associations. This new emphasis on renting also led to the deregulation of the private rented sector as part of a strategy to revive investment in that market.

By the early 1990s housing policy had been significantly reshaped: the commitment to home ownership remained firmly at the centre of policy, but alongside it there was a new strategy for rented housing based on support for private renting, and for housing associations as the main providers of new social rented accommodation. The local authorities were marginalized; they were not expected to build new houses and were encouraged to dispose of their remaining stock to sitting tenants or other landlords, becoming enablers rather than providers.

Continuity, innovation and change

Ball (1985) has argued that:

Thatcherism has not changed the basic tenets of traditional Tory housing policy. Instead it has tried to bring them to reality in a time period so short that no previous government would have dared to try for fear of the outcry.

This statement raises two sorts of questions: about the balance between continuity and change in housing policy since 1979, and about how it was possible to press ahead with such haste. It is clear that the enthusiasm for home ownership was a continuation of well established Conservative policy, although on this issue there was little disagreement between the main political parties (Merrett 1979: 269). What separated the parties was the degree of their enthusiasm rather than the principle of support for home ownership. The Government's positive attitude to the private rented sector and its less favourable approach to council housing were also consistent with traditional Tory policies.

It can, however, be argued that the policies pursued in the early 1980s did represent a real break with the past, in the sense that previous Conservative governments since the end of the First World War had all accepted that councils had a role to play in meeting the need for new housing, and since the end of the Second World War they had appeared to accept that council housing was a permanent and growing part of the housing stock. Since 1979 this has ceased to be the case; 1980 marked a real turning point in the development of council housing in Britain: whereas from 1919 to 1979 the number of council dwellings increased every year, since 1980 the number has declined every year. By the late 1980s Ministers were beginning to question whether there was a continuing need for local authorities to be involved with the direct provision and management of rented housing. William Waldegrave (1987), for instance, went on record as saying:

> I can see no arguments for generalised new build by councils, now or in the future ... The next great push after the right to buy should be to get rid of the state as a big landlord and bring housing back to the community.

Thus, during the 1980s and early 1990s there was evidence of a new hostility towards council housing, going far beyond anything seen from previous Conservative governments. The reasons for this are extremely complicated and a full explanation would need to range from the rise of the new right in the Conservative Party in the 1970s through to the long-term restructuring of the housing market, the delegitimation of council housing and the growth of working-class home ownership (see also Forrest and Murie 1990). The point to be brought out here is that the growth of owner occupation had been sustained for many years by the transfer of dwellings from the private rented sector, but by the late 1970s private renting was reduced to little more than 10 per cent of the stock and could no longer be relied upon to provide a substantial flow of dwellings suitable for transfer. The introduction of measures to boost the sale of council houses can therefore be seen as a tactical response from a government committed to a policy of expanding home ownership. From the point of view of a focus on implementation, it can be said that the introduction of a right for council tenants to buy their homes at substantial discount represented resort to a new policy instrument to pursue an established objective in circumstances where the preexisting mechanisms could no longer be relied upon.

Turning to the question of the Conservatives' commitment to rapid progress towards their goals, an interest in implementation raises questions about why it was thought to be possible to make changes more quickly than in the past, and how the pace of policy action could be increased to such an extent; what did the desire for rapid change mean for the way that the Government sought to implement its policies? On the issue of the feasibility of rapid change it can be argued that in the early 1980s the Government seized an opportunity to implement a policy, the right to buy, which was electorally popular and attractive in terms of public expenditure. The success of the right to buy lay in its appeal to individual self-interest, while opposition to it was grounded in more esoteric arguments about the collective benefits of council housing. As Griffiths and Holmes (1984) ruefully put it: 'The Labour Party's opposition appeared defensive and curmudgeonly.' The general point here is that the ease with which rapid and radical change can be introduced is a reflection of both the determination of the Government and the propitiousness of the circumstances. It is important to add that the Conservatives have been very selective in the policies which they have pushed through; the reform of mortgage interest relief, for instance, which has been canvassed by a wide range of expert opinion, has been rejected, even by a government whose housing policy has in many respects been driven by Treasury concerns, because it is perceived to be electorally unpopular. It is also worth saying that the Government has not always judged the mood of the public correctly, as the fate of the tenants' choice and HATs proposals in the late 1980s clearly shows.

On the issue of how rapid change can be achieved, the first point to make is that the Thatcherite approach was characterized by a willingness to take firm action to deal with any opposition. The overall approach of the Government since 1979 has been one of deep hostility to local government in general, accompanied by a willingness to confront disagreements head-on, and to impose policies on local authorities. The second point is that since 1979 the Government has been willing to innovate in terms of policy instruments deemed to be necessary to achieve its objectives. The right to buy, tenants' choice, HATs, and the new financial regime for local authority housing all come into the category of innovative policy instruments.

Many of the Government's new policy instruments have been designed with implementation problems in mind. The introduction of the right to buy illustrates the approach of a government committed to a particular objective and sensing opposition from many of those upon whose co-operation policy action would depend, i.e. the local authorities. The new policy instrument, the right to buy, contained features which were to become characteristic of the strategy to implement demunicipalization in the 1980s and 1990s:

- it removed local authority discretion with respect to an important aspect of local housing policy, and equipped the Government with powers to penalize councils which refused to comply
- it placed the onus on tenants to initiate action
- it was accompanied by other measures designed to give tenants incentives to take that action.

Coercion, incentive and leverage emerged as three important aspects of housing policy under the Thatcherite Conservatives in the 1980s. Where it was expected that local authorities would oppose Government policy, powers were taken to insist on their compliance, although, in the context of a focus on implementation, it must be added that insistence was not always sufficient to secure outcomes which the Government wanted. The Housing Act 1980 included provisions which enabled central government to simply take over local authority functions if a council was found to be in default of its duties concerning the right to buy. And in the case of Norwich City Council these powers were invoked in December 1981 (Forrest and Murie 1985). The 1980 Act left tenants to initiate the sale of council houses, but gave them the clearest possible incentive to do so, in the form of a carrot and stick approach. The carrot was the offer of substantial discounts from the market price, together with a guaranteed mortgage from the local authority, and the stick was the imposition of higher rents. Rent increases were secured by means of leverage on local authorities' housing revenue accounts (HRAs). A new subsidy system for local authority housing,

based on notional HRAs had the effect of giving the Secretary of State considerable leverage on rents without having formally to instruct councils to make
specific rent increases. Actual subsidy was based on notional HRA deficits,
giving the centre considerable scope for subsidy withdrawal while leaving the
authorities with the choice of higher rents, lower levels of service or higher rate
fund contributions to support housing.

Another way of looking at innovation and change since 1979 is to recognize
that the Government put itself in the position of having to introduce new
measures in response to situations created by its own promotion of owner
occupation and disinvestment in local authority housing. By raising rents in real
terms, reducing the rate of new building and selling off the existing stock, the
Government created two new problems: what to do about HRA surpluses and
the accumulation of capital receipts. Both of these issues were to feature in
struggles between central and local government in the post-1979 era of disinvestment in council housing.

Initial policy responses were contained in the Local Government, Planning
and Land Act 1980. The issue of revenue surpluses was addressed through
measures designed to enable the Treasury to recoup them from local authorities
in the form of lower levels of rate support grant as authorities deemed to be in
surplus were assumed to transfer funds from the HRA into the general rate fund
(Malpass 1990a: 142–4). In the case of capital receipts, the 1980 Act set out
provision for a proportion of receipts, known as the prescribed proportion
(initially 50 per cent but later reduced to 40 per cent and then 20 per cent), to be
available for re-investment in capital projects. With respect to both surpluses
and capital receipts the struggle between central and local government for
control of these resources was resolved during the 1980s in favour of the local
authorities, with the result that the government sought new legislative powers
for the 1990s (see below and Chapter 7).

The private implementation of public policy

A feature of housing policy in recent years has been the growing reliance on
private-sector institutions for the achievement of policy objectives. The growth
of home ownership is clearly dependent on private-sector, commercially motivated organizations and the judgements that they make about the profitability of
new developments or the credit-worthiness of prospective house buyers. Private-sector implementation of public policy raises particular problems for
government, especially for a government publicly committed to a hands-off
approach. The Thatcher and Major governments have differed from both
Conservative and Labour governments in the 1970s in that they have refused to
become involved in measures to maintain stable interest rates for home buyers,
but the price that has had to be paid for that position has been the political
unpopularity arising from periods of very high interest rates and unprecedented
levels of mortgage arrears (Dwelly 1991). However, recent Conservative
governments have been prepared to subsidize individual home owners in other

ways. The refusal to confront the issue of mortgage interest relief has meant the retention of a highly expensive and regressive subsidy, amounting to £7800 million in 1990/91 (Newton 1991: 58). To this can be added the value of discounts under the right to buy, totalling £2700 million in 1988/89 (Forrest *et al.* 1990: 162).

Reliance on the private sector has an effect on the nature of the policy instruments used by governments. The use of incentive devices is particularly noticeable in the private rented sector. Three relevant measures were included in the Housing Act 1980. First, all remaining controlled tenancies were brought within the scope of rent regulation, thereby enabling landlords to seek a higher return through fair rents; second, the phasing of fair rent increases was speeded up, and, third, private landlords were given an incentive in the form of shorthold tenancies, which enabled landlords to let their property for fixed periods of at least one year and to obtain vacant possession at the end of the agreed time. In addition to these changes the Government was persuaded to introduce the concept of assured tenancies, outside the protection of the Rent Acts. This was in response to an initiative by the Abbey National Building Society, and the scope of assured tenancy lettings was initially very restricted: freedom to establish assured tenancies, let at market rents, was restricted to institutional landlords investing in new building. The importance of this initiative is that, although it made very little impact in the short term, by 1987 the assured tenancy idea had become the model for the deregulation of the private rented sector as a whole. Deregulation of private renting was accompanied by an innovation in the form of the extension of the business expansion scheme to cover investment in rented housing. This involved the provision of generous tax breaks as an incentive to investors and gave a clear signal to the market. It also represented a major change of policy in the sense that no previous British government had been prepared to subsidize private landlords directly (see Chapter 5).

Meanwhile, housing associations, which began the 1980s with little more than 2 per cent of the total housing stock, went through a period when their future looked rather precarious. Whilst they were technically private organizations, housing associations relied heavily on Exchequer support in the form of Housing Association Grant (HAG), which meant that in the climate of the early 1980s they were seen as part of the public sector and were affected by the drive to cut public spending. In addition, the Government's enthusiasm for the expansion of home ownership led it to want to include housing associations within the scope of the right to buy, although in the event the right to buy was restricted to tenants of non-charitable associations (Best 1991). A moratorium on new building by associations was introduced for a while in 1980/81, and although completions did recover in later years the output of associations throughout the 1980s remained below what was achieved in the late 1970s. It was not until the 1990s that housing associations were given a clear indication that they were to play a much enhanced role in the provision of new housing in the social rented sector. The housing associations have been subject to a process of privatization, being required to set higher (but still 'affordable') rents, and to raise more of their development capital from private sources. They have become subject to the incentives generated by market forces and by the prospect of becoming very much more significant players in the provision of social rented housing (see Chapter 4).

'A fundamental and much needed review'

The question was posed at the beginning of this chapter, why should a government which had been in office for eight years feel it was necessary to conduct a fundamental review of housing policy? There are various responses to that question. First, there were some clear examples of policies which were not working as the Government had intended – local authority capital and revenue finance were in this category. Defective legal drafting and local authority resistance had resulted in central government losing control of a significant amount of capital spending, and surrendering its leverage on council rents in most parts of the country.

Second, there were some areas where existing policy instruments had not failed, but where it could be argued that their very success in itself made it necessary to look at what new instruments might be needed in the circumstances created by that success. The right to buy had clearly been a successful policy from the Government's point of view, but the prospects of sales to individual owners continuing to yield large-scale reductions in the council stock in the 1990s seemed slim. And the success of the right to buy had made the Government eager for yet more cuts in council housing.

Third, the Government's growing recognition of the need for a substantial rented sector, combined with its hostility to council housing and its traditional support for private renting, pointed to a strategy for reviving investment in private renting. It was also necessary to develop a clear position in relation to the housing associations, which had been given conflicting messages about the Government's attitude.

Fourth, there was the emergence of a new approach to the provision of public services in general, involving the state becoming essentially a puchaser of services rather than a provider. Le Grand (1990: 351) has suggested that 1988 may come to be seen as a major turning point in the development of the Welfare State because in that year across a range of services similar reforms were introduced:

In particular, the proposed reforms in primary and secondary education, health, housing, and social services all involve the introduction of what might be termed 'quasi-markets': the separation of state finance from state provision and the introduction of competition for provision from independent agencies. If these reforms are carried through to their logical conclusion, the welfare state in the 1990s will be one where local authorities will not own and operate schools, houses, and residential homes, and where health authorities will not own and operate hospitals. Instead local authorities and, increasingly, central government will be financing a growing number of private and voluntary institutions, all competing for custom:

opted out and other independent schools, housing associations, private landlords, trust hospitals, private and voluntary residential homes.

This, then, was the context within which the review of housing policy took place. It included an attempt by ministers and their supporters to undermine council housing by means of attacks on the quality of housing management, and more broadly to depict council housing as a failed solution. The attempt to problematize council housing can be seen as a way of persuading tenants to opt for different landlords, and more broadly as a reformulation of the housing problem in a way which made sense in terms of the sorts of policies that the Government was committed to.

The new housing policy was presented in a brief White Paper in September 1987. Four main objectives were set out (HMSO 1987: 3):

First, the Government will continue to spread home ownership as widely as possible, through encouraging suitable market conditions, continuing tax relief on mortgage interest, and pressing ahead with the right to buy ...

Second, the Government will put new life into the independent rented sector. The letting of private property will again become an economic proposition ...

Third, the Government will encourage local authorities to change and develop their housing role. Provision of housing by local authorities as landlords should gradually be diminished, and alternative forms of tenure and tenant choice should increase ...

Fourth, the Government will focus the use of scarce public money more effectively so that tenants are given a better deal.

The White Paper was followed by two major Acts, the Housing Act 1988 and the Local Government and Housing Act 1989. The first introduced the deregulation of private renting, the new financial regime for housing associations, tenants' choice and housing action trusts. The 1989 Act introduced the new financial regime for local authority capital expenditure in general and for the revenue side of local authority housing. The main elements of the new housing policy are the subject of subsequent chapters.

Conclusion

This review of housing policy and the housing system since 1979 indicates that policy has been a blend of continuity and change. The Conservative administrations led by Margaret Thatcher were clearly committed to the conventional Tory goal of a 'property owning democracy', yet they appeared at times to lack confidence while at other times their enthusiasm for change seemed to run ahead of the capacity of the housing system to keep pace. Beneath the overarching goal of a bigger owner occupier sector the Thatcher governments proved to be enthusiastic innovators in terms of policy instruments, some of which were more thought out and effective than others. New instruments varied considerably in the extent to which they reflected anticipation of implementation problems. In a sense, therefore, housing policy since 1979 has been a curious mixture of unyielding ideological commitment and the appearance of being made up in an almost casual, reactive way.

The outcome, however, is that housing policy in the 1990s is operating in a substantially different environment from that of the late 1970s. This is important not only in terms of the sorts of policies which are likely to be brought forward, but also in terms of appropriate implementation strategies and the kinds of organizations that are involved in delivering policy objectives. The increasing importance of market institutions in the housing system is particularly significant in terms of government's ability to achieve its policy objectives and the methods at its disposal. The political consequences of tenure restructuring cannot be ignored here, and in this connection Kleinman (1991) has made the interesting suggestion that housing policy has become bifurcated:

> To talk about 'housing policy' means to talk about two very different sets of concerns, issues and possible solutions. One set relates to the circumstances of the majority, who are mostly well-housed and can reasonably expect to be better housed in the future. The other set relates to the circumstances of the disadvantaged minority, who are badly housed or homeless, whose prospects of future betterment are uncertain, and whose residential segregation, in many cases, compounds social and economic inequality. For the majority of the population, their interests are served by the state intervening to ensure continuity and reasonable market conditions. This means providing a legal framework for the enforcement of contracts; ensuring the supply of finance; supplying output to some degree, especially counter-cyclically; providing a land-use planning framework; maintaining affordability through subsidies, especially to owner-occupiers; and, perhaps most importantly, ensuring steady economic growth and *relatively* full employment.
>
> Other aspects of housing policy, e.g. homelessness, social housing provision and renovation, means-tested housing allowances, etc. are provided to a minority of the population, a minority which is increasingly segregated or at least differentiated from the majority geographically, ethnically or in terms of household type. Whatever the formal appearance, such policies and their associated expenditure are consented to by the majority, not as a type of collective provision but as a form of altruism (helping the poor); or as an insurance payment against riot, theft or social disorder; or as socially necessary expenditure (because low-paid but essential workers need to live somewhere).

This can be criticized for over-simplifying the situation, but it is probably on the basis of such over-simplifications that politicians base their housing policies. The shape and direction of housing policy in the remainder of the century will tend to reflect these broad divisions.

References

Balchin, P. (1989) *Housing Policy: An Introduction*, Basingstoke, Macmillan.

Ball, M. (1985) 'Coming to terms with owner occupation', *Capital and Class*, No. 24: 15–44.

Ball, M. (1990) *Under One Roof*, London, Routledge.

Best, R. (1991) 'Housing Associations: 1890–1990', in S. Lowe and D. Hughes (eds) *A New Century of Social Housing*, Leicester, Leicester University Press.

Blunkett, D. and Jackson, K. (1987) *Democracy in Crisis: The Town Halls Respond*, London, Hogarth.

Boddy, M. (1989) 'Financial deregulation and UK housing finance', *Housing Studies*, Vol. 4, No. 2: 92–104.

Boddy, M. and Fudge, C. (1984) *Local Socialism? Labour Councils and New Left Alternatives*, Basingstoke, Macmillan.

Butcher, H. *et al.* (1990) *Local Government and Thatcherism*, London, Routledge.

Clapham, D. (1989) 'The new housing legislation – what impact will it have?' *Local Government Policy Making*, Vol. 15, No. 4: 3–10.

Clapham, D. and Maclennan, D. (1983) 'Residualisation of public housing: a non-issue', *Housing Review*, January–February.

Coleman, D. (1989) 'The new housing policy – a critique', *Housing Studies*, Vol. 4, No. 1: 44–57.

Donnison, D. and Maclennan, D. (1985) 'What should we do about housing?' *New Society*, 11 April: 43–6.

Dwelly, T. (1991) 'No rest on arrears', *Roof*, September–October: 11.

English, J. (1982) 'Must council housing become welfare housing?' *Housing Review*, September–October.

Ford, J. (1991) 'Mortgage misery deepens', *Roof*, July-August: 9.

Forrest, R. and Murie, A. (1983) 'Residualisation and council housing: aspects of the changing social relations of housing tenure', *Journal of Social Policy*, Vol. 12, No 1: 453–68.

Forrest, R. and Murie, A. (1985) *An Unreasonable Act?* University of Bristol, School for Advanced Studies.

Forrest, R. and Murie, A. (1990) *Selling the Welfare State*, 2nd edn, London, Routledge.

Forrest, R. Murie, A. and Williams, P. (1990) *Home Ownership: Differentiation and Fragmentation*, London, Unwin Hyman.

Gamble, A. (1988) *The Free Economy and the Strong State: The Politics of Thatcherism*, Basingstoke, Macmillan.

Griffiths, D. and Holmes, C. (1984) 'To buy or not to buy, is that the question?' *Marxism Today*, May.

Hall, S. and Jacques, M. (eds) (1983) *The Politics of Thatcherism*, London, Lawrence and Wishart.

HMSO (1979) Cmnd. 7746 (1984) *The Government's Expenditure Plans 1984–85 to 1986–87*, London.

HMSO (1987) Cm. 214 *Housing: The Government's Proposals*, London.

HMSO (1991) *Housing and Construction Statistics*, London.

House of Commons (1980) *First Report of the Environment Committee, Session 1979–80*, HC 714, London, HMSO.

House of Commons Debates (1979) *Hansard*, col. 407, 15 May.

Kavanagh, D. (1987) *Thatcherism and British Politics: The End of Consensus?* Oxford, Oxford University Press.

Kleinman, M. (1991) 'Housing and Urban Policies in Europe: Towards a New

Consensus?' Paper presented to the Housing Studies Association Conference, Oxford, September.

Lansley, S. Goss, S. and Wolmar, C. (1989) *Councils in Conflict: The Rise and Fall of the Municipal Left*, Basingstoke, Macmillan.

Le Grand, J. (1990) in J. Hills (ed.) *The State of Welfare*, Oxford, Clarendon Press.

Malpass, P. (1983) 'Residualisation and the restructuring of housing tenure', *Housing Review*, March–April.

Malpass, P. (1990a) *Reshaping Housing Policy: Subsidies, Rents and Residualisation*, London, Routledge.

Malpass, P. (1990b) Housing Policy and the Thatcher Revolution, in P. Carter, T. Jeffs and M. Smith (eds) *Social Work and Social Welfare Yearbook 2*, Milton Keynes, Open University Press.

Malpass, P. and Murie, A. (1990) *Housing Policy and Practice*, 3rd edn, Basingstoke, Macmillan.

Merrett, S. (1979) *State Housing in Britain*, London, Routledge and Kegan Paul.

Newton, J. (1991) *All in One Place: The British Housing Story 1971–1990*, London, CHAS.

Newton, K. and Karran, T. (1985) *The Politics of Local Expenditure*, Basingstoke, Macmillan.

Stoker, G. (1988) *The Politics of Local Government*, Basingstoke, Macmillan.

Waldegrave, W. (1987) Speech in Bristol, 28 August, Conservative Central Office, London.

Wilson, E. (1992) *A Very British Miracle*, London, Pluto.

Young, G. (1991) 'Our shared commitment', *Roof*, November–December: 8.

CHAPTER 4

The re-privatization of housing associations

BILL RANDOLPH

Introduction

The Conservative Government intended the Housing Act 1988 to stimulate a major shift in the orientation of housing associations. The objective was to move them firmly away from the quasi-public housing sector which associations had become as a result of the Housing Act 1974 and back towards the private, or more precisely, 'independent' rental sector. The deregulation of new housing association tenancies paralleled that in the rest of the private rented sector. The associated introduction of mixed funding and private finance had the objective of reducing the proportion of public grant committed to new development and pushing rents towards market levels. Both these aimed to reduce the perceived imbalance between housing associations and the private rental market and, in doing so, at least potentially opened the door for other private landlords to eventually obtain public funding in competition with associations.

A closely related policy objective was to stimulate greater cost efficiencies in associations through greater exposure to private-sector 'disciplines'. This was to be achieved by the reduction in grant levels which would stimulate associations to pare the costs of development and management to ensure rents were kept affordable. It was also to be aided by the introduction of 'value-for-money' criteria in the allocation of funds between associations. Quite simply, those associations which could produce housing at the lowest unit cost to meet stated needs objectives would receive public funding. In effect, associations were now to compete for funds on a cost efficiency basis.

In one sense, then, the 1988 Act moved associations back towards the position they were in before the 1974 Act effectively brought them into the public housing sector. The 1988 Act therefore has led to a partial re-privatization of associations.

The mechanisms the Government used to encourage associations to comply in the implementation of the Act were a mixture of incentive and leverage. Given that associations are basically private organizations, the Government had no power to enforce the desired funding changes on them. But if an association wished to develop with the benefit of public grant, then it would now have to do so under the new rules of mixed funding. The incentive to play by the new rules was straightforward: a tripling of the Housing Corporation's annual Approved Development Programme by the mid-1990s. Associations had the choice of taking advantage of this expansion in funding or not. Most associations chose to play.

But in accepting to play under the new rules, it can be argued that associations have become subject to greater central control as they move into the mainstream of central government social housing policy. A clearly stated aim of the Act was to facilitate housing associations to become the main provider of social housing within a re-invigorated 'independent' rented sector (i.e. independent of local government). In this sense, housing associations have moved closer to the centre of the social housing stage, responding more directly to the policy demands of government. At the same time, the changes to the capital subsidy system and the shift in subsidy balance toward housing benefit have strengthened central control on the funding of the sector.

These points will be explored in the following discussion, which attempts to assess the major repercussions of the Housing Act 1988 and the associated introduction of private finance and lower grant rates on housing association activity. It also considers some of the main implementational problems that have accompanied the introduction of the new funding regime and whether the objectives of the Act have been achieved.

The Housing Act 1988 – what did it set out to do and what were the reactions?

The changes to the housing association financial regime introduced with the Housing Act 1988 had two stated objectives. The first was to lay the ground for a larger 'independent' rented sector, of which housing associations were to play the major part in the provision of new social rented housing through a greatly expanded development programme. The second was to introduce 'market' disciplines into housing association activity as a spur to additional development and to maximize 'efficiency' and value for (public) money.

But just as important was the desire to lower public subsidy levels and push rents in the sector nearer to 'market' levels. These related objectives were not implemented through the Act itself, but were largely introduced by subsequent changes in the funding regulations. A central plank of this policy was the introduction of private funding to replace the fully public funding system set up under the Housing Act 1974.

In essence, the new mixed funding regime, which took effect from 1 April 1989, imposed a limit on the proportion of scheme costs covered by Housing Association Grant (HAG) which was now to be fixed at the start of the scheme, not calculated at the end, as before. Initially, HAG was to average 75 per cent nationally. For most schemes the remaining costs would need to met by a loan from private sources, such as a bank or building society. The Government argued that the addition of private money would result in a higher level of output for any given amount of public funding. Together with the promise of a much expanded funding programme, fixed HAG, as the system came to be known, would stimulate a rapid growth in new housing association development.

To effect this change, the Act deregulated rents for most new lettings from 15 January 1989. Rents for new assured lettings would be determined by associations themselves rather than Rent Officers. Deregulation was essential for two reasons. First, private funding would only be forthcoming if lenders were sure that any future changes in loan terms or potential deficits could be met by rents free from external regulation. And secondly, the reduced grant percentage for new schemes would ensure that rents for these schemes would rise substantially above prevailing fair rent levels. The removal of Major Repair HAG from new schemes would also mean that provision for future major repairs would need to be built into the rent calculation, further pushing up rents.

In essence, then, the 1988 Act set the legislative framework in which the remainder of the policy, introduced though a series of procedural and funding changes, has operated. Details of the changes introduced by the Act and other associated initiatives have been summarized elsewhere (see NFHA 1989, 1990; Cope 1990; Smith 1990; Walentowicz 1990; Hills 1991).

Few in the housing association movement seriously questioned the opportunity for an increase in development opportunities or of the need for cost effectiveness. But serious doubts were raised concerning how the implementation of the 1988 Act and its related funding changes would affect the viability of associations and their ability to continue to provide good standard housing to those in greatest need at a price they could reasonably afford (Hills 1987; NFHA 1987; National Housing Forum 1988). In particular, there was an underlying unease concerning the repercussions of marrying the private-sector ethos of commercial efficiency and public-sector ethics of meeting housing need. The Act itself had little to say on the latter subject. These doubts centred on five main areas:

- the affordability of rents that were likely to be produced under the new mixed funding regime and the impact on the type of tenant housed
- the adequacy of housing benefit in protecting tenants against rent increases
- the greatly increased financial risks the new system placed on associations and the impact this might have on the development programme, standards of provision and diversity
- the costs and availability of private funding and the funding of major repairs
- the reduced rights new tenants would face under the assured rents regime.

In practice, the latter issue was effectively diffused by the promotion of the 'Tenants' Guarantee' by the Housing Corporation which minimized the impact of assured tenancies on tenants' rights. Consequently, the main interest has been focused on the first four issues.

The following sections will assess how far these doubts have been confirmed.

But first, we will consider the question of whether mixed funding has actually led to an increase in housing association output.

The promised development boom

As we noted above, the introduction of the mixed funding regime following the Housing Act 1988 has been accompanied by a substantial increase in the amount of public funding for housing associations. Trends in the Approved Development Programme funding for new rented housing over the period 1986/87 to 1994/95 are shown in Figure 4.1. Mixed funding, which was piloted in 1987/88 with the 'Challenge Funding' scheme using 30 per cent HAG, will represent 91 per cent of the annual allocation of £1.169bn in 1992/93. The total level of funding is predicted to reach £2.075bn by 1994/95.

But the level of output in terms of units approved for development did not matched the increase in funding in the first two years after the Act. Figure 4. 2 shows approvals for rent over the period 1978/79 to 1994/95. The Corporation had predicted that approvals would increase substantially from 17 600 in 1989/90 to 24 500 by 1990/91. But in fact the actual numbers approved were 16 200 in 1989/90 and just 8900 in 1990/91. This was lower than that achieved during the temporary moratorium on spending in 1980/81.

The reason for this slump in approvals stemmed from an unforeseen consequence of the switch to mixed funding. The Housing Corporation simply failed

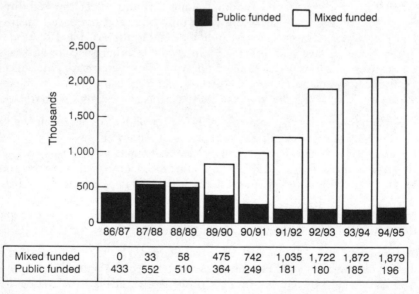

Figure 4.1   The Approved Development Programme, 1986/87–1994/95, new housing for rent

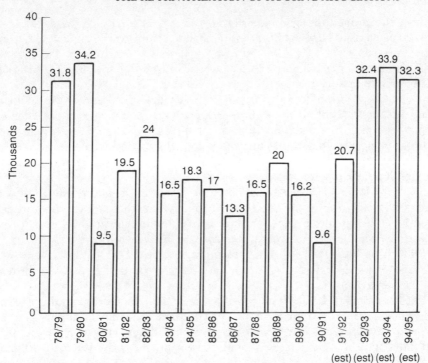

Figure 4.2   Annual Housing Corporation approvals for rent, 1978/79–1994/95

to predict a rapid, and one-off, acceleration in the rate of grant claims by associations which the new funding system encouraged. In the past, associations submitted schemes for scrutiny and approval at both acquisition and tender (scheme on site) stages. This multiple approval process built an element of inertia into the system which tended to slow the grant drawdown process. The new funding regime telescoped the scheme scrutiny process by removing the need for Corporation approval at the second stage of the development process.

Moreover, mixed funding encourages associations to speed up the development period to minimize costs, especially from any short-term private finance borrowed for the development. As a consequence of both these factors, mixed funding has resulted in a more rapid rate of grant drawdown as schemes proceed through the development process faster than in the past. During 1989/90 associations also appeared to bring forward grant claims on schemes already in the development pipeline, but funded under old HAG, possibly in order to minimize outstanding cost commitments and risks by completing schemes more quickly.

Finally, the 1989/90 period also coincided with the beginnings of the property slump. Associations, especially in the south of England and London, were able to purchase 'off-the-shelf' schemes from developers who could no longer rely on the home ownership market to complete their sales. Such purchases are, of course, encouraged under mixed funding as they entail much lower levels of development risk. They result in an immediate claim for the entire HAG payment, however.

Whatever the precise reason, there was a substantial speeding up of grant drawdown by associations in the year following April 1989. As a result, the Housing Corporation literally ran out of money before the end of the financial year. By January 1990, the Corporation were forced to take the unprecedented step of bringing forward £120 million of the agreed 1990/91 spending programme to meet the shortfall. This money could only be taken out of that part of the programme reserved for new approvals in 1990/91, as schemes already in the development pipeline had to be protected.

By the end of the 1989/90 financial year, the level of funding shortfall was such that the Corporation was forced to take two further steps. It first pruned back 1989/90 scheme approvals as far as possible and then announced a drastic cut in the planned new programme for 1990/91 to allow the outstanding 1989/90 programme to go through. In all, an estimated 14 000 homes were 'lost' over these two years as a result of the cash crisis, representing almost a third of planned approvals.

The cash crisis of 1989/90 represents a major implementational failure of the new Act, effectively stalling its impact by two years. The indications are that the promised expansion is now underway, however. Latest Housing Corporation estimates of the numbers of rented units to be approved show a rise to 34 000 by 1994/95. Whether or not this level will be achieved remains to be seen. But the development boom heralded by mixed funding, if it arrives, should be placed in perspective: 34 000 approvals will only return associations to the levels achieved in the late 1970s under old style HAG (Walentowicz 1991b).

Rents and affordability

Rents for most new lettings are now set by individual associations. However, following the Act no official guidance was given as to what constituted an appropriate rent other than a series of vague and possibly contradictory directives. The *overriding* requirement was one of affordability, namely that 'rents should be set and maintained within the reach of people in low paid employment'. But at the same time associations are 'expected to maximize rental income on all their properties . . .' (Housing Corporation Circular: HC 60/89). A further proviso was that rents should be 'significantly below the free market level' (DoE 1987: para. 14). Rents were at the same time to be both deregulated but restrained!

The logic behind deregulated rents was summarized by the Corporation. 'There is no point in promoting housing which cannot be afforded, but equally there is no point in keeping rents *below* affordable levels' (Housing Corporation 1990: p. 7; original emphasis). But as to what an affordable rent might be, this was '. . . for associations to determine' (Housing Corporation Circular: HC 60/89). Naturally, all this left associations rather confused as to the levels at which rents should be set or how they might assess their affordability for prospective tenants.

The lack of guidance on rent setting and affordability was widely interpreted as a recognition by the Government that the cost rents required for mixed funded schemes were considerably above prevailing fair rents and would represent a significant proportion of the incomes of the average tenant. The issue of affordability rapidly became, and indeed remains, the major issue surrounding the 1988 Act.

The fear was that increases in rents would either force associations to move 'up market' and house households who could afford the higher rents without difficulty, or concentrate on households in receipt of housing benefit (NFHA 1987). The former would contradict the charitable traditions of the movement while the latter would lead to greater residualization of the sector. It is worth noting in relation to the latter point that a subsidiary objective of rent deregulation was that higher rents would encourage those with the ability to buy a home to move out of the social rented sector altogether. Deregulation can therefore be seen as part of a general policy to speed the residualization of the social rented sector.

Rents after deregulation

Rent deregulation and lower grant rates have had a major impact on associations, in terms of management practice, and tenants, in terms of rent levels. Evidence on rent trends drawn from the NFHA's CORE monitoring system for new lettings show that rents have risen considerably since 1988 (Randolph 1992a; 1992b).

Average rents in new lettings rose from £18.16 in the second quarter of 1988 to £32.89 by the second quarter of 1991, an increase of 81 per cent. Rents for lettings of newly developed homes (new-lets) increased by 104 per cent. In comparison, the RPI increased by 26 per cent over this period. Average rents have therefore risen at three times the rate of general inflation. At the same time, between 1988 and 1991, average fair rents for all housing association tenancies registered with Rent Officers increased by an average of 26 per cent. Rents for new lettings have therefore increased much faster than they would have done under the fair rent regime.

At the same time there has been a marked divergence in rent structures since 1989. For example, in the second quarter of 1988 the average new-let rent (£20.32) was 18 per cent higher than the average rent on re-lets of existing properties (£17.51). But by the second quarter of 1991, the gap had widened to 42 per cent (£41.44 compared to £29.65 respectively).

Similarly, average assured rents rose by 45 per cent between the first quarter of 1989 and the second quarter of 1991 (from £23.21 to £33.93) while average fair rents had risen by just 28 per cent (from £20.35 to £26.64). Consequently, the gap between fair and assured rents has risen from 13 per cent to 27 per cent over this period.

There is also evidence that rents are beginning to diverge between smaller and larger units and between high- and low-cost regions. The switch to assured tenancies and mixed funding is breaking down the rather uniform rent patterns produced under the fair rent system.

Figure 4.3 shows that the divergence only began to open up at the end of 1989, almost a year after the introduction of assured tenancies. This reflects two underlying effects. To begin with, less then a third of associations had implemented a permanent rent setting policy by this time. Most associations had adopted interim policies in which rents were set in relation to prevailing fair rent levels. The introduction of more permanent policies after this date is likely to have been accompanied by more realistic assessments of necessary rent levels (Stevens 1992).

But the trends also reflect the lag between the implementation of mixed funded development and the outturn of this policy in terms of rent levels of completed schemes. Schemes coming into management up to the end of 1989 will almost entirely have been funded under the old HAG regime or the transitional arrangements for schemes started before April 1989. There was little pressure to increase rents in these schemes substantially above the prevailing fair rent level. Only from the beginning of 1990 have schemes approved under the

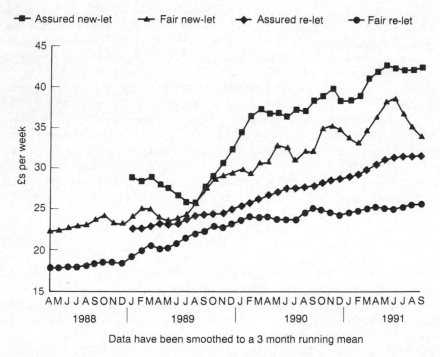

Data have been smoothed to a 3 month running mean

Figure 4.3   Rents by letting type, April 1988–September 1991

new funding arrangements entered management in any numbers. The upward pressure on new-let rents from this date is a clear reflection of this.

Whatever happened to affordability?

Without any clear guidance, the implementation of the concept of affordability stimulated a somewhat confused reaction amongst practitioners, academics and commentators alike. The main issue of contention centred on what proportion of income should constitute a reasonable amount to pay in rent. The NFHA recommended 20 per cent as a guideline, based on evidence from other tenures, and calculated a matrix of Indicator Rents to show what affordable rents might be for properties of different size and location (NFHA 1990; Treanor 1990). The grant rates themselves implied a figure nearer 33 per cent. Others criticized the proportional income approach as ignoring the absolute levels of income households might be left with after paying rent (Kearns 1990; Maclennan et al. 1990). But they gave little practical advice on alternative measures or appropriate rent levels. This debate is unlikely to be resolved.

Regardless of what the appropriate level of affordability should be, the evidence is that rent levels have become more steadily more unaffordable as the incomes of new tenants have fallen well behind the rise in rents. In fact, average rents have risen at three times the rate of average incomes of working tenants and rents in new developments increased by four times incomes (Figure 4.4). This has had two major repercussions for tenants. First, rapidly rising rents have resulted in deteriorating affordability trends. Figure 4.5, which is based on NFHA CORE data for new tenants with at least one person in work, shows monthly trends in the proportion of 'available' income (i.e. net income plus any estimated Housing Benefit (HB) entitlement) taken in gross rent (rent plus eligible service charges) for new tenants from April 1988 to September 1991. The upward trend lines confirm that rents are taking greater proportions of tenants' incomes. Starting at 20 per cent, the proportion had risen to nearly 25 per cent by the middle of 1991. Affordability rates for tenants in newly developed homes ended the period at 28 per cent. Rates for new-let rents began to move steadily upwards at the beginning of 1990, corresponding to the period when schemes developed with mixed funding would have started to come into management.

At the same time, Figure 4.6 suggests that the 'residual' incomes left to tenants once they have paid their rents and an allowance is made for basic living costs (calculated as Income Support plus 20 per cent) have fallen. This decline in residual incomes is particularly noticeable for tenants moving into new-lets.

On the basis of these two measures, it is clear that rents have become steadily less affordable for new working tenants over three years since the beginning of 1989, and that this deterioration has been most marked for tenants moving into newly developed homes.

Have higher rents changed the type of tenant housed? In fact, fears that the new regime would force associations to house more affluent tenants have not

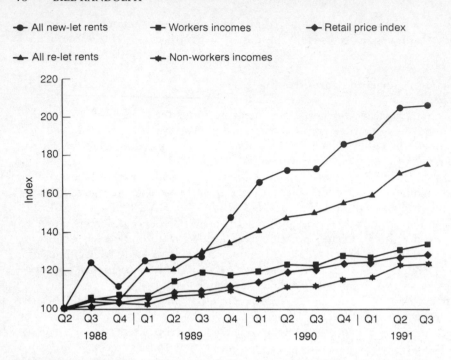

Figure 4.4   NFHA Rents and Incomes indices, Quarter 2 1988 to Quarter 3 1991

been fulfilled. The evidence points to a stable pattern of income distribution. The major consequence of the differential changes in rents and incomes has been the growing proportion of new working tenants who qualify for housing benefit, particularly for newly developed homes. The proportion of working tenants eligible for housing benefit moving into new units has increased dramatically, from 32 per cent in the first quarter of 1989 to 46 per cent in the third quarter of 1991. Average housing benefit paid per new-let unit has also risen sharply, from approximately £5.50 to over £14 during the same period (Randolph 1992a; 1992b).

Without doubt, deregulated rents and mixed funding have drawn more new tenants into the benefits trap. For the 22 per cent of new tenants who are unemployed, of course, higher rents have simply deepened the benefit trap further, giving even less encouragement to seek employment. In effect, the new funding regime has encouraged the extension of the dependency culture so often decried by Government ministers. But even so, the growth of housing benefit take-up has not stopped the proportion of income spent on rent for new tenants rising steadily since the Act. Housing benefit has only partially 'taken the strain' of higher rents.

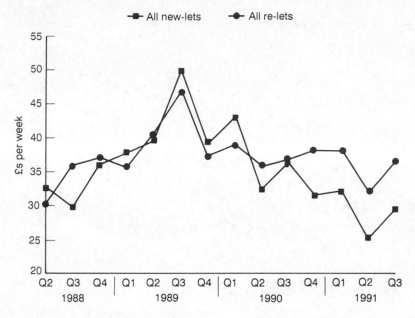

Figure 4.5 Affordability rates by letting type, April 1988 to September 1991

Risk and the development process

The Act introduced a new word to the housing association vocabulary: risk. Risk was the *quid pro quo* of lifting the Treasury convention that the entire costs of HAG-funded schemes be regarded as public expenditure. In return for this dubious concession, the risk of cost overruns on new developments would no longer be underwritten by the final HAG payment. Similarly, Revenue Deficit Grant, which could be claimed if there were any future revenue losses on the scheme, and Major Repair Grant, which paid for future major improvements, were abolished for new schemes. Future deficits or major repairs on the scheme are now the association's responsibility.

In contrast, the 1974 funding system was to all intents and purposes risk free. Under the 1974 system, the final HAG payment at the end of the development period was adjusted to cover agreed cost overruns. Cost control and the prediction of final costs at scheme approval stage was therefore not crucial to the success of a scheme as overruns would be met with the final HAG payment. And the Grant Redemption Fund arrangements, introduced in 1980 to recoup any rent surpluses, gave no incentive for associations to closely control costs.

The 1988 HAG system reversed the role of HAG in the funding equation and in doing so introduced risk. Grant levels are now predetermined for any given scheme. For tariff schemes this means a cash amount fixed at the prevailing total cost limits. Financial risks resulting from any cost overruns are entirely borne by the association. For non-tariff schemes HAG is a fixed percentage of estimated

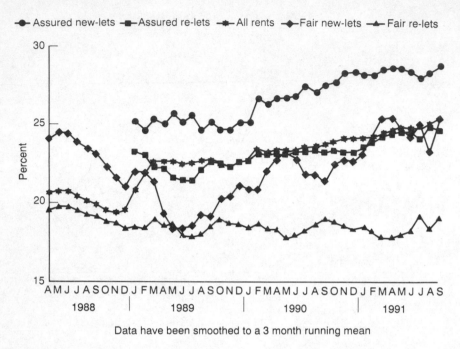

Data have been smoothed to a 3 month running mean

Figure 4.6   Residual incomes, re-lettings and lettings, Quarter 2 1988 to Quarter 3 1991

scheme costs, although limited cost overruns, and hence risk, can be shared between the association and the Corporation through a final grant adjustment.

Together, these changes mean that associations which want to develop using mixed HAG need to adopt risk avoidance strategies to ensure future viability. Schemes or development methods involving higher risk are less likely to be pursued. It was predicted that in practice this would mean a shift away from higher-risk schemes such as rehabilitation of older inner city property, where development costs were not always easy to predict and schemes tend to be more complex administratively. Green field, new build developments would be a better risk and could often be cheaper.

Similarly, the traditional procurement method, known as 'contract with variations', which left any risk entirely at the door of the association, was also likely to decline. Instead, there would be a move to fixed price design and build or 'off-the-shelf' packages in which the risk of cost overruns would lie with the builder. Unfortunately, scheme design and specification are more likely to be determined by the developer, with the implicit threat that space and design standards will fall, reflecting those prevailing in the private sector.

The evidence from the first two years of the new programme has confirmed many of these predictions (Walentowicz 1991b; Randolph 1992a; 1992b). There has been both a relative and an absolute decline in the number of units in

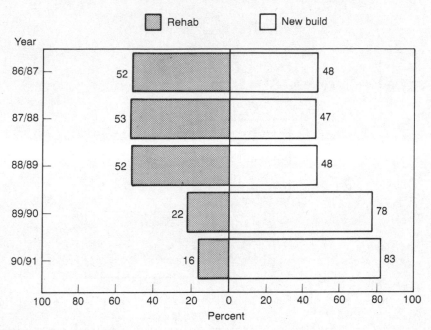

Figure 4.7   The proportion of units by scheme type (rehabilitation or new build), 1986/87–1990/91

rehabilitation schemes. Rehabilitation averaged a very stable 50 per cent of the annual programme throughout the 1980s, an average of 9 500 units per annum. This proportion fell sharply to 22 per cent in 1989/90 and to 16 per cent in 1990/91 while numbers slumped to below 2 000 units per annum (Figure 4.7). Significantly, the largest associations have seen the proportion of rehabilitation approvals fall fastest as they have made a rapid switch to new build development.

The shift from rehabilitation has also been linked to a shift away from inner urban areas. The proportion of approvals in the 57 Urban Programme authorities, i.e. those local authorities considered by the DoE to have the greatest levels of deprivation, fell from 68 per cent in 1987/88 to 52 per cent in 1989/90 and to 43 per cent in 1990/91 (Figure 4.8). The decline has been absolute as well as relative. While both new build and rehabilitation programmes have fallen in these areas, the rehabilitation proportion has declined fastest. Space and design standards also appear to be under threat. The average floorspace area per unit in newbuild schemes approved in the first year of mixed funding 1989/90, was 9 per cent below the equivalent Parker Morris standard. Moreover, the average floorspace of these schemes was 11 per cent lower than that achieved in schemes approved in 1987/88, i.e. before mixed funding (Walentowicz 1992).

In addition to the introduction of private funding and the encouragement this

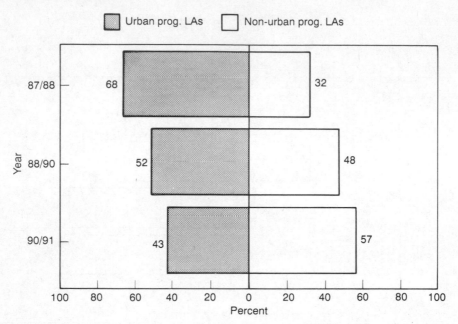

Figure 4.8   The proportion of units by urban programme status, 1987/88, 1989/90 and 1990/91

might give to associations adopting a more cost conscious attitude, the Housing Corporation has promoted a clear message that only the most 'efficient' associations will be considered suitable for HAG-funded development activity in the future. 'Efficiency' in this context means quite simply the ability to produce housing at the lowest cost. The establishment of a 'two-tier' development procedure in which 'fast-track' tariff arrangements contrast to the more heavily scrutinized non-tariff scheme-by-scheme procedure was an explicit attempt to promote cost-efficient production.

Tariff programmes allow the possibility of averaging out costs between different schemes in the package, with lower cost schemes in effect cross subsidizing high costs. Tariff was specifically aimed at the larger associations with sufficient financial strength to sustain a large-scale rolling programme and who might be expected to exploit the advantages of bulk production to keep development costs to a minimum. Associations who did not meet the financial requirements for tariff status – mainly smaller and specialist – remained subject to the scheme-by-scheme approval system with more stringent cost supervision. Implicit in the tariff/non-tariff division was the view that small-scale production was inherently less cost efficient and could not be relied on to minimize costs.

But tariff procedures largely failed to make any headway in high-cost areas. In 1989/90 tariff schemes accounted for 66 per cent of all Housing Corporation funded units in the West Midlands, North West, Merseyside, North and York-shire and Humberside regions, but only 21 per cent in the higher-cost regions of London, West, East and East Midlands. The respective proportions were 73 per cent and 20 per cent in 1990/91. There were no tariff schemes at all in the South East in either year.

The regional bias in tariff funding largely stems from the inability of associations in high-cost areas to exploit the cost-limit system sufficiently to make the additional risks involved worthwhile. It has been much harder to find schemes where total costs are significantly below the Total Cost Indicator level in the South compared to the North. The failure of tariff in much of the southern half of the country represents yet another major setback for the implementation of mixed funding.

What price private finance?

Private finance lay at the heart of the Housing Act 1988. Initial reactions largely concentrated on whether private lenders would offer terms to enable affordable rents to be charged. The Act was introduced as interest rates were rising. The implications for rents were clear. In the event, while affordability remains a central concern, private finance has run into a number of more protracted difficulties. Principal amongst these has been the relative paucity of both funding and funders (Couttie 1991; European Capital 1991; Pryke and Whitehead 1991). Whether this is the result of fears over the future re-introduction of rent control, the collapse of the property market, competition for funds from voluntary transfers or simply misconceptions about the activities of housing associations – social housing was as much a novel concept to City financiers as was private finance to many in associations – is unclear. But the net result was that just as associations were gearing up for private finance, private lenders were becoming much less inclined to lend.

Of the 23 banks with whom associations had arranged funding by March 1991, one accounted for almost half of all committed loans (Duckworth 1992). Similarly, of the 21 building societies with outstanding loan commitments at this time, just three accounted for 86 per cent of the total. There was also a virtual absence of any direct lending from insurance and pension funds. The relatively small sums required by most associations were insufficient to interest them. However, access to these funds has been made possible through The Housing Finance Corporation (THFC), a financial intermediary set up with Housing Corporation and NFHA backing in 1988 to act as a conduit for City funding into associations. In fact, THFC has been a major source of hard cash for mixed funded development. While only contributing a minority of committed funding, THFC drawdowns (as opposed to committed lending) by 31 March 1991 were more than double any other lender, at £157 million (with a further £100 million in late 1991). Without this level of 'self-help', mixed funding might well have stalled.

Other areas of concern include the exposure of associations, particularly smaller ones, to variable interest rates. Variable rates increase financial uncertainty and hence risk. The evidence also pointed to a relatively high volume of short-term lending: a quarter of the total value of committed lending on loans of less than five years, with attendant refinancing risks. And there is some evidence of loan terms hardening in the deteriorating financial climate of the early 1990s.

The role of low-start finance has also proved problematic. A fundamental principle of the new grant system is the use of low-start private finance to achieve affordable rents in the early years of the scheme. However, these loans are more risky than conventional loans. Deferred or stepped interest rate loans expose associations to risk if inflation is lower than predicted. In contrast, index-linked loans expose associations to risk if inflation is higher than predicted. At the same time, falling inflation is a disincentive for lending index-linked funding, and vice versa for deferred.

Associations can minimize their risk exposure by developing a mixed loan portfolio in which a range of high-risk low-start money is balanced by low-risk conventional loans. This works against smaller associations with more limited borrowing potential. In mid-1991 just over half of committed private funding was on a range of low-start bases, with less than 10 per cent conventional funding. Moreover, the proportion of lending on deferred interest terms for smaller associations was three times the level of other associations, compounding their risk exposure.

But there are added problems. The Corporation's grant model assumes all loans are on a low-start basis. Risk avoidance requires a mix of loan types, including initially more costly conventional loans. This means that outturn rents produced from a balanced loan portfolio will need to be higher than the Corporation's grant model assumes. Thus risk management and prudent financing result in higher rents than the post-1988 Act grant structure predicts.

The mix of loan types also has repercussions on the ability of associations to build up major repairs provisions. The low-start model assumes that a major repair fund can build up relatively quickly in the early years of the loan when repayment costs are lower. Conventional funding involves higher initial repayment costs and reduced capacity to build up repair provisions if rents are to be kept down. This could be risky, especially for small associations without the reserves to cover unforeseen repairs bills. Indeed, predicting the outcome of the complex relationship between funding method, major repairs provision, rent levels, inflation and repair costs over the lifetime of the scheme is a further area new to associations and fraught with uncertainty.

The period since 1988 has hardly been a propitious one for introducing private finance into social housing. Real interest rates have been at record levels and funding has become much harder to obtain. Whether the demands for private funding over the next three years, if the programme expands as predicted, will be met, and from whom and on what terms, is a major question mark overhanging the whole 1988 Act funding regime.

Control and centralization

Part of the Government's rhetoric accompanying the 1988 Act concerned a desire for an 'independent' rented sector, with housing associations becoming less heavily controlled and scrutinized by the Government and its agents. This greater independence would allow associations to respond more flexibly in an evolving rental market, albeit at the price of additional risk. This desire was reflected in the reduced scheme scrutiny system and the 'fund-and-forget' approach to association activity, particularly cost overruns, development risk and rent setting.

But it can also be argued that there were a number of alternative goals of the 1988 Act which have led to an increasing degree of overall central government influence on the sector, both administratively and in terms of the flow of subsidies. Perhaps most significant of these was the objective to promote housing associations as vehicles for a (reduced) social housing sector which would be outside the influence of local authorities and could be developed as centrally controlled agencies. An additional element in this is the only partly concealed desire to see new development concentrated into a smaller number of the biggest associations. These would deal directly with the Housing Corporation and could, in effect, become the development arms of the Corporation. Associations have therefore moved into a much more central role in social housing policy. With it has come increasing government attention.

The concentration of control on association activities has been aided by the declining ability of local authorities to fund housing associations directly due to much tighter controls on council capital spending since the early 1980s. The 1988 Act also drew local authority HAG funding development into the Housing Corporation approvals system.

But the Act also heralded a greater degree of concentration of central government influence over the funding of housing association activity than previously. First, the new HAG system allows for much greater control over the actual level of capital subsidy. With predetermined HAG, it is much easier to manipulate the grant percentages to regulate expenditure. There can be little doubt that the intention was to reduce capital subsidy from the 75 per cent initially settled on. Indeed, the first opportunity to take advantage of lower development costs resulting from the property slump was not translated into lower rents or more units but into lower HAG (now estimated to average approximately 70 per cent as from 1992/3). The 1988 capital funding system therefore allows the grant percentage, and hence the capital subsidy, to be easily ratcheted downwards. Reversing this, should rents prove unaffordable, is likely to be much more difficult.

Secondly, the funding changes shifted the balance of housing subsidy in the sector away from capital subsidies and toward the housing benefit system. The impact of rising rents resulting from lower grant rates has been partially cushioned by higher housing benefit payments. However, the degree to which the current housing benefit system has been increasingly fine tuned to 'target' the beneficiaries as well as to regulate the overall level of the subsidy is well documented (Walentowicz 1991a). Clearly, shifting the balance of the total subsidy package towards a centrally controlled individual housing subsidy further increases the total control the Government is able to assert on the housing associations system.

The net outcome of both these moves is to establish a firmer grip on both ends of the subsidy equation. The open-ended nature of the old HAG system has been largely removed and subsidy balance has shifted towards housing benefit, which, although in theory open-ended, is subject to considerable regulation and manipulation. Beneath the rhetoric of independence, flexibility and efficiency contained in the 1988 Act lay the sub-text of greater control. Indeed, it could be argued that the 1988 Act had more to do with an attempt to create a 'quasi-market' *within* a centrally directed housing association sector (Le Grand 1990). The abandonment of agreements on zoning which limited the areas where associations could operate and the introduction of competitive bidding procedures for cash allocations in the early 1990s represents an overt attempt to establish an 'internal' market with associations competing on a value for money basis. As such, the changes in housing association activity heralded by the 1988 Act have clear similarities with the Government's policies towards the education and health services. Perhaps the term 'pseudo-privatization' should be used to describe this situation of a move away from full public subsidy, the creation of internal markets and greater central government control.

Mixed funding – mixed blessings

The implementation of deregulation and mixed funding has certainly proved a mixed blessing on the ground. At one level, the Government's basic objective of drawing in private capital to make the public subsidy go further has succeeded. In excess of £2 billion in loan commitments had been made up to the end of March 1991, a substantial amount by any measure. Schemes approved by the Housing Corporation in the first two years after the introduction of mixed funding incorporated £443 million of non-HAG funding, equivalent to some 6 300 extra homes.

There is also no doubt that associations are much more cost conscious. Predetermined HAG, financial viability tests, cash limits and, more latterly, competitive bidding, have seen to that. Further benefits include a more sophisticated approach to financial planning, a greater appreciation of the role of management information and greater integration of corporate decision making as development, management and finance functions have become much more intertwined. Small and specialist associations are still developing, albeit often in partnership with larger associations. In many respects, then, associations have been relatively successful in adapting to and implementing the objectives of the Housing Act.

But there have been significant difficulties. First, the cash crisis robbed the new funding regime of its impact during the first two years after 1989. Output stalled, despite the escalation in funding levels. Second, there is no hard evidence as yet to suggest that the pressure from lower grants has stimulated any real efficiency gains in terms of lower procurement costs. If cost efficiencies have been achieved, then they have been swamped by the impact of the falling property values over the period since 1988. It is possible to argue that the new grant regime has led to an increased flexibility in procurement methods which has allowed associations to take better advantage of the opportunities to purchase schemes on a package deal and 'off-the-shelf' basis. But in any event, whatever cost efficiencies have been achieved, they have certainly not reduced costs to the extent that outturn rents are anywhere near levels that could be deemed reasonably affordable.

Third, the full effects of the 1988 Act have taken time to filter through and have been felt mainly on the margins so far. The problems inherent in the Act itself are only now becoming clear. Most of these problems have been felt by tenants, in the form of more unaffordable housing, threatened standards and a reduction in new provision in high needs areas. And as rents have risen, more tenants have been drawn into the benefits trap, thereby increasing the level of benefits dependency.

Fourth, if the cash crisis robbed the new system of its initial impetus, then subsequent development has switched towards lower risk new build outside the main areas of urban deprivation. The Act has effectively removed associations as major players in inner-city renewal, the basis of their post-1974 growth. Established space and design standards are also under threat.

Fifth, while private funding has been attracted to the sector, there has been a worrying lack of lenders and long-term costs and risks associated with low-start funding seem high. And there are still major unresolved difficulties over the funding of future repairs.

Sixth, smaller associations who wish to develop are clearly now operating at a disadvantage on a number of fronts. Whether they will be squeezed out of development activity altogether or turn to development agreements with a limited number of larger associations who would take on the bulk of the development work, remains to be seen.

Finally, rather than stimulate a move towards greater variety and choice, the re-privatization of associations is more likely to lead towards a more homo-geneous housing association sector relying on large-scale production to the detriment of small-scale, one-off and specialist development. The creation of an 'internal' market for development work can only help this tendency. And at the same time, there has been an increase in centralized control on the level of total public subsidy and an increase in the direct influence the Government is having on associations' activities.

All these changes are undoubtedly changing the way associations operate and the housing services they offer. Under the new Major administration the effects of the 1988 Act will continue to push associations towards the private sector. Much will also depend on how far associations are able to resist implementing policy objectives many have questioned.

References

Cope, H. (1990) *Housing Associations: Policy and Practice*, London, Macmillan.

Couttie, D. (1991) *Institutional Investment for Rented Housing*, York, Joseph Rowntree Foundation.

Department of the Environment (1987) *Finance for Housing Associations: The Government's Proposals*, London, DoE.

Duckworth, S. (1992) *Private Finance after the Act, NFHA Research Report 20*, London, NFHA.

European Capital Co. (1991) *Housing Associations – Improved Access to the Capital Markets*, York, Joseph Rowntree Foundation.

Hills, J. (1987) *Finance for Housing Associations: A response to the Government's Proposals*, Welfare State Programme Research Note No. 8, London School of Economics.

Hills, J. (1991) *Unravelling Housing Finance*, Oxford, Clarendon Press.

Housing Corporation (1990) *Into the Nineties*, London, Housing Corporation.

Kearns, A. (1990) 'Strategies for Affordable Housing', Paper presented to the NHFA Annual Conference, 21–23 September 1990.

Le Grand, J. (1990) *Quasi-Markets and Social Policy*, DQM No. 1, School for Advanced Urban Studies, University of Bristol.

Maclennan, D., Gibb, K. and More, A. (1990) *Paying for Britain's Housing*, York, Joseph Rowntree Foundation.

National Federation of Housing Associations (1987) *Rents, Risks and Rights*, London, NFHA.

National Federation of Housing Associations (1989) *The Housing Act 1988*, London, NFHA.

National Federation of Housing Associations (1990) *Paying for Rented Housing*, NFHA Research Report 12, London, NFHA.

National Housing Forum (1988) *The Affordability File*, London, NFHA.

Pryke, M. and Whitehead, C. (1991) *An Overview of Recent Changes in the Provision of Private Finance for Social Housing*, DP 28, Department of Land Economy, University of Cambridge.

Randolph, B. (1992a) *Rents, Incomes and Affordability after the Act*, NFHA Research Report 18, London, NFHA.

Randolph B. (ed.) (1992b) *Housing Associations after the Act*, NFHA Research Report 16, London, NFHA.

Smith, M.E.H. (1990) *Supplement to the Third Edition of the Guide to Housing*, London, The Housing Centre Trust.

Stevens, S. (1992) *Rent Setting after the Act*, NFHA Research Report 17, London, NFHA.

Treanor, D. (1990) *Housing Association Rents*, London, NFHA.

Walentowicz, P. (1990) *Caught in the Act Again*, London, SHAC.

Walentowicz, P. (1991a) *Of Little Benefit*, NFHA Research Report 9, NFHA, London.

Walentowicz, P. (1991b) *Development after the Act*, NFHA Research Report 14, NFHA, London.

Walentowicz, P. (1992) *Design Standards after the Act*, NFHA Research Report 15, NFHA, London.

CHAPTER 5

Rebuilding the private rented sector?

PETER KEMP

Introduction

This chapter examines the policies of the Conservative administrations of 1979 to 1992 towards the private rented sector. This form of housing provision has been in decline since the First World War. Its role has been substantially replaced by owner occupation and council housing. While the Conservatives have been enthusiastic supporters of the growth of home ownership, they have only reluctantly conceded – in the face of the continuing decline of private renting – a role for local authority provision.

The publication of the 1987 Housing White Paper (DoE 1987a) signalled a new approach to rented housing provision by the Conservatives. As well as setting out a strategy for the demunicipalization of rented housing, the White Paper – together with other changes introduced in 1987 and 1988 – heralded a new determination to revive the private rented sector. This new approach needs to be understood within the context of the long history of decline of the sector, the limited success of the initiatives introduced by the first Thatcher administration to revive private renting, and its policies towards the other housing tenures.

The next section sets the scene by briefly reviewing the legacy of decline and decay of private renting with which the Conservatives were faced when they came to office in 1979. This is followed by an outline of the policy towards the sector followed by the 1979 Conservative administration and an examination of the impact which it had up to 1987. Then we examine the new approach to the sector pursued by the Conservatives and assess its impact to date. A final section draws conclusions about the implementation of policy in the sector and more generally.

Reasons for decline

The long decline of private renting has been the outcome of a complex set of factors, the relative importance of which has varied over time (Kemp 1988a). These causes have operated on both the demand and supply side and, inevitably, also reflect elements of both choice and constraint. One crucial nexus of factors in this decline has been the housing finance system – that is, the ways in which housing has been taxed, subsidized and priced – and, therefore, the way in which the state has intervened in housing provision. Thus the state has been deeply implicated in the decline of private renting.

One of the more salient features of the housing finance system which has affected decline is rent controls. These have existed in one form or another since 1915 and affected more or less of the sector. Rent control has helped to reduce the rate of return from private letting. It has given landlords an incentive to sell their property on vacant possession to the owner-occupied sector and place the proceeds in more remunerative investments.

The provision of tax reliefs to the owner-occupied sector has helped to shift demand away from private renting and to home ownership. Further, to the extent that tax relief has been capitalized into house prices, it has increased the rent that a landlord would require in order to continue letting the accommodation rather than sell it to the owner-occupied sector.

Quite apart from any inherent advantages which ownership may have over renting (see Whitehead 1979), it has had two important financial attractions for much of the post-war period. First, inflation has meant that, while rents tend to increase over time, mortgage repayments on loans taken out in previous years will fall in real terms. Second, average house prices have broadly increased in line with average earnings and faster than the rate of inflation for most of the post-war period. Consequently, home owners have been able to make significant capital gains, a possibility not open to those who remain as tenants (Saunders 1990). The result has been that most people who could afford to buy their own home have done so rather than rent it privately. Many of the people who remain as tenants of private landlords cannot afford to pay a rent that would give landlords an economic rate of return.

In combination, rent control, the tax incentives to home ownership and the low incomes of many private tenants, have helped to create a value gap between vacant possession and sitting tenant prices (Doling and Davies 1984; Hamnett and Randolph 1988). This has given landlords an incentive to sell when they get vacant possession. It has also meant that landlords seeking to disinvest will make less money by selling with a sitting tenant than they would with vacant possession. Landlords' inability to regain possession at the time of their choosing as a result of the security of tenure provisions of the Rent Acts has therefore been a disincentive to investment in rental property.

Further, the value gap has also given an incentive to speculators to buy tenanted property and then sell to owner occupiers – sometimes after renovation works have been carried out, often with the aid of an improvement grant (Crook and Martin 1988) – as soon as the tenant can be persuaded to leave. The value gap has therefore helped to create the problem of insecurity of tenure and harassment for private tenants (Kemp 1988a).

Rent controls, the low incomes of many private tenants and the lack of a depreciation tax allowance (Nevitt 1966) have made it difficult for landlords to adequately maintain or improve their properties. Although improvement grants have been available in one form or another since 1949, the extra rent which landlords have been able to charge after improvement has tended to be insufficient to cover their share of the cost of improvement works. Moreover, improvement policy has been remedial in nature, that is, concerned with remedying defects rather than with preventing them from arising in the first place (SHAC 1981).

The private rented sector, and especially houses in multiple occupation, shows up very badly on the three main house condition indicators of lack of basic amenities, unfitness and disrepair. The 1981 English House Condition Survey found that one in seven privately rented dwellings lacked one or more basic amenities, one in six were unfit and two fifths needed repairs of more than £2500 (in 1981 prices). Yet because landlords have been letting in a seller's market since the Second World War they have been able to let even dwellings in very poor condition (DoE 1977).

Since 1919, governments have provided subsidies to social housing landlords which have enabled them to provide housing at a lower rent (for comparable accommodation) than private landlords have been able to do. In Britain, governments (even Conservative ones) have generally been reluctant to provide subsidies to private landlords. Leaving aside improvement grants, prior to 1979 the only subsidies provided to private landlords were Exchequer grants payable on new housing built for letting under Labour's Housing Act 1924 (Kemp 1984).

One reason for the reluctance to provide such subsidies has been the negative image of private landlords in Britain. This image is encapsulated in the phrase 'Rachmanism', defined in the *Concise Oxford Dictionary* as the 'Exploitation and intimidation of slum tenants by unscrupulous landlords'. In this imagery, poor or unwilling tenants are perceived to be renting substandard property from inefficient or even disreputable landlords. In turn, this poor image has reduced both the demand for private renting from those able to afford owner occupation or gain access to social rented housing and the willingness of 'lily-white' organizations such as pension funds to invest in new supply within the sector.

The private rented sector has also been the subject of at times intense and emotionally charged political debates about its future and appropriate policy responses to its decline. While housing to let is essentially a long-term investment, governments and their polices come and go. The political uncertainty surrounding the future of private renting has added an element of political risk to investment in the sector. This will almost certainly have increased the rate of return (and hence the rent) that a landlord will require in order to invest in private housing to let (Whitehead and Kleinman 1989).

This brief résumé of some of the causes of decline of the sector serves to illustrate the complex and deep-seated nature of that decline. It also suggests that the problems of the sector are not amenable to simple policy prescriptions.

It follows that 70 years of decline would not be easily or quickly rectified when the Conservatives came to power in 1979.

The legacy

When the Conservatives returned to office in 1979 the private rented sector accounted for about 2.3 million dwellings or 11 per cent of the housing stock in Britain. The rate of decline during the 1970s was approximately 80 000 dwellings per annum.

Not only had the private sector declined considerably over the years, its role within the housing market had also changed. The decline had been concentrated in unfurnished lettings, so that a growing proportion of the sector was comprised of furnished accommodation. Increasingly, the sector was providing less long-term unfurnished housing and more short-term, immediate-access furnished accommodation. A review (Kemp 1988a: 28–29) of the composition of tenants within the sector concluded that:

> Many private tenants are elderly, have low incomes, rent unfurnished houses or flats and have lived at their present address for many years often dating back to when private renting was the majority tenure. By contrast, a high proportion of private tenants, particularly in the furnished subsector where relettings are concentrated, are young, often single, usually without children, rent rooms or flats and have lived at their present address for at most only a year or two.

A survey of private tenants in England in 1978 found that just over two thirds had a regulated tenancy under the Rent Act 1965, of whom one-third (or about one-fifth of all tenants) had a fair rent registered with the Rent Officer service. Seven per cent of private tenants had a controlled rent extant from the pre-1965 Rent Acts. About one in twenty private tenants was renting from a resident landlord, one in six were either living in rent-free accommodation or otherwise renting tied accommodation (Todd *et al.* 1982).

The 1978 survey also found that the ownership of privately rented housing was diverse and relatively small in scale. Over three-fifths of private lettings in 1978 were owned by individuals and only one-tenth by property companies, while just over one-fifth were employer landlords (Todd *et al.* 1982). A survey of landlords in densely rented areas of England and Wales in 1976 found that the median size of holding of non-resident individual landlords was only five to nine lettings, while for companies it was 50 to 99 lettings. Thus, private letting in Britain in the late 1970s (as had always been the case) was a fragmented, small-scale and largely unmodernized sector of the market economy (Kemp 1988a).

Housing Act 1980

Policy objectives are notoriously difficult to pin down. Nevertheless, the housing goals of the first Thatcher administration can be interpreted as being (i) to increase home ownership, (ii) to cut and make more effective use of public expenditure in housing, (iii) to minimize the role and size of the council housing sector (not least by giving council tenants the right to buy their house at a discount), and (iv) to revive the private rented sector. Extending home ownership had an evident priority for the Conservatives over reviving the private rented sector.

The Minister for Housing and Construction, John Stanley, set out the Government's intentions and hopes for the private rented sector (Crook 1986: 1031–32):

> We believe that the private rented sector has got a significant role to play in the provision particularly of accommodation which is required by those who are mobile, those who want accommodation for a relatively short period. There is an enormous demand amongst people who may be saving up to buy sooner, or later, who may have relatively low incomes at this particular time but can see income growth coming, for the availability of short term accommodation. All the various changes that I have referred to in the 1980 Housing Act are meant to try to increase the availability of that accommodation. As far as the other wing of the private sector is concerned, the long stay accommodation, our view is that we have to try and strike as equitable a balance as we can between the landlord interest and the private tenant interest and we have no further proposals to bring forward in that area at the moment.

The Housing Act 1980 included a package of measures aimed at stimulating the private rented sector. First, easier rules for regaining possession were introduced for resident landlord lettings. Second, the remaining controlled tenancies, extant from the pre-1965 years, were converted into regulated tenancies. Third, the phasing in of increases in fair rents and the interval between fair rent increases, were both reduced from three years to two. Fourth, a new form of tenancy known as 'shorthold' ('short tenancies' in Scotland) was introduced. These were regulated tenancies of from one to five years which gave landlords the power to regain possession after the fixed term. Initially, all shortholds had to have a fair rent registered, but this requirement ceased to apply outside Greater London from December 1981 and in London from May 1987.

Finally, in England and Wales (but not in Scotland) a new form of tenancy known as 'assured tenancies' were introduced. These were lettings by approved landlords of newly built property at market rents. They thus represented a form of deregulation. New construction had been subject to rent regulation since the 1965 Rent Act.

Impact of the 1980 Act

The House of Commons Select Committee on the Environment investigated the private rented housing sector in 1981/82. It doubted whether the changes made by the 1980 Act would have more than a marginal impact on the sector. The measures failed to address what it referred to as the 'central dilemma' for the sector, namely the gap between what tenants could afford to pay in rents and what landlords needed to charge in order to get an economic rate of return. This could only be achieved by altering the distribution or the amount of housing subsidies (HCEC 1982).

In attempting to give landlords of property which was registered with the rent officer more regular rent increases and to raise rents nearer to market levels, the 1980 Act initially had some effect. In the five years to 1980, the average registered rent increased by less than the retail prices index, average earnings, average house prices and the index of repair and maintenance costs. But in the five years following the 1980 Act, registered rents increased by more than these other indices (Crook 1986; Kemp 1988a).

The introduction of shortholds was a response to the complaint that the inability of landlords to regain possession was a disincentive to investment in rental property. This complaint reflected the gap between vacant and sitting tenant house values. The view of many people giving evidence to the House of Commons Select Committee in 1981/82 was that shorthold would have little impact (HCEC 1982). This was partly because many landlords had already found ways to avoid or evade the security provisions of the Rent Acts, for example, by using non-exclusive occupation agreements or licences (Crook 1986).

The attractiveness of shortholds to landlords appears to have increased after the House of Lords *Street* v. *Mountford* ruling in 1985, the effect of which was that many lettings thought to be outside the Rent Act were in fact probably covered by it. While shorthold tenants had the right to get a fair rent registered, landlords at least had the right to regain possession at the end of a definite term of years. The evidence from a survey of private renters in 1988 was that about one in 20 lettings in England were shortholds by that date. Two-thirds of these had commenced in 1988 or the previous year (Dodd 1990).

An important feature of assured tenancies was that they did not come within the fair rent system. From 1965 to 1980 newly built property had come within the regulated tenancy arrangements, hence a fair rent could be registered on such property. This was seen by the Government as a major reason for the lack of new building within the sector.

When the Secretary of State for the Environment announced the approved landlord scheme, he made it clear that he had in mind as approved bodies the financial institutions such as the pension funds, insurance companies, and the building societies (who, because prior to 1986 they were not allowed to own houses or land, would operate through unregistered housing associations). This list was subsequently widened to include other organizations that were 'suitably qualified to build and manage homes for renting' (DoE 1984: 2).

In order to stimulate interest in assured tenancies, the Chancellor, Geoffrey Howe, introduced capital allowances in the 1982 budget for an experimental five-year period. Research on approved landlords found that the capital allowances were an important reason why many of the approved firms had become interested in the scheme (Kemp 1988b). However, in the 1984 Budget, the Chancellor, Nigel Lawson, phased out the allowances after only two years. According to a Minister for Housing, the DoE was not alerted to this abolition until it was too late to prevent it from happening (Young 1989). Thus, the Chancellor's objective of simplifying the tax system conflicted with the objective of attracting private investment back into the rented sector.

In fact, by April 1987 only 217 organizations had applied for and received approval, of which only a small minority were financial institutions of the type the Secretary of State had been particularly keen to attract (Kemp 1988b). Moreover, only 742 assured tenancies had been built for letting by that date (a further 2256 had been built as part of shared ownership and long leasehold schemes, almost all of them by McCarthy and Stone (Developments) Ltd, a builder of leasehold schemes for the elderly).

By the mid-1980s it was becoming clear that the measures introduced in the Housing Act 1980 were having only a very limited impact on the sector and had failed to halt or reverse decline. Although registered rents had increased in real terms, they were still providing uncompetitive rates of return. While shorthold was having more impact than many commentators believed would be the case when it was introduced, it tackled only the symptom and not the cause of the security of tenure problem for landlords. Finally, deregulation of new construction was clearly failing to have much impact at all.

Towards a new approach

During 1985 the Conservatives contemplated removing rent controls on new lettings but, in the event, shrank back from doing so. The reasons for this appear to be not only that it would appear to be giving succour to the unpopular private landlord, but also the cost implications for housing benefit of rising rent levels which deregulation seemed to imply. Housing Minister William Waldegrave (1987: 10) noted that the block on decontrol had come from a

> ... dubious alliance of those who absurdly believe that all private landlords are bound to be like Rachman and those who fear housing benefit costs rising if there are to be real market rents.

The responsibility for housing benefit lay with the (then) Department of Health and Social Security – who were under pressure from the Treasury to contain their rising budget – while housing was the responsibility of the Department of the Environment. Here again, there was an inter-departmental conflict of objectives in government which affected the prospects of reviving the private rented sector.

However, during 1986 the Conservatives introduced a range of initiatives aimed at paving the way for the introduction of new private investment into rented housing provision. These can be seen as precursors to the more fundamental changes announced in 1987 (Kemp 1988c). The assured tenancy regime was extended to include refurbished property. The restriction on building societies owning houses and land was removed. Discussions were held with the building societies about the possibility of them taking over the ownership of council housing estates, though it soon became clear that this was not likely to develop in a significant way (DoE 1987b). And the Local Government Act 1987 gave local authorities discretionary power to provide financial assistance to private landlords letting on assured tenancies.

As well as these measures, the Government also attempted to promote a new image for private landlordism. The Secretary of State for the Environment talked of the need to 'exorcise the ghost of Rachman', while the Minister for Housing, John Patten spoke of wanting to create a new breed of 'model landlords' (1987: 24):

> I can understand all the objections to old-style renting outside the council sector, but I'm trying to outflank that opposition by creating a form of 'new model renting' – tenancies ... This isn't people with Alsatian dogs trying to kick down the front door and evict you. It's like motherhood and apple pie. After all who could possibly object to renting from organizations like the Halifax or the Woolwich?

The Housing White Paper 1987

Following their election for a third term of office, the Conservatives published their first Housing White Paper under Prime Minister Margaret Thatcher (DoE 1987a). The White Paper was significant not merely because it outlined an extensive array of policy innovations, but also because it signalled a shift in the focus of attention in housing policy, away from the extension of home ownership – although that was still the most important objective – and towards the demunicipalization of rented housing provision.

The White Paper set out four objectives for housing policy, the second of which was to 'put new life into the independent rented sector', by which it meant private rented and housing association accommodation (DoE 1987a: 3). The role which was envisaged for private renting in the White Paper was very much to do with its immediate access characteristics and its ability to facilitate labour mobility (DoE 1987a: 2):

> ... private renting offers a good option for people who need mobility or who do not wish to be tied by ownership ... The private sector can offer greater flexibility and responsiveness to market demand. It can provide housing in a way that encourages labour mobility and meets changing needs of individuals and the economy as a whole. Restoring an active private rented sector will allow individuals to take advantage of improved prospects in different parts of the country. It will help progress towards a better match between supply and demand for labour.

Underlying the decontrol of private lettings was not only an ideological distaste of regulation but also an apparent belief that rent control and security of tenure legislation – in addition to the attractions of home ownership – had been the main reason for the decline of private renting (DoE 1987a).

To further this objective, new lettings by private landlords were to be deregulated. This, it was claimed, would mean that the letting of private property 'will again become an economic proposition'. Even so, the White Paper (DoE 1987a: 10, emphasis in original) took care to explain that the Government

> ... does not propose to make any substantial changes in the regime for *existing* tenancies subject to the Rent Acts. It would not be right to disturb these existing tenancies, though minor amendments will be made to the succession rules. As and when such tenancies come to an end, landlords will be free to relet on the new basis.

The Housing Act 1988

The proposals for private renting in the 1987 White Paper were included in the subsequent Housing Act 1988, which came into force in January 1989. Under the 1988 Act, all new private lettings were to be either new style, 'assured tenancies' or 'assured shorthold tenancies' (called 'short assured tenancies' in Scotland), both of which were modified versions of those introduced in 1980.

As well as strengthening landlords' grounds for possession, the approved landlord arrangement was abolished under the new style assured tenancies. Assured shorthold tenancies could no longer be referred to the Rent Officer for a fair rent to be registered and the minimum term was reduced from one year to six months. A new offence of harassment was also introduced by the 1988 Act, largely to allay fears that deregulation would echo the alleged effect of the 1957 deregulation and herald a return of 'Rachmanism' (Kemp 1987).

Finally, in order to prevent private-sector rents increasing on a sea of housing benefit subsidy, rent officers were given a new role of policing housing benefit claims. Since April 1989 local authorities have had to refer new claims for housing benefit on deregulated tenancies to the Rent Officer to determine whether the rent is above a 'reasonable market rent' or the accommodation 'over large for the claimant's reasonable needs'. If the rent or the accommodation are unreasonable, the Rent Officer has to determine what a reasonable market rent would be for the property. This determination is then used by the Department of Social Security (DSS) when it reimburses local authorities for their housing benefit expenditure. However, the landlord is not required to reduce the rent accordingly (Kemp 1990).

Thus, the policy conflict between the DSS and Treasury on the one hand and the DoE on the other was resolved by using the Rent Officer as a form of rent regulation for private tenants on housing benefit.

The Business Expansion Scheme

In the 1988 Budget statement, the Chancellor, Nigel Lawson, announced an extension of the Business Expansion Scheme (BES) to include companies letting on assured tenancies, for a limited period, until the end of 1993. It is clear from ministerial statements (e.g. Lamont 1988; Young 1991) that this was meant to act as a kick-start to investment in the private rented sector. It apparently did not reflect a view that the sector needed subsidies to make letting competitive. Rather, it was intended to be a demonstration project, showing that competitive returns could once again be made now that lettings had been decontrolled and the market set free (Crook *et al.* 1991).

The BES was originally introduced in 1983 with the objective of encouraging small businesses as part of the 'enterprise culture' which the Conservatives were hoping to encourage. It provided tax relief to investors on the purchase of share in BES firms and exemption from capital gains tax if the shares were held for at least five years. The generous tax relief provided under the scheme was intended to compensate for the high level of risk involved in investing in small and new firms.

The extension of BES to include companies providing rental housing let on assured tenancies had an immediate impact. In the first two years during which the scheme applied (1988/89 to 1989/90) £543 million was invested in assured tenancy BES companies. This produced approximately 10 000 dwellings, two-thirds of them newly built (Crook *et al.* 1991).

While investment continued in the third and fourth years, much of it was linked to housing associations and university halls of residence rather than to mainstream private renting. This development partly reflects a key feature of the BES, namely the fact that it in effect gives investors an incentive to disinvest after the minimum five-year holding period for the shares. Consequently, many companies sought to guarantee an 'exit route' for investors. Housing associations and universities – who saw the BES as a way of securing additional accommodation on cheaper terms than conventional loans – were able to 'guarantee' that they would buy back the property at an agreed uplift from the price at which they had originally sold them to the BES company. In several cases, the housing association schemes were linked to mortgage rescue packages aimed at preventing home owners in arrears from being evicted.

New lettings

The BES represents only a small share of the new private lettings market, albeit a high profile one. It is too early to assess the impact of deregulation on the supply of and demand for non-BES privately rented dwellings. Moreover, the position is complicated somewhat by the slump in the owner-occupied housing market which began at the very end of the 1980s and continued into the early part of the 1990s. It appears that because of the state of the property market, considerable numbers of home owners are unable or unwilling to sell while the property

slump continues and are letting their homes out (and, in turn, themselves renting other dwellings) until such time as the property market picks up. This
may therefore prove to be only a short-term boost to the private lettings
market.

Preliminary results from an OPCS survey of private tenancies in 1990 nonetheless provide some information on the sector one and a half years after the
1988 Act came into force. This can be compared with the results of a similar
survey carried out in 1988. The 1990 survey found that the number of private
lettings had fallen by 43 000 or 2. 5 per cent over this two-year period. However,
the total number of recent lettings, that is those taken out in 1987 or 1988 for the
earlier survey and in 1989 or 1990 for the later survey, had increased. In the
1988 survey it was 641 000 or 37 per cent of all lettings, while in the 1990 survey
it was 690 000 or 41 per cent of lettings.

This increase in recent lettings seems to reflect the continuing decline of
long-term unfurnished lettings and the growing proportion of short-term furnished lettings, rather than a response to deregulation. For a given stock size, the
greater the proportion of lettings that are of short duration, the more of them
that will be taken out recently. Indeed, the OPCS survey suggested that the
average duration of lettings had decreased between 1988 and 1990 (OPCS
1991).

Rapid turnover within the private rented sector meant that a high proportion
of lettings were now deregulated. This is shown in Table 5.1. By the summer of
1990, 28 per cent of all private lettings were either assured or assured shorthold
lettings created under the 1988 Act. The proportion of lettings which had a
regulated tenancy fell from three-fifths in 1988 to one-third in 1990. The
proportion of lettings which had a fair rent registered with the Rent Officer fell
from one-quarter to one-sixth.

Table 5.1   Types of private letting in England 1988 and 1990

Type of letting*	1988 (per cent)	1990 (per cent)
Resident landlord	6	4
No security	4	5
Not accessible to the general public		
rented	13	13
rent free	15	14
Regulated		
with registered rent	26	18
without registered rent	33	15
Protected shorthold and pre-1989 assured	4	2
Assured shorthold	–	8
Post-1988 assured	–	20

* Totals in 1988 and 1990 were 1 741 000 and 1 698 000, respectively.
Source: OPCS (1991)

Table 5.2   The size of the private rented sector in England 1980 and 1990

Year	No. of dwellings (000s)	Percentage of all dwellings	Percentage of rented dwellings
1980	2 084	12	27
1990 (provisional)	1 507	8	25

Source: DoE (1991)

Overview

During the 1980s, the private rented sector continued to decline in size. The number of privately rented dwellings in Britain fell by more than one-quarter. The sector also decreased both its share of the total housing stock and, though only slightly, its share of the stock of rented houses (see Table 5.2). Thus, measured in terms of the number and proportion of dwellings that were rented from private landlords, the objective of reviving the sector can be seen to have failed. Nevertheless, the second half of the 1980s did witness a significant slowing down of the rate of decline of the sector. As Table 5.3 shows, during the early 1980s the sector was declining at about 80 000 dwellings or four per cent per annum. By the end of the 1980s, the rate of decline had almost halted, though whether this was due to deregulation, temporary letting for the duration of the property slump or other factors, is not known.

While it will be several years before the full impact of deregulation will become clear, the BES has provided some clues. Research into the short run impact of this fully deregulated subsector found that the rental income from BES lettings was below that which appears to be necessary to attract new, non-subsidized investment into the private rented sector. As a result, without subsidies of the sort provided by the BES, significant new investment in the sector is unlikely to be forthcoming. As a demonstration project, therefore, the BES appears not to be working (Crook *et al.* 1991).

Table 5.3   The rate of decline of the private rented sector in Britain 1980

Year	Dwellings (000s)	Percentage of PRS stock
1980/81 (estimate)	−91	−3.8
1981/82	−86	−3.8
1982/83	−80	−3.6
1983/84	−80	−3.8
1984/85	−79	−3.9
1985/86	−77	−3.9
1986/87	−71	−3.8
1987/88	−58	−3.2
1988/89	−34	−1.9
1989/90	−8	−0.5

Source: DoE (1991)

Conclusion

Although by no means the most important or pressing objective for the post-1979 Conservative governments, creating a commercially viable private rented sector was nonetheless something which they sought to achieve. This aim was largely pursued by a gradual process of deregulation, beginning with new construction by approved landlords from 1980 and thereafter widening in scope. Especially towards the end of the period, the Conservatives supplemented this strategy with the provision of subsidies, mainly in the temporary form of tax reliefs under the BES. Despite these measures, the private rented sector continued to decline, though the rate at which it did so began to slow in the late 1980s.

The measures taken during the 1980s to revive the sector had a symbolic significance for the Conservatives. Nevertheless, in so far as the purpose of these measures was to create a commercially viable private rented sector, their impact fell short of the objectives. The reasons for this apparent failure are relatively easy to discern.

While the reasons for the decline of the sector are complex and interrelated, the policy instruments used to solve the problem dealt with only limited aspects of these causes, in particular rent regulation and security of tenure, but left many other factors such as the tax subsidies to home ownership largely untouched. Moreover, even the issues which were addressed were less important than some of the other factors behind the continuing decline of the sector. Thus, rent regulation was not as important a reason for decline as it had been when private renting was a major housing tenure. Only one in ten new lettings in the early 1980s – the market deregulated by the Housing Act 1988 – had a registered rent (Todd 1986). Even within the stock of private lettings, only a quarter had a registered rent in 1978 (Todd et al. 1982). Again, security of tenure was itself only a symptom of the lack of profitability of rented housing rather a cause of it (Kemp 1988a).

Thus, deregulation and weakening tenants' security did not adequately serve to close the gap between what tenants could afford to pay in rent and what landlords needed to charge in order to get a competitive rate of return. While subsidies were provided, the BES was seen only as a kick-start to attract investment and not as a continuing support for private renting. Apart from the cost which such subsidies would mean if kept in place for a substantial period, the provision of subsidies would be an acknowledgement that the market, left to itself, was not capable of providing affordable and acceptable housing to rent. To that extent, the Conservatives' approach was based on an inadequate causal theory.

In addition, the policy to revive private renting was in apparent conflict with two other Conservative objectives. First, for reasons discussed above, the provision of tax reliefs to home owners was an important factor behind the continuing decline of private renting. But abolishing or phasing out these tax reliefs would have, at the very least, appeared to undermine their most important housing goal, which was the growth of home ownership. Second, the revival of private renting was in conflict with the objective of reducing, or containing the growth of, public expenditure. The growing cost of housing benefit was contained by numerous cuts in housing benefit levels during the 1980s (Hills 1991). These cuts, particularly in 1988 when those under 25 – the key demand group for private renting – were especially affected (Kemp 1990), will have reduced the ability of private tenants to afford to pay their rent.

Much of the problem for the Conservatives in attempting to revive the private rented sector was that they were, almost by definition, reliant on non-government actors – private investors and private organizations – to implement their policies for them. Market-led policy implementation is almost bound to be more difficult to control than policies which are implemented via public-sector agencies. Unlike local authorities, the private sector could not be compelled to invest in housing to let. Rather, the attractiveness of private renting on either the demand or the supply side had to be improved compared with the available alternatives. Despite making some progress in that direction, the measures taken did not go nearly far enough to tackle the fundamental causes of the problem.

References

Crook, A.D.H. (1986) 'Privatisation of housing and the impact of the Conservative Government's initiatives on low-cost home ownership and private renting between 1979 and 1984 in England and Wales: 4. Private renting', *Environment and Planning A*, Vol. 18: 1029–1037.

Crook, A.D.H. and Martin, G. J.(1988) 'Property speculation, local authority policy and the decline of privately rented housing in the 1980s: a case study of Sheffield', in P.A. Kemp (ed.) *The Private Provision of Rented Housing*, Aldershot, Avebury.

Crook, A.D.H., Kemp, P. A., Anderson, I. and Bowman, S. (1991) *Tax Incentives and the Revival of Private Renting*, York, Cloister Press.

Department of the Environment (1977) *Housing Policy Review, Technical Volume III*, London, HMSO.

Department of the Environment (1984) *Assured Tenancies*, Housing Booklet, No. 17, London, HMSO.

Department of the Environment (1987a) *Housing: The Government's Proposals*, London, HMSO.

Department of the Environment (1987b) *New Directions for Council Housing*, London, HMSO.

Department of the Environment (1991) *Housing and Construction Statistics 1980–1990*, London, HMSO.

Dodd, T. (1990) *Private Renting in 1988*, London, HMSO.

Doling, J. and Davies, M. (1984) *The Public Control of Privately Rented Housing*, Aldershot, Gower.

Hamnett, C. and Randolph, B. (1988) *Cities, Housing and Profits*, London, Hutchinson.

Hills, J. (1991) *Unravelling Housing Finance*, Oxford, Oxford University Press.

House of Commons Environment Committee (1982) *The Private Rented Housing Sector, Volume 1. Report*, London, HMSO.

Kemp, P.A. (1984) 'The Transformation of the Urban Housing Market in Britain c1885–1939', DPhil Thesis, Brighton, University of Sussex.

Kemp, P.A. (1987) 'The ghost of Rachman', *New Society*, 6 November.

Kemp, P.A. (1988a) *The Future of Private Renting*, Salford, University of Salford.

Kemp, P.A. (1988b) 'The impact of the assured tenancy scheme, 1980–1986', in P.A. Kemp (ed.) *The Private Provision of Rented Housing*, pp.78–95, Aldershot, Avebury.

Kemp, P.A. (1988c) 'New proposals for private renting: creating a commercially viable climate for investment in rented housing?' in P.A. Kemp (ed.) *The Private Provision of Rented Housing*, pp. 175–185, Aldershot, Avebury.

Kemp, P.A. (1990) 'Deregulation, markets and the 1988 Housing Act', *Social Policy and Administration*, Vol. 24.

Lamont, N. (1988) 'The business of renting', *Housing Review*, November–December.

Nevitt, A.A. (1966) *Housing, Taxation and Subsidies*, London, Nelson.

OPCS (1991) 'The 1990 private renters survey: preliminary results', *OPCS Monitor SS91/2*.

Patten, J. (1987) 'Interview with John Patten, Minister for Housing', *Roof*, January–February.

Saunders, P. (1990) *A Nation of Home Owners*, London, Allen and Unwin.

SHAC (1981) *Good Housekeeping: An Examination of Housing Repair and Improvement Policy*, London, SHAC.

Todd, J.E. (1986) *Recent Private Lettings*, London, HMSO.

Todd, J.E., Bone, M.R. and Noble, I. (1982) *The Privately Rented Sector in 1978*, London, HMSO.

Waldegrave, W. (1987) *Some Reflections on Housing Policy*, London, Conservative News Service.

Whitehead, C. (1979) 'Why owner-occupation?', *CES Review*, No. 7: 37–50.

Whitehead, C. and Kleinman, M. (1989) 'The private rented sector and the Housing Act 1988', in M. Brenton and C. Ungerson (eds) *Social Policy Review 1988–9*, pp. 65–84, London, Longman.

Young, G. (1989) 'Review of "The Future of Private Renting"', *Search*, No. 1, February: 27–28.

Young, G. (1991) 'Speech by Sir George Young', presented to a seminar on *The BES and Rented Housing: What Next?'* July, London.

CHAPTER 6

Remodelling a HAT: the implementation of the Housing Action Trust legislation 1987–92

VALERIE KARN

Introduction

In 1987, in the Conservative Party's election manifesto, Nicholas Ridley, the Secretary of State for the Environment, announced his intention to introduce Housing Action Trusts (HATs). He later described them as 'the cutting edge of the Government's inner city regeneration drive' (Dennis 1990: 14).

These HATs were to be corporations appointed by the Secretary of State to take over large, run-down, local authority housing estates, to 'secure the repair and improvement' and 'proper and effective management and use' of the housing (Housing Act 1988: 63, 1a,b) and then transfer ownership to new private or voluntary sector landlords. In the initial formulation, a re-transfer to the local authority was not envisaged. The idea was that in future the HATs programme would be substantially financed from the proceeds of sales of land and renovated property. In this way, public expenditure would be minimized and private finance could be channelled into renovation.

HATs were to be subject to very streamlined, rapid procedures, by-passing local government. The HAT areas were to be selected by the Secretary of State and, though local authorities and tenants would be consulted, there was to be no tenant ballot and no local authority veto. The Chair and members of the HAT Board would be appointed by the Secretary of State as individuals, not as representatives of other bodies, e.g. tenants' associations or local authorities.

The White Paper on Housing was published in September 1987, followed by the Consultation Document on Housing Action Trusts, on 18 October (Department of the Environment 1987). The Housing Bill containing the HATs legislation was introduced by Nicholas Ridley on 19 November. On 11 July of the following year, William Waldegrave, the Housing Minister, announced the 18 council estates in six areas (Leeds, Southwark, Sandwell, Sunderland, Tower Hamlets and Lambeth) where the Government proposed to establish the pilot HATs. Consultants were subsequently appointed to do feasibility studies in these areas. In fact, none of the six selected HATs came to fruition and by mid-1990 it looked as if no HATs at all might be declared. However, behind the scenes, Waltham Forest and Hull had started negotiations with the Government about HATs in their areas. By late 1991, HATs had been confirmed in both these areas, and, even more significantly, HATs were under discussion by a number of local authorities, including Brent, Liverpool and Birmingham, and a proposal in Tower Hamlets had been revived.

To understand what went so wrong with the implementation of HATs from 1987 to 1990 and why this position changed so dramatically, we need to look at the aims and character of the legislation, its presentation and the responses of local authorities and tenants.

The aims of HATs and their impact on implementation

The HATs policy's primary aim was the renewal of local authority estates, but it had two strong supplementary aims. The first of these was openly stated in the legislation, namely to introduce diversity in ownership of housing and in particular 'diversity in the identity of landlords' (Housing Act 1988: 63, 1c). HATs were an integral part of the policy of eliminating, or at least minimizing, local authority ownership of rental housing and substituting 'independent landlords'.

The second aim was made clear in the confrontational way in which the legislation was presented: it was clearly intended to 'diminish and humiliate local authorities' (Lord McIntosh of Haringey 1988). The original HATs legislation has, in fact, to be seen in the wider context of the Thatcher Government's attack on local government and in particular on Labour-controlled, urban local authorities.

The Government's presentation of HATs as a way of rescuing tenants from incompetent local authorities came out very clearly in exchanges in the House of Commons on 11 July 1988 (*House of Commons Debates* 11 July 1988: cols 24–28):

> MR JOHN HEDDLE (MID STAFFORDSHIRE): Will my Hon. Friend accept the congratulations of all the tenants in the areas that he has mentioned, as the opportunity that he has just announced will enable them to release themselves from the clutches of unsympathetic local authority landlords? ... Does my Hon. Friend also agree that HATs will produce better housing management and more sympathetic living conditions for those who are currently homeless?
>
> MR WILLIAM WALDEGRAVE: I welcome my Hon. Friend's support for this extremely important matter. To put it politely, it is perfectly obvious that some local authorities that cover the estates cannot grapple with the severity of the problems they presently face.
>
> MR ROBERT G. HUGHES (HARROW WEST): Does my Hon. Friend accept

that his statement today will bring real relief and help to people in Labour-controlled areas who have been left to rot by successive Labour councils in places in which no Labour Members would wish to live?

SIR GEORGE YOUNG (EALING, ACTON): Is my Hon. Friend aware that his statement will be widely welcomed, not least by tenants in difficult-to-let estates throughout the country, who have been failed by their local authorities?

But tenants, far from feeling rescued, were alarmed at the prospects of HATs, which they saw as 'yet another attack on public sector housing, local democracy and the emerging tenants movement' (*Community Action* 1988, 80: 22). For them, the welcome promise of resources for renewal was submerged by the fear of privatization and the loss of democratic accountability. The budget announced for the first six HATs was £125 million, over three years, or about £20 million per area. It was abundantly clear that this would only go a small way to meeting the cost of renovations in the sorts of areas being discussed and the tenants feared that the balance would be met by transferring property to the private sector.

The local authorities were placed in an invidious position. They badly needed resources to renew their run-down estates, especially as Housing Investment Programmes had been savagely cut. Some would have agreed to hand over their property to a HAT in order to be relieved of the managerial and financial strain that they represented, particularly as they were about to face the ring fencing of housing revenue accounts. However, the confrontational manner in which HATs were presented made it politically impossible for them to accept them. In doing so they would be seen to be both accepting humiliating terms for themselves and colluding with central government in putting tenants at risk of being priced out of the areas in which they lived.

The combination of these factors was therefore to make HATs, in their original form and style, unacceptable both to tenants and to local authorities. As a result, an alliance of local authorities and tenants sprang up with the apparently unlikely aim of rejecting substantial HAT investment for the renovation of some of the most run-down estates in Britain. This was despite the fact that the Secretary of State and his Ministers made it abundantly clear that, however bad their conditions, estates that turned down a HAT could not expect any extra resources to be channelled through the local authorities:

MR WILLIAM WALDEGRAVE: ... if additional allocations were made to a number of boroughs ... the way in which that money would be spent would be extremely unpredictable, to put it politely, and it may be wasted. [*House of Commons Debates* 11 July 1988: col. 27]

MR NICHOLAS RIDLEY: It will be for individual tenants to decide whether they want to proceed. If they do not want a Trust, then the available resources can be used to tackle areas and problem housing elsewhere. [*House of Commons Debates* 16 March 1989, Written Answers: col. 324].

On their side, the Government appeared to be convinced that tenants would welcome HATs and that they could be used as a weapon to help impose these arrangements, should local government not succumb to the financial pressures to accept them.

The political naivety of this was remarkable on three counts. First, government appeared to have overlooked the threat that tenure diversification, loss of secure tenure and the likelihood of raised rents presented to local authority tenants. Even housing association tenancies were regarded with alarm because, under the new legislation, they became subject to assured not secure tenancies and a new financial regime with severe implications for rent levels.

Second, ministers grossly exaggerated the degree of hostility of tenants of such areas towards their local authorities, as compared with their hostility to the Conservative Government's own housing policies. Even in badly managed estates there were strong elements of 'better the devil we know'.

And finally, it seems extraordinary that government thought that, even if HATs could have been imposed against the will of local authorities and tenants, they could have operated effectively in such a confrontational climate. Even though the legislation allowed HATs to take over many local authority powers within the HAT boundary, the opportunities for local authority obstruction would have been manifold, both during and after the handover period. The complexity of the preparations needed for the handover of GLC estates to the London boroughs, in a collaborative climate, should have provided a warning. Indeed, this very point was made by civil servants during the consultation around the White Paper, but ignored.

But, as Hyder (1984: 1), Metcalfe (1984: 116) and others have observed, governments have a tendency to believe that once a policy has been announced, its implementation is assured. In the case of the HATs policy, as in so many others (Hyder 1984: 1),

> an easy assumption prevailed that, once a decision had been taken, its execution was a simple and mundane affair that did not merit a great deal of attention.

With its very large Commons majority, the Government was clearly tempted to feel that it could with impunity introduce and enforce any policy it chose, including HATs. But over a period of time, it had to come to terms with the fact that there are other forms of effective democratic opposition than defeating the government in the House of Commons. Government had eventually to concede that HATs could not be imposed; they had to be negotiated both with tenants and with local authorities. Only after this had happened did any HATs appear.

Phases of implementation

It is possible to identify four distinct but overlapping phases in the implementation of HATs, which mark their progression from confrontation to negotiation, and from coercion to incentive (see Chapter 3).

Phase one

The first can be called the *legislative phase*. This lasted from the introduction of the White Paper in September 1987 until 11 November 1988, when the Housing Act became law. From the very first, there was strong tenant opposition to HATs. In the original legislation, as mentioned earlier, there was no provision for a tenant ballot. This proved to be both an issue in its own right and one that exacerbated worries about other factors, such as security of tenure, rent levels, rehousing rights, privatization, etc. and deepened suspicions that the whole programme was more about the forcible imposition of privatization than renewal of the estates for the existing occupants (Woodward 1991).

There quickly grew up national networks of tenants' groups from estates that felt under threat. Rumour was rife about which areas were to be selected. Every deteriorated council estate in a Labour-controlled urban authority regarded itself as a target. The atmosphere of doubt was made worse by the vagueness of the legislation about what constituted 'consultation' and at what stage this could occur. Questions were constantly being put in Parliament about secret discussions that were supposed to have been taking place on the suitability of particular estates.

Despite all this public anxiety, the Government at first rejected all requests to modify the HATs legislation to be more acceptable either to tenants or to local authorities. For instance, negotiations between the tenants of the Hulme estate in Manchester and William Waldegrave, between December 1987 and May 1988, about an 'agreed HAT', collapsed when he felt unable to meet any of their conditions (Shaughnessy 1989). Having failed to gain acceptance of their 'charter' the tenants mounted a successful campaign to persuade the minister to exclude them from the 'target' list (Dibblin 1988; *Community Action* 80: 23–24).

However, during the Committee stage of the Bill the Government began to make some concessions to the tenants and local authorities. In particular, it was agreed that property could be re-transferred from the HAT to the local authority, if the tenants wanted that, and if the local authority agreed. This allayed some fears about privatization but anxiety and mistrust remained, partly because of the implications of such repurchases for local authority borrowing, but largely because the stated aim of HATs was to 'diversify' ownership away from local authorities.

In 1988, however, most tenant opposition focused on the refusal of the Government to allow a tenant ballot. Though the House of Lords defeated the Government on 28 July 1988, by 102 votes to 95 on an amendment to introduce a ballot, the Government refused to accept this amendment on the grounds that there was no chance of balanced and informed opinion amongst tenants, as a result of being 'misinformed' by Labour-controlled councils (*House of Commons Debates* 2 November 1988: col. 1156).

But suddenly, on 7 November 1988, the day before the amendments to the Housing Bill had to be tabled, Lord Caithness, 'cornered by Dimbleby on TV, blurted out that the tenants in HAT estates would get a ballot' ('On the Record',

BBC Television: 6 November 1988). This was greeted as 'one of the most significant victories for organized tenants in the Thatcher era' (*Community Action* 1988, 81: 9). Why the concession was suddenly made, was not explained. After all, ministers had been long aware of tenant hostility to HATs. Some said it was 'just a monumental blunder by the Minister, others that the Government's business managers decided they couldn't risk the bill running out of time if there was a further rebellion in the Lords' (*Community Action* 1988, 81: 9).

Government still maintained that the lack of a ballot was the sole cause of real complaint and that other tenant opposition was merely whipped up by Labour Party campaigning and 'municipal harassment' (*House of Commons Debates* 2 November 1988: col. 1005). As Nicholas Ridley stated in the House of Commons on November 11, the day the Housing Act was passed (*House of Commons Debates* 11 November 1988: cols 676–77):

> We have heard wildly exaggerated fears that have been sown in their minds, and the absence of a ballot was the one clear point to unite opposition. I came to the view that real arguments were impossible to get across if the ballot question was obscured. Let there be a ballot. I am proposing that there should be a ballot. Then there will be only one issue: which is more important – the political opposition of the Labour Party, or greatly improved living conditions for the people in these areas?

However, the concession of a ballot was to solve nothing for government. It did not significantly reduce hostility and it made the imposition of a HAT impossible.

Phase two

The second, or *feasibility studies*, phase overlapped the 'legislative phase' and began on 11 July 1988, when William Waldegrave announced the names of the six pilot HAT areas and the appointment of consultants to do feasibility studies on them.

It is said that there were two schools of thought amongst officials in the Department of the Environment about the types of areas which should be selected. The first thought that the policy would lack any credibility as a vehicle for tackling urban renewal if it did not target the very worst estates. The other favoured selecting less deteriorated areas where successes could be more easily and quickly demonstrated. There was an additional criterion to be considered, namely the potential attractiveness of estates to private-sector investment. In the end, the Department came up with a rather mixed looking group. The Sunderland and Leeds estates certainly were not amongst the worst in Britain, and in Sandwell local authority plans for redeveloping the selected estates were already well under way (Grant 1988: 22). Some of the estates in Lambeth, Southwark and Tower Hamlets were very deteriorated but others had already received substantial improvement and their choice was described by tenants as 'eccentric' (Woodward 1991: 48). There were also very strong overtones of potential for private development particularly in those estates bordering Docklands (Woodward 1991: 48).

The local authorities were not consulted about the choice of areas and the Government's dismissive approach maximized their hostility. As William Waldegrave replied to Mr Chris Mullin, the MP for Sunderland South (*House of Commons Debates* 11 July 1988: col. 29):

> There were no formal consultations with local authorities before the estates were designated. That has always been made clear. The time for consultations is now ... It is right that the proposals should be put to the House before they are discussed with outside interests.

From the tenants' side, the first round of public meetings produced large turnouts, 700 in Sunderland, 100 in Leeds, 90 in Southwark and over 1000 in Tower Hamlets (Woodward 1991: 46; *Community Action* 80: 25).

Even after the ballot issue was resolved, the consultants found that there were many other causes for uncertainty and hostility. The tenants were worried that tenanted property was going to be sold to private landlords: 'who were only interested in maximising their profits' (PIC/Peat Marwick McLintock 1989: 31); that rent levels would 'skyrocket and become unaffordable'; that the estates would 'move up-market' and that the existing tenants would be 'long-term losers' in that process; that they would lose their right to transfer out of the estate into other local authority housing after the designation of the HAT and that their security of tenure 'would be materially and adversely affected'. Although, under the legislation, tenants of the HAT actually had secure tenancies, it was unclear what would happen after the property was sold to other landlords (Woodward 1991: 47).

In essence, people did not really know what they would be letting themselves in for. As PIC/Peat Marwick McLintock put it (1989: 31–32):

> There was a critical problem here, namely that the 1988 Housing Act provides that the HAT itself develop the plans for the estates *after* it has been created.

Residents would not know what HATs would mean for them until after they had committed themselves by a ballot to the HATs process. In addition, while they would be consulted about plans after the HAT had been declared, they had no veto on the form that future plans would take. This insecurity was to lead tenants to demand major representation on the Board of the HAT to ensure that plans were not carried through that were detrimental to their interests. But here again there was a problem. Since HAT board members were to be appointed as individuals and not as representatives of particular bodies such as residents' associations, they would not be accountable to any tenant body and not removable by them. The Secretary of State, on the other hand, could remove or replace members at will and could reverse decisions of the Board.

The consultants came to the view that if the HATs policy were to have any chance of implementation a number of things had to be done. First of all, the confrontational approach to local government needed to be dropped. Central government had to 'procure the understanding and support of the local authorities' for the designation of a HAT in their area. The first step in 'bridging the divide which exists between central and local government over the HAT programme' should come from central government offering discussions and consultation (PIC/Peat Marwick McLintock 1989: 32).

Secondly, because residents did not know what the HAT was going to do, illustrative plans should be distributed to all households affected by a HAT proposal, before any ballots were held. These plans should be specific to individual estates and should cover physical renovation, financial arrangements, costs, rent policies and likely rent levels, future management structure and consultation and participation procedures. The consultants also advised that there should be statements about what sort of arrangements might be made after the HAT finished, which landlords the HAT would be likely to be handed on to, and what the rent structure of those landlords was likely to be. Although HATs were housing-only operations, the problems of these estates were of course much wider than just housing, so it was also considered important to lay out how such issues as employment, education and race relations were to be dealt with.

The third and final recommendation of PIC/Peat Marwick McLintock was that, given the tremendous hostility, at least six months should be allowed for consultation processes after these plans had gone out, to give time for the bitter feelings to heal and to allow time to involve tenants in making plans 'their own' before endorsing them in a ballot (PIC/Peat Marwick McLintock 1989: 33).

Just as crucial as the consultants' comments on the acceptability of HATs were their estimates of costs. By November 1988 the original budget for the HATs programme had been raised to £192 million, spread over three years, but the consultants' reports suggested that this would still be inadequate and that subsequent years would require even larger investment. The consultants' estimates of costs were: Southwark, £112 million; Lambeth, between £93 and £132 million; Leeds £135 million; Sandwell, £13.5–£22.4 million; Tower Hamlets, £231 million including the cost of dealing with overcrowding; and Sunderland, between £51 and £75 million, depending on the scale of Right to Buy sales. The overall costs for the six areas were estimated at £404.5–£476.4 million, including the cost of dealing with rehousing to reduce overcrowding in the Tower Hamlets estate (Burrows 1989: 52). PIC/Peat Marwick McLintock (1989: 59–75) estimated that £97 million would be recoverable by sales of the property at the end of the HAT, either to local authorities or housing associations/co-operatives. Even phased over ten years, these costs were clearly far beyond those originally projected and the prospects of recycling profits from sales to fund later rounds of HATs relatively limited.

Finally, in terms of the suitability of the areas they were asked to review, PIC/Peat Marwick McLintock expressed reservations about the wisdom of designating a HAT in the estate in Sunderland, where problems 'were clearly of a lower order of magnitude than those found to be present in London'. They considered that 'the HAT programme would be more coherent and logical, and more widely accepted within the housing community if it was confined to situations that would be described as 'an exceptional response to an exceptional situation' (PIC/Peat Marwick McLintock 1989: 58).

It had been the Government's intention to proceed with declaring HATs by April 1989. Instead, in view of the consultants' warnings, in March 1989 the Secretary of State announced, more cautiously, that he had decided to 'proceed towards the declaration of HATs' in nine estates in five areas, but that consultants would be re-appointed to carry out further consultations in preparation for the ballots. The areas selected were: Lambeth (Loughborough and Angel Town Estates); Southwark (North Peckham and Gloucester Grove Estates); Sunderland, (Downhill, Townend Farm, Hylton Castle and part of Red House Estates); and Leeds (Gipton Estate). In Sandwell, where Price Waterhouse said that conditions on the Lion Farm Estate did not justify a HAT, the Windmill and Cape Hill Estates were selected. In Tower Hamlets, it was decided not to proceed with the designation of a HAT in the suggested estates. The official reason given was that the over-crowding problem could not be relieved within the designated area or within the cost constraints of the programme. However, the extraordinary level of tenant hostility and turnout at meetings may also have been a factor (Woodward 1991).

Phase three

The third, or *ballots phase*, began in March 1989. To try to defuse opposition the Government wrote to all five areas giving written guarantees that the local authority would be allowed supplementary credit approvals to buy back the estates when the HAT was wound up, if that is what the tenants wanted. But despite this, in most areas, the minds of both tenants and local authorities were already effectively made up.

In September 1989, Lambeth commissioned its own MORI poll which showed that 72 per cent of tenants in the Angel Town and Loughborough estates would reject a HAT (Frew 1990: 13). In March 1990, the tenants of the Gipton Estate in Leeds, backed by the council, organized their own ballot. In response to a question about whether the tenants' group should negotiate with the Government over proposals for a HAT or ask the Government to withdraw the proposals, 92 per cent voted for withdrawal on a 53 per cent turnout (*Inside Housing* 9 March 1990: 7).

In Sandwell, the tenants had formed SHOC (Sandwell HAT Opposition Campaign) to demonstrate their active opposition. But, right from July 1988, the local authority had its own independent strategy, namely 'to show the DoE that we could achieve what a HAT aimed to without a HAT being imposed' (Dwelly 1990: 25). It had immediately opened local housing offices to demonstrate its commitment to management reform and sold 240 of the worst properties on the Lion Farm Estate to a construction firm, on the condition that they should be 'razed to the ground immediately'. This had resulted in the Lion Farm Estate being dropped from the list of HAT estates but the Windmill Lane and Cape Hill Estates were still affected. The council proceeded with more demolitions and sales to housing associations and hired their own consultants to work out improvement schemes. However, the tenants felt excluded and suspicious and demanded participation in the plans. Eventually new consultants worked with the tenants to produce an Estate Action proposal and the campaigns of the tenants and local authority came together with increasing coherence.

In effect, only Southwark and Sunderland appeared to offer a real possibility of a 'Yes' vote. Government therefore concentrated attention on these, putting huge resources into consultancies, and offering vastly increased financial allocations, £80 million in Sunderland and £112 million in Southwark, more than the entire budget for the six original ones. In addition further concessions about rent levels, etc. were made to try to win over the tenants.

In Sunderland the council neither publicly supported nor opposed the HAT. They would accept it if the tenants voted in favour (Bright 1990: 8). The main tenants' organization (STAND – Sunderland Tenants Against No Democracy) which had lobbied Parliament about the ballot, campaigned for a say in the running of the HAT, but, once these government undertakings had been given, did not oppose it. However, in the end, in April 1990, there was an 80 per cent 'No' vote in Sunderland (*Inside Housing* 1990, 5: 5). The explanation was worry about the reliability of government's assurances. A number of individuals and agencies including the local MP, Bob Clay, had obtained legal opinion that the assurances would be unenforceable (Bright 1990: 8). Legal opinion by Hodge, James and Allen was that:

> The local authority could not enter a legally binding agreement to buy back property when it has not even been transferred to a HAT and a HAT is not in existence. A local authority could make a policy statement that it would repurchase housing stock from a HAT if possible. Such a statement is of little use as it would not bind future councils and the HAT could not be bound to sell back to the local authorities.

At this point, between April and June 1990, the Government, recognizing that if Sunderland was not winnable, Lambeth, Leeds and Sandwell were hopeless, withdrew its HATs proposals in all four areas. In Sandwell the Government said they had withdrawn because the local authority was making progress in dealing with the problems and a £7 million Estate Action programme was approved.

Like the Sunderland tenants, the Southwark tenants' representatives, especially those on the North Peckham estate, had adopted a negotiating stance with the Government rather than just outright opposition. But in Southwark, the negotiations went much further. Working with PIC, the tenants' associations prepared a package that in the end they felt able to recommend. This included (Dwelly 1991: 25):

> better rights of repair, a rent arrears policy, the promised establishment of estate management boards, guarantees that no private landlords or non-social landlords would appear and no emptied homes would be sold, individual household vetoes over change of landlord during the HAT, decanting and arbitration procedures and a rent freeze until rents equal 80

per cent of the borough average, and four places for tenants on the eleven member HAT board.

The Government became fairly confident of getting a favourable response at least in the North Peckham estate. However, in the event, the ballot in Southwark produced a 'No' vote; 67 per cent against on North Peckham Estate and 73 per cent against on Gloucester Grove. This was announced on 5 October 1990. The explanation of this 'No' vote, varied according to the source. One side said PIC had only ever talked to tenants' associations and not won people over by door-to-door visits. The other said that it was largely to do with Southwark's opposition (Frew 1990: 12):

> Southwark council's eleventh-hour decision to campaign against the HAT undoubtedly had an important influence on the outcome of the ballot. The council's opposition was not on the substance of the proposals but rather on the possibility that the commitments would not be honoured by the Government and the HAT board.
>
> The council correctly pointed out that it was not possible to make many of the key pledges on the HAT legally binding. It argued that there was no certainty that the Government or HAT board would not depart from these pledges at some future date, adding that such a danger was made all the more real by the fact that the Government nominees would form a clear majority on the HAT board.

Again, lack of certainty and lack of trust in central government had prevented a HAT. Whatever government's assurances, there was no getting away from what the legislation entitled the Secretary of State to do, if he chose.

Not surprisingly, by this point people were asking whether the Southwark result would 'bring down the final curtain on the entire HAT programme' (Frew, 1990). There had been recent press publicity about a leaked internal government memo indicating that the Department of the Environment was coming under pressure to abandon the HAT programme. Certainly by this time, the programme did not look like very good value for money. Although no HATs had been started, the cost in consultants' fees had reached £2 923 000 by 31 October 1990, £667 000 of which was spent in Sunderland and £1 411 000 in Southwark. A further £93 000 had been spent on information materials and the two ballots (*House of Commons Debates* 20 November 1990, Written Answers, col. 62). In Lambeth, Leeds, Sandwell and Southwark the local authorities had also hired their own consultants, and so did the tenants in Leeds and Tower Hamlets, at a total cost of over £200 000 (Frew 1990: 13).

However, the HAT programme was not dead. In parallel with the dying throes of the 'famous five' HATs, there had already arisen some new possibilities, which we discuss in the next section.

Phase four

The fourth, or *local authority HAT*, phase began behind the scenes in November 1989 when discussion started about the possibility of using a HAT to finance the renewal of four estates of panel concrete construction housing in Waltham Forest LBC (Cathall Road, Oliver Close, Chingford Hall and Boundary Road). The problem of what to do about these four estates had been exercising Waltham Forest for the last five years or more. The very high cost of refurbishment and associated decanting problems had led Waltham Forest to engage the architects, Hunt Thompson, to investigate, in close consultation with tenants, the feasibility of phased redevelopment. However, Waltham Forest could not finance such a project through its Housing Investment Programme, and in 1988 a proposal for a joint council/tenant company to redevelop the estates floundered when the Government changed the rules about leasebacks. Similarly the idea of a tenant-controlled housing association acquiring the estates from the council through Tenants' Choice, failed when the DoE, in September 1989, refused to allow the council to pay the association a 'dowry' reflecting the negative value of the unimproved estates (Owens 1992: 18). Embarrassingly for the Government, the scheme had received wide publicity and, in particular, the tenants' and Hunt Thompson's efforts had come to the notice of the Prince of Wales, who had publicly praised it as an example of 'community architecture'. Now he declared his concern about the absence of funding. After 'strenuous lobbying, involving local MP Norman Tebbit', the HAT solution was offered in November 1989 (Owens 1992: 18). In February 1990, Waltham Forest confirmed that it would be initiating formal negotiations with the DoE about a HAT, the first local authority to do so.

Waltham Forest itself took a neutral stance on the HAT, letting the very well established tenants' organizations negotiate terms and make up their own minds. The tenants drew up a lengthy 'tenant expectations document' (TED), setting out how they would like the HAT to operate (Owens 1992: 17; *Inside Housing* 1991, 28: 3; 31: 3). There were a number of important requirements, notably about tenants' ability to decide their final landlord. But perhaps most important, the tenants won strong representation on the HAT board (four out of eleven places, along with one councillor and five DoE nominees, plus the Chair). The negotiations about the TED took from December 1990 until July 1991, when there was an 81 per cent vote in favour of a HAT. The HAT, carrying with it £170 million of investment, started in April 1992.

But Waltham Forest, though the first to negotiate about a HAT, was not the first to finalize one; they were overtaken by Kingston upon Hull. Hull had started private negotiations about a HAT in North Hull in early 1990, and had carried out their own feasibility study but this had been a very well kept secret. The official announcement didn't come until November 1990 (Bright 1991: 8–9). After that, the procedures were so expedited that the consultations and ballot were all completed in four months. In March 1991, the ballot produced a 69 per cent majority for the HAT (*Inside Housing* 1991, April 19: 1).

The HAT area comprised about 2000 unimproved pre-war houses on the North Hull estate. The other 1800 houses on the estate had already been improved by the local authority but dwindling resources meant that the rest would have a long wait. As Dwelly comments, 'despite the homes' obvious need for improvement, it is hard to square the condition of these properties with the

Government's assertion that HATs are meant to urgently remedy Britain's worst estates' (Dwelly 1991: 22). North Hull was not even, according to Hull officers, the worst estate in Hull. It was chosen, according to the Chair of Housing, John Black, for purely expedient reasons, because of its size: 'We needed an area with the scale for a HAT. The council has to maximize investment and we believed £50 million was the minimum amount the DoE would look at under the HAT arrangements' (Dwelly 1991: 22). The authority also wanted an estate which would bring in a capital receipt from its sale to the HAT, part of which could be used to improve other housing.

The Hull HAT was a compromise between an authority that wanted housing resources and the DoE, which was desperate to find 'a pragmatic local authority willing to persuade its tenants that a HAT was in their interests' (Dwelly 1991: 23). The DoE did not even do its own feasibility study, but accepted Hull's study and raised no objection that the area was not sufficiently run-down. Clearly, the main aim of the HAT programme by this time was to have any HAT at all; the coherence of a HAT strategy was a dispensable luxury.

Nationally, the Hull HAT was much more controversial than Waltham Forest's because in Waltham Forest the tenants were highly organized and active and the local authority, after initial discussion, left the decision to them. In North Hull there was no tenants' association and the local authority campaigned hard for a 'Yes' vote, allowing only a very short preparatory period and limited opportunities for the tenants to take external advice. The authority made a promotional video in which it emphasized that the 'North Hull Voluntary HAT' was an entirely different prospect to the HATs rejected elsewhere. In reality, the agreed concessions for tenants were not as great as those in Southwark; North Hull tenants have only two board members out of the eleven. (The council had in fact argued for only one tenant and four councillors on the Board, but Sir George Young and the tenants pressed for two tenants and three councillors.)

The distinctive thing about the Hull HAT is that it is very clearly a local authority vehicle. Apart from the fact that there are three councillors on the board, the Chair of Housing of the local authority, John Black, is the deputy Chair of the HAT and the chief executive of the HAT was formerly the director of Housing of Hull (*Inside Housing* 1991, 36: 6). The first housing association development in the HAT area has gone to a housing association of which John Black is the Chair; the city treasurer is the treasurer and the town clerk is the secretary (*Inside Housing* 1991, 45: 1). The council has also won two contracts for architectural and legal work on the estate and the direct services organization is bidding for the repairs contracts. The council is also initially handling the housing management and repairs on an agency basis after the handover in January 1992 (*Inside Housing* 1991, 45: 1). So the Hull HAT is far removed from Nicholas Ridley's original brainchild.

The announcement of the Hull HAT negotiations and the progress in Waltham Forest led other authorities to consider the merits of seeking this funding for run-down estates. The first to announce its intention to do so was Liverpool in April 1991, with a plan to deal with all its tower blocks in this way

(*Inside Housing* 1991, 15: 5; 25: 1). Consultants were hired to advise the tenants and a vote was due for May/June 1992 (*Inside Housing* 1991, 36: 5; 42: 3). Other schemes were progressing in Tower Hamlets, Brent, and elsewhere (*Inside Housing* 1991 38: 1; 40: 7).

The HATs policy shift towards collaboration with local authorities was finally made official on 10 July 1991, when Sir George Young in issuing new guidelines for HATs declared that (*House of Commons Debates* 10 July 1991: col. 960):

> The government are now anxious to work as hard as possible to ensure that, where HATs are proposed, that is done on the basis of collaboration and partnership. We do not want any of the adversarial politics that, sadly, were injected into some of the earlier proposals, mainly by people who were politically dogmatic and committed against HATs.

This placatory tone has to be seen not just as a product of the difficulties in implementing HATs but in the context of the arrival of the Major administration, the previous November. Although Sir George asserted that 'it is not the Government but Labour Members who are shifting their positions on Housing Action Trusts' (col. 959), the tone of his announcement could not have been in greater contrast to that of himself and his colleagues on 11 July 1988. Instead of the minister announcing the areas in which HATs were to be imposed, he was 'courting bids from local authorities for next year's programmes' (col. 956). Local authorities were described as sharing in the search for solutions rather than just as the cause of the problems; 'we must look to local authorities to propose solutions ...'. And the whole HATs programme was presented as providing (col. 957–8):

> a basis on which central and local government, with the active involvement and support of tenants, can work together over the coming years to eliminate the worst concentrations of run-down local authority housing.

On that occasion, Sir George Young also made clear that in future HAT schemes would have to be for areas which are 'so severely run down and present such exceptional problems that they are likely to be beyond the resources and capacity of the local authority, even with the support of the estate action and other programmes' (col. 957). Purely expedient schemes such as Hull's were now able to be a thing of the past.

Conclusion

An essential ingredient of robust policy design must clearly be either its acceptability to the 'beneficiaries' or the ability to enforce the legislation if it is not acceptable. The original HATs policy failed on both counts. The history of its implementation is marked by the process of modification of the presentation and substance of the programme and increase of the financial incentives to make it more acceptable, first to tenants and then to local authorities. Early attempts to placate tenants by conceding a ballot, ironically had the effect of making the policy unenforceable by central government, because tenants remained deeply uneasy about the programme and were now armed with the ability to prevent it. It then became necessary to placate local authorities, and use them to carry tenants along, as a means of achieving any implementation at all. Ultimately, the only HATs declared have been at the instigation, or with the agreement of local authorities and with the incentive of hugely increased allocations of public money. The allocations for the Waltham Forest and Liverpool HATs are worth £160 million and £190 million, respectively, each more than the original budget for all six. The budget for the Hull North HAT is £50 million, hardly exemplifying the policy to 'focus scarce public money more effectively' which the White Paper of September 1987 had heralded (*HMSO* 1987: 3).

Clearly, HATs evolved radically between 1987 and 1992, although the legislation upon which they are based remained the same as in 1988, and on the face of it the Hull and Waltham Forest tenants might have had the same misgivings as the tenants of Southwark and Sunderland. In the end, like the local authorities, they had to weigh the risks against the resources.

As Hyder (1984: 15) has said,

Implementation is the ... attempt at realising policy, its trial solution. It is more than the mechanical carrying out of policy. The process of implementation is capable of affecting policy or altering the policy process itself. The study of implementation often assumes fully formed, complete policies as the starting point. Most policies that are to be implemented are in fact unclear, tentative and subject to negotiation, and it is precisely because of their unsettled and unfinished nature that the implementation process has a close and creative interaction with policy. Thus the whole process may be regarded as evolutionary.

David Liggins, the Chair of the North Hull HAT, has said that, 'HATs are not viable. I think there will only be another three or four at most. In five years' time they will all be gone' (Bright 1991: 9). The form that HATs have taken to make them acceptable to tenants and local authorities has involved such a high level of direct government investment and such a small local authority contribution that they are unlikely to be repeated around the country (*Inside Housing* 1991, 48: 7).

The Government seems unlikely to permit or need more than a handful of 'face-saving' HATs. After the Major administration arrived, the Conservative Government became far less confrontational with local government, but just as effective in getting local authorities to accept policies such as 'diversification' of tenure. As Peter De Leon has remarked, 'the reformer's zeal brought to the political stage can be easily turned aside with a counter-zealot's parry' (De Leon 1987: 191); a more subtle approach can be more productive. Financial constraints, introduced by the Thatcher Government but retained by John Major, have been combined with incentive programmes, such as City Challenge, which are presented as partnerships between central and local government and the private sector. The combination of carrot and stick is being used to lever local authorities into types of renewal schemes which are little different from those which HATs were initially intended to produce. Hulme, as a potential HAT, was initially offered £50 million for housing renewal, but this figure would undoubtedly have risen dramatically had there been any chance of a favourable ballot. As a City Challenge area, Hulme will receive about £7 million a year over five years, for a whole range of renewal activities (not just housing) and the only new housing in the area will have to be produced by housing associations. In addition, all the hostility from tenants about raised rents, loss of social housing and lack of democratic control will be vented on the City Challenge local authorities and housing associations, not on central government.

It could be argued that, by 1992, Labour local authorities needed HATs (or at least the HAT funds) more than the Conservative Government did.

The author wishes to thank Hannah Moore for her invaluable assistance in tracing material for this chapter.

References

Bright, J. (1990) 'The down to earth approach to a HAT', *Inside Housing*, 30 March: 8–9.

Bright, J. (1991) 'Hull's HAT: a footnote in housing history', *Inside Housing*, 17 May: 8–9.

Burrows, L. (1989) *The Housing Act 1988: A Shelter Guide*, Shelter.

De Leon, P. (1987) 'Policy termination as a political phenomenon, in D.J. Palumbo (ed.) *The Politics of Program Evaluation*, Vol. 15, London, Sage Year Books in Politics and Public Policy

Dennis, F. (1990) 'HATs. Who needs them?', *Housing*, November: 14–15.

Department of the Environment (1987) *Housing Action Trusts. A Consultation Document*, DoE.

Dibblin, J. (1988) 'Hulme won't wear a HAT', *Roof*, July–August: 25–26.

Dwelly, T. (1990) 'More than bricks and mortar', *Roof*, July–August: 24–26.

Dwelly, T. (1991) 'Too much trust', *Roof*, March–April: 22–25.

Frew, R. (1990) 'A HAT's last stand', *Roof*, November–December: 12–13.

Grant, C. (1988) 'Old HAT', *Roof*, July–August: 22–24.

HMSO (1987) *Housing: The Government's Proposals*, Cmnd. 214, London.

Hyder, M. (1984) 'Implementation, the evolutionary model', in D. Lewis and H. Wallace (eds) *Policies into Practice: National and International Case Studies in Implementation*, London, Heinemann.

Lewis, D. and Wallace, H. (eds) (1984) *Policies into Practice: National and International Case Studies in Implementation*, London, Heinemann.

Lord McIntosh of Haringey (1988) *The Times*, Friday 29 July: 10, col. 3.

Metcalfe, J.L. (1984) 'Industrial strategy 1975–1979: the strategy that never was?' in D. Lewis and H. Wallace (eds) *Policies into Practice: National and International Case Studies in Implementation*, London, Heinemann.

Owens, R. (1992) 'If the HAT fits', *Roof*, January–February: 17–19.

PIC/Peat Marwick McLintock (1989) *Housing Action Trust Studies, Overall Report: Southwark, Lambeth, Tower Hamlets, Sunderland*, Department of the Environment.

Shaughnessy, H. (1989) 'Housing Action Trusts and communications structure: A study of state–tenant negotiations in a Manchester housing estate', *International Journal of Urban and Regional Research*, Vol. 13: 339–354.

Woodward, R. (1991) 'Mobilising opposition: the campaign against Housing Action Trusts in Tower Hamlets', *Housing Studies*, Vol. 6, No. 1: 44–56.

CHAPTER 7

The new financial regime for local authority housing

PETER MALPASS AND MATTHEW WARBURTON*

Introduction

The new financial regime for local authority housing in England and Wales, introduced by the Local Government and Housing Act 1989 has been in operation since 1 April 1990. (The new regime does not apply in Scotland which has its own legislation; see Gibb and Munro 1991: 98–104.) In the first two years of the new system, council rents in England rose by an average of 30 per cent, while in London rent increases of 50 per cent have been common, and in the London Borough of Ealing rents doubled between 1990 and 1991 (ADC 1991; AMA 1991; DoE 1991). At the same time capital spending has been cut significantly compared with the levels achieved in 1989–90. These have been the most obvious and dramatic effects of the new regime, but there are also other less obvious, although no less significant, repercussions for local authority housing and for central–local relations.

Most work on housing finance (Hills 1991; Garnett et al. 1991; Gibb and Munro 1991; Maclennan et al. 1991) falls within the boundaries of applied economics. However, the research reported here adopts a different perspective, which can be described as a policy approach to housing finance. This approach represents a more appropriate way to study the local implementation of central government legislation, and reference to implementation and its vicissitudes is an essential supplement to conventional work on housing finance and its reform. Much has been written about the level of rents which, in the view of those proposing reform, ought to be charged by local authorities (for a review see Hills 1990: chapter 16), but much less about how local authorities are to be

* The research on which this chapter is based was supported by the Joseph Rowntree Foundation between April 1990 and July 1992.

persuaded or coerced to set rents at these levels. To illustrate the point, the Second Report of the Inquiry into British Housing (Joseph Rowntree Foundation 1991: 49–50) puts forward a proposal for rents based on capital values but notes only that, 'there are difficulties . . . in enforcing rent regulation on local authorities' and contents itself with the hope that its proposal would 'commend itself on grounds of fairness'. The history of local authority housing finance strongly suggests that this is most unlikely, since councillors are jealous of their autonomy in matters of rent setting, and because a consensus on what constitutes fairness in this context is very hard to achieve. Past experience also suggests that implementing local authority housing finance policy poses problems which are neither insignificant nor easily resolved.

Rents and subsidies: the issues

This chapter and the research on which it draws are mainly concerned with aspects of the revenue side of local authority housing, namely questions of rents and subsidies. However, it is important to acknowledge that the revenue side cannot be understood in isolation from the capital side, because capital and revenue interact in significant ways. For most local authorities a significant proportion of revenue expenditure (averaging over 27 per cent in 1991–92 (CIPFA 1991: 5)) is accounted for by debt charges arising from borrowing for capital investment. The level of investment, in terms of the number and quality of houses built or improved, influences the amount which needs to be raised in rents. The issues raised by this vary according to whether the stock is growing from a small or large base, or if houses are being sold more rapidly than new ones are being built.

The basic problem in housing finance policy is that houses are expensive relative to earnings, because they occupy land and require large amounts of labour in their construction. As a result very few people can afford to buy outright, especially at the start of their independent adult lives. Renting provides one way of tackling this problem; it represents a method of spreading the cost of housing over time, giving access to a necessary item of consumption which cannot be paid for in full. Nevertheless, the implications of high costs on the one hand, and on the other a political commitment to an adequate supply of socially acceptable housing at affordable rents are generally accepted to include some degree of subsidy. The policy issues here are to do with questions of pricing and forms of subsidy: should rents be set at sub-market levels, with subsidy channelled to housing suppliers, or should rents be set by the market, with subsidy given to consumers? These are not mutually exclusive approaches and it is possible to have systems in which subsidy is channelled to both consumers and suppliers at the same time. The debate about different approaches to the level and delivery of subsidy is as old as council housing itself (Malpass 1991a).

Overlying these financial issues are questions about who decides the rate of investment and the level of rents. These are essentially aspects of the relationship between central and local government (see Chapter 2), and lie at the heart of the policy approach to housing finance. A feature of the history of council housing in Britain is the high level of real autonomy enjoyed by local authorities in relation to patterns of investment, rents, allocations policies, management structures and accounting practices. This freedom was never completely unbounded, and central government always sought to influence (rather than direct) local policies, and in particular to limit the Treasury's financial liability. But over the last 20 years, successive governments have adopted measures designed to restrict local autonomy, although it would be a mistake to see this as a simple, unproblematic and wholly successful exercise for the centre (Houlihan, 1988; Forrest and Murie 1990; Malpass 1990; Malpass and Murie 1990).

Part of the explanation for this changing relationship between the centre and the localities lies in the changing role played by council housing in the overall housing system. Apart from the Housing and Town Planning Act 1919, all subsidy legislation from the end of the First World War to 1972 gave assistance in the form of fixed amounts per dwelling per year for a certain number of years. In this sense, government assistance in that period can be seen as investment subsidy, since it was related to the rate of new building over time, rather than to the state of the housing revenue account (HRA) in any particular year. The old system of fixed annual payments combined three important features which enabled it to endure for so long. First, it meant that the Treasury's financial liability was quite highly predictable from year to year, the only element of uncertainty being the level of local authority house building. Second, it gave local authorities considerable freedom over rents, whilst also giving them an incentive to control costs (since any increased costs would not be reflected in higher subsidy). It should be remembered here that authorities could draw on their own local tax base to enhance central subsidy, although the use of such rate fund contributions became generally confined to high-cost areas, especially in London. Third, the old system enabled central government to influence local authority rent levels by means of financial leverage, without breaching the convention that authorities had full responsibility in this area (Malpass 1990, 1991b).

Over the last 20 years successive governments have adopted policies which have moved council housing more towards a residual role in the housing system, concentrating on accommodating those who cannot afford to buy their own houses. Implicit in the residualization of council housing is a shift in the basis of rents and subsidies policy. This has involved the abandonment of the investment subsidy approach and the search for an effective and politically acceptable alternative based on the current deficit on the HRA. A key problem thrown up by the preference for deficit subsidy is that it creates new tensions in the central–local relationship. A shift to deficit subsidy inevitably raised questions about what were the appropriate levels of income and expenditure, and who was to decide.

This move also raised the issue of rent setting. Under the old system the total rental income was set by reference to the expenditure incurred in providing the service, but deficit subsidy implied setting rents independently from expenditure. Thus the shift from investment to deficit subsidy systems can be seen as embracing a parallel move from historic cost pricing to current value pricing, and this can in turn be related to a move away from concern with the supply of council housing towards preoccupation with tenure restructuring.

The first legislative attempt to introduce a deficit subsidy system to British local authority housing was the Housing Finance Act 1972 when a Conservative government brought in a system based on 'fair rents', deficit subsidy and a mandatory rent rebate scheme. This can now be seen as a false start which foundered on local opposition and inadequate legal drafting. A key problem was the complete removal of local autonomy in relation to rent setting, and reliance on administrative and judicial means of enforcing rent increases.

The Housing Act 1980 represented a new approach to the same basic set of issues. This time the problem was implicitly formulated in terms of the desire to obtain control of the volume of subsidy, without completely eroding local autonomy. Whereas the 1972 Act had placed the emphasis on a principled approach to rent setting, the 1980 system contained no such principles, and instead the emphasis was placed on giving the centre the power to reduce subsidy. This was achieved by an important breakthrough in the form of the notional HRA which became the basis for the calculation of subsidy, irrespective of the state of the actual HRA. The use of the notional HRA permitted a return to financial leverage as the means of exerting central government pressure on local rents. The advantage of this approach was that it preserved both limits to central government's financial liability and an element of local autonomy.

Under the 1980 Act system, subsidy was paid according to the centre's assumptions of year-on-year changes in income and expenditure, while local authorities remained free to set their own rents and expenditure on management and maintenance. Authorities were also free to draw on the rates to supplement rent income, and were permitted to budget for HRA surpluses, which could be transferred to support rate fund expenditure. In terms of central–local relations the adoption of a notional HRA gave the centre considerable power whilst providing local authorities with no opportunity for public defiance of the exercise of that power. It was, therefore, a highly potent and successful device for reducing subsidy and raising rents: in the first year of operation 1981/82, council rents rose by 48 per cent on average, and in three years the real value of general subsidy fell by over 80 per cent.

However, the 1980 Act system soon began to lose its potency, because leverage on rents was dependent upon there being some subsidy which could be withdrawn. It very quickly became clear that a majority of authorities were 'going out of subsidy', and the Government in the early 1980s lacked the political will to utilize other powers which it possessed to put further financial leverage on rents, by reducing the rate support grant of those authorities whose notional HRAs were in surplus. In the face of opposition from Conservative-controlled councils, the Government gave way and conceded both that a majority of councils would be released from direct central government pressure to raise rents and, where authorities chose to raise rents to levels which produced HRA surpluses, then those surpluses would be available to enhance local expenditure on non-housing services, with no reduction in rate support grant. This concession was good for local authorities but it fatally undermined the coherence of the revenue side of council housing finance, which meant that eventually the Government would move to reform it.

To conclude this section it can be said that in terms of implementation the key issues in relation to rents and subsidies are to do with both the principles of pricing public services and the politics of central–local relations. In the context of a culture of local autonomy the centre has relied to a large extent on the provision of subsidy as a mechanism for influencing local decisions on investment and rents. In the past the emphasis was more on investment and in recent times it has shifted to rents (investment now being controlled by different mechanisms). The long-term trend towards consumer subsidies is associated with declining levels of new building. However, the past exercise of local autonomy in relation to investment and rent setting means that it is now very difficult for the centre to achieve a coherent pricing structure based on a simple subsidy system; because there is considerable variation in circumstances from place to place, and local authorities are unwilling to give up their control of rents. Finally, it is important to refer back to the point made in Chapter 3, concerning the changing politics of local authority housing. For many years the key issues were about output levels and how to deal with the consequent income deficits on the HRA. Since 1980 sales have exceeded new building, giving rise to high levels of capital receipts, and rents have risen in real terms, with the result that HRA surpluses have appeared in many areas. The new issues, which the new financial regime is designed to confront, are therefore to do with the ownership and control of capital receipts and HRA surpluses. These are clearly issues with important implementation implications.

The new financial regime

The new financial regime for the revenue side of local authority housing was introduced in Part VI of the Local Government and Housing Act 1989. This consisted of new accounting arrangements and a new subsidy system, based on, but in certain crucial respects very different from, the previous system. Part IV of the Act introduced a new system for the control of local authority borrowing and capital expenditure on all services. This has important implications not only for housing capital expenditure but also for rents and revenue spending on management and maintenance.

In the consultation paper on the new financial regime the Government set out three objectives for the new regime (DoE 1988: 5–6):

(i) It should be simpler, so that subsidy works in a more intelligible way and gives consistent incentives.

(ii) It should be fairer towards tenants and charge payers alike, and fairer between tenants in different areas. Rents generally should not exceed levels within the reach of people in low paid employment, and in practice they will frequently be below market levels. They should, however, be set by reference to these two parameters: what people can pay, and what the property is worth, rather than by reference to historic cost accounting figures.

(iii) It should be more effective, directing the available subsidy to those areas where it is needed, and providing an incentive for good management rather than a cover for bad practice and inefficiency.

The first of these objectives is uncontroversial, although more easily stated than achieved. The second is by no means new; it has been a continuing theme of government policy since the late 1960s that councils should be persuaded to charge rents closer to market levels, while remaining in some sense affordable. The aim is both to reap the claimed efficiency advantages of market pricing, and assist the revival of the private rented sector, while at the same time economizing on Exchequer support in the form of subsidy. The third objective refers to the reconstitution of the HRA as a 'landlord account', separated ('ring fenced') from the other accounts of the local authority, and establishing a closer relationship between the rents paid by tenants and the cost of the services provided.

There was considerable consultation with the local authority associations during 1988/89 and certain quite significant changes were made, but the basic principles outlined in the consultation paper were enshrined in the Act. Space permits only a brief outline of the new system, although fuller accounts are available elsewhere (Hills 1991; Malpass 1990; Garnett et al. 1991; Gibb and Munro 1991). The new system is clearly a development from the 1980 Act system, retaining the notional HRA as the basis upon which subsidy is paid, although the way that the HRA is composed and calculated is different in certain crucial respects. The essence of the system is very simple: the HRA is now ring fenced, so that authorities cannot make discretionary payments to or from the general fund, and subsidy is the difference between notional income and expenditure (although the calculation of these amounts can be very complicated).

The system includes new ways of setting notional rents and notional expenditure on management and maintenance. Since 1990/91 the Government has produced annual assumptions about the rate of change in income and expenditure which are specific to each authority. This is a development from the 1980 system, in the sense that during the 1980s the Government had the statutory power to assume different rates of change in different places, but never did so. The basic objective of differentiation is to allow the Government to relate rent increases to variations in capital values from place to place, and to vary management and maintenance allowances according to differences in stock characteristics.

Whereas in the past an authority could have had up to three forms of subsidy (centrally funded housing subsidy, rent rebate subsidy, and local rate fund contributions) now there is only one, the housing revenue account subsidy. By eliminating rate fund contributions and combining the two central subsidies the Government has, in effect, widened the definition of what counts as the deficit on the HRA, thereby bringing virtually all authorities back into subsidy. The effect of these moves is both to restore government leverage on rents across the country and to give it complete control of subsidy income to local HRAs.

The first two years

The first point to be made about the introduction of the new financial regime, and it is an important point in the context of a focus on implementation, is that local authorities did not idly wait for the new system to take effect on 1 April 1990. They engaged in a variety of anticipatory action, the most significant form of which was an increase in capital expenditure. Authorities had accumulated capital receipts to a greater or lesser extent during the 1980s and the consultation paper of July 1988 revealed that they would lose their ability to spend up to 100 per cent of their receipts. As a result 1989/90 saw a 25 per cent increase in local authority capital spending.

The second point concerns the Government's determination to press ahead with implementation of the new financial regime in 1990/91, even though certain key aspects of the system had not been finalized. Thus, the 1990/91 management and maintenance allowances were based directly on actual spending levels from 1986/87 to 1988/89, and in 1991/92 'targeted' allowances were introduced for maintenance, but not for management. Detailed specification of the 'ring fence' – what items of expenditure should be included within the HRA – will not be complete before 1994/95. This represents a very clear example of implementation preceding completion of policymaking.

At the aggregate level, capital spending fell sharply in 1990/91 (DoE 1991: 95) and again in 1991/92 (ADC 1991; AMA 1991). The compulsory setting aside of 75 per cent of accumulated capital receipts resulted in an estimated £3 200 million reduction in local authority housing debt in 1990/91, and this helped to produce subsidy savings for central government.

Guideline rent increases have been subject to 'damping', and this seems set to become a continuing feature of the system. Damping is a way of limiting maximum guideline rent increases and preventing any actual decreases in guideline rents. Without damping the attempt to relate rents to capital values would produce some very large rent increases in London and the South East, and some large decreases in the North. The range of guideline rent increases in the first three years of the system was: 1990/91, 95p–£4.50; 1991/92, £1.38–£2.50; 1992/93, £1.20–£4.50. No real explanation has been forthcoming from the Government for the changes in the upper and lower levels from year to year, but it is clear that the reduced value of the upper level in 1991/92 had the effect of dragging up the lower limit. This was because of the way in which the system is related to public expenditure planning totals; the use of capital values in rent differentiation is about the distribution of guideline rents designed to raise a given aggregate level of income. Thus, the more that large rent increases are damped, the greater is the share of the total that has to be raised from authorities which would have reduced rents without damping. In 1990/91 57 per cent of authorities were given guideline increases at the top or bottom of the range, and in 1991/92 the proportion was 68 per cent. In both years there was a clear regional pattern, with large majorities of northern authorities being given the minimum increase, and the maximum increases being concentrated in London and the South East.

In practice, most authorities in both years raised their rents by more than their guideline. Seven managed to make no increase at all in April 1990, but others produced some of the highest rent increases ever recorded in British public housing. The London Borough of Redbridge, for instance, went for an increase of £15. 68 per week, compared with a guideline of just 95p. In 1990, 65 per cent of authorities raised rents by more than the guideline amount, and only 10 per cent by less. By April 1991 almost 84 per cent of English local authorities had actual rents above their guidelines. Some increases in 1991 were spectacular, with the London Borough of Ealing leading the field with an average increase of over £28 per week. While most increases were much more modest than this, there was still a marked divergence of the overall actual average rent from the average guideline rent, to an extent which had not been observed in the 1980s. In the period 1983/89 actual rents tended to lag a little behind notional rents, and in 1989/90 average actual rents were 2 per cent below notional rents, but by 1991/92 they were almost 10 per cent above guidelines.

Behind the national picture lies a pattern of variation which reflects the Government's intention to raise rents more in areas of high capital values. All the authorities in the list of the top 20 rent increases in 1990 were in the South of England, and 19 of the top 20 in 1991. Looking at the top 20 rents (as distinct from rent increases) in 1991, all 20 were in the South of England, with 14 in London. In the case of the bottom 20, however, all were in the Midlands or the North, with distinct concentrations in Staffordshire and Cheshire and the North East counties. Although the widening of regional variations is broadly in line with the Government's policy, it is also clear that the authorities with the highest rents tend to have increased by substantially more than was assumed for subsidy purposes, while the authorities with the lowest rents tend to have raised rents by less than guideline.

As might be expected, there is a close relationship between rents above guidelines and management and maintenance spending above allowances. In 1991/92 aggregate spending on management and maintenance was planned to be 30 per cent higher than the Government's aggregate allowances. The management and maintenance allowances for each authority in 1990/91 were based on the average of actual spending by the authority in 1986/87, 1987/88 and 1988/89. Thus in the first year there was no attempt by government to differentiate allowances, but in 1991/92 an element of redistribution was introduced into the allowances for maintenance spending (but not for management). Differentiation of allowances proved to be a tricky implementation problem, since it required a comprehensive and reliable database on which to base the calculations. In 1991/92 it was decided that there was no readily available technique to permit differentiation of management allowances (and research was commissioned to try to overcome the problem).

However, differentiation of maintenance expenditure was deemed to be possible, and target spending levels, based on stock characteristics, were calculated for each authority. The 44 authorities whose allowance for 1990/91 was more than 60 per cent above their target for 1991/92 received the same cash allowance in 1991/92 as in the previous year. The resources so released were distributed to the 34 authorities whose allowances would otherwise have been furthest below them. Eighteen of the gainers were in London and the remainder were evenly spread through the regions. Of the losers, 27 were in the South and nine in the North.

There are a number of implementation issues here. Local authorities vary very considerably in their management and maintenance expenditure, as measured by the Government. The 1990/91 allowances, reflecting actual spending in the late 1980s, varied from just over £500 per dwelling per year to over £2 000. Previous subsidy systems had never required local authorities to justify their spending levels; however, the new financial regime implies the problem of not only deciding what is the 'correct' level of spending in each area but also bringing widely divergent authorities into line with the centrally determined levels. This produced the rather ironical situation in which a Conservative government found itself encouraging some (often Labour) authorities to increase their management and maintenance expenditure, while at the same time freezing the allowances of others (often Conservative controlled) on the implied grounds that they were spending 'too much'. In fact it has to be made clear here that the targeting exercise was not based on any genuine assessment of need to spend; targeting is essentially an exercise of redistribution, rewarding some at the direct expense of others. In any event, local authorities themselves continue to make decisions about rents and spending which are based on their own assessments of what it is reasonable to charge and what needs to be spent.

The dramatic deviation of actual rents and spending decisions made by local authorities from the guidelines and allowances set by the Government is the most striking feature of the new regime to date. This has important consequences for central government, and draws attention to the extent to which the centre is involved in implementation. In the annual round of central government budget planning the DoE has to estimate the cost of the rent rebate element of housing subsidy, and is clearly under some obligation to assume that the sum will be close to that which is implied by the assumptions about rent increases. But if councils subsequently raise rents by more than the guideline levels then the actual amount claimed in rent rebate subsidy will increase, and may exceed the amount included in the public spending estimates. This is what happened in both 1990/91 and 1991/2. In 1990/91 the DoE had to seek a supplementary estimate approaching £600 million, which was the largest single such estimate since the unbudgeted Falklands War in 1982. From the point of view of the DoE this is clearly a problem in terms of its relations with the Treasury, to the extent that the Department appears to be unable to remain within its agreed budget.

The policy approach

It would be a mistake to take the Government's claimed objectives at face value. The White Paper and other Government statements from which the stated objectives are taken cannot be assumed to be part of a rational structure wherein objectives and policies are logically and closely related. They have at least in part a polemical purpose, concerned with securing and confirming support for legislative change. In this connection objectives may be included and benefits claimed for reform on the 'pork barrel' principle that it is necessary to show that the legislation offers some positive outcome for every interest whose support is needed to secure its passage. Particularly where local government will be largely responsible for implementation, central government can adopt policies and claim benefits for them, secure in the knowledge that it will not be held responsible when outcomes fail to match up to claims except where the causal chain leads undeniably back to the centre.

Consequently, stated objectives may conflict, may vary in priority, and some may be purely symbolic; other objectives may be unstated but crucial. This has implications for the evaluation of the implementation process. Whether, from the Government's point of view, the system is a 'success' or 'failure', can only be judged against the objectives they actually regard as important. What these are cannot be read off from policy statements, which are only one source of evidence about objectives and may be supported or contradicted by other sources.

It is also important to recognize that the government is not the only policymaker in the field. In the case of the new financial regime, the legislation primarily provides a framework within which various actors – most importantly the Secretary of State for the Environment and local housing authorities – both make policy and seek to implement it. In one sense the Secretary of State is an agent through which the Government seeks to implement the policy objectives which motivated the legislation; in another sense he or she is a key policymaker since the legislation gives him or her sufficient power to dilute or amend those objectives. The local authorities, too, are policymaking institutions pursuing their own objectives, which will often not coincide with those of the central government. The success or failure of the new regime, for the Government, hangs on whether it is successful in so constraining the policymaking activities of the local authorities that their many and various decisions deliver outcomes consistent with central government's objectives. For the local authorities themselves, the success or failure of the system depends on how far they can continue to pursue their own locally determined objectives within or despite it.

Nor can the relationship between the Government's policy objectives and the new financial regime, as it has emerged from the legislative process and been operated in practice, be taken for granted. Legislation does not begin with an otherwise blank sheet of paper at the top of which are written the desired objectives; it amends and adapts a pre-existing framework of legislation in ways that are governed as much by practicability as by the objectives in mind. Like other policymaking processes, it is a process of negotiation. As Barrett and Fudge (1981: 24–25) have argued, 'policy is not a "fix" but a series of intentions around which bargaining takes place and which can be modified as each set of actors attempts to negotiate to maximize its own interest and priorities'.

To this it should be added that the initial negotiating stance of a set of actors may already incorporate concessions to other parties, recognizing what realistically can be achieved in the negotiating process, bearing in mind the power of the other actors and what is practicable. A considerable number of amendments were made to the proposed structure and operation of the new financial regime as the Local Government and Housing Bill passed through Parliament, some in response to local government representations. But there are also clear signs that the initial proposals, before any amendment, fell short of a system which could guarantee delivery of the objectives claimed by the Government.

Accordingly, the research on which this chapter is based looked first at the system's structural characteristics – what it is capable of delivering, and what it cannot – and how it has been operated by the Secretary of State and civil servants in the Department of the Environment. This analysis provides some clues as to the objectives which underlay the introduction of the system, and their relative importance for the Government, then and as the political priorities of the Government have changed over time.

The impact on central–local relations

It was argued above that the turn in the early 1970s from an investment to a deficit subsidy system had important implications for central–local relations. From then on the Government found it necessary to take a closer interest in what local authorities spent on managing and maintaining their stock, and in the rents that they charged. On one view, the new regime can be seen as the culmination of this process, with the Government specifying for individual authorities the guideline rents they 'ought' to charge, and the amounts they 'ought' to spend on management and maintenance, and, through ring fencing, severely restricting authorities' freedom to deviate from these guidelines. On this view, the new regime is a response by government to the fact that local authorities were using their freedom under the old system to follow rent and spending policies which failed to correspond to government objectives. Government, in retaliation, has tightened control from the centre in order to ensure that its objectives are met.

What is missing from this account is any explanation of why it is only now that government has moved to ring fence the HRA, and why the new regime leaves an important degree of freedom available to local authorities – freedom to set rents and spending levels which deviate from the government guidelines. The short answer is that increased central control has costs as well as benefits for government. The Housing Finance Act 1972 still stands as a warning of the problems which arise for government from central control (Malpass 1989). Where rent setting powers are removed from local authorities, government is seen as responsible for any increase, and local authorities lose any incentive to constrain spending, since it will not affect rents. Central government then faces the unpalatable choice between an open-ended commitment to subsidize spending and central control of spending as well as rents.

Central control of spending would be a nightmare for central government because of the multiplicity of local factors influencing the 'need to spend', which cannot be reflected in a simple formula applicable to all authorities. Fine tuning the formula to fit each local situation would be a time consuming and costly process, while ignoring local variation in costs would leave the Government open to the charge of underfunding the service to tenants.

Linking subsidy to a notional HRA, while leaving authorities free to determine actual rents and spending levels, mitigates these problems, but does not avoid them altogether. Now that virtually all authorities are brought back within the scope of the subsidy system, and given ring fencing of the HRA, the annual subsidy determination is a much more significant element in local authority's annual budgeting process. Authorities are much more vulnerable to an unfavourable subsidy determination than when they could use rate fund contribution to compensate. Consequently, they are much more motivated to renegotiate the determination if they can. Conversely, civil servants at the Department of the Environment and Welsh Office have greater interest in avoiding determinations which can be represented in public as arbitrary in their effects, and are motivated from their side to negotiate. Moreover, the method of calculating subsidy leaves plenty of scope, at least in the early years, for negotiation, since it is based on local authority supplied data, which authorities can, to some extent, influence.

Some authorities have been able to take advantage of particular circumstances and to renegotiate the basis on which subsidy is calculated; Sandwell, for instance, re-opened its accounts for 1988/89 in order to decapitalize £15 million in repairs spending, with the effect that the subsidy allowance for management and maintenance in 1990/91 and 1991/92 was significantly increased.

However, the use of a notional HRA is not without its disadvantages. It means that, in effect, government has a single policy instrument with which to influence local authority behaviour – the amount of subsidy provided. Although the subsidy determination is based on a guideline rent and management and maintenance allowance, the amount of subsidy is related to the difference between the two. The same amount of subsidy is therefore equally consistent with the combination of a high guideline rent with a high management and maintenance allowance, or a low rent increase low management and maintenance allowance.

The notional HRA approach offers the local authority a trade-off between rent levels and management and maintenance spending, the terms of which can be varied by central government giving or withholding subsidy. But its basic limitation is that one policy instrument cannot deliver more than one policy objective. Government can use withdrawal of subsidy to force up rents, provided local authorities wish to maintain the same real level of spending on management and maintenance. Alternatively, the provision of additional subsidy may encourage higher spending on management and maintenance, on the assumption that authorities are not likely to prefer to reduce rents, although there is no guarantee that authorities would use the extra resources efficiently. But government cannot use the subsidy system to induce authorities to raise rents in order to finance higher spending and a better standard of service.

This analysis suggests, and the history of the first two years of the 1980 Act system bears out, that this type of system works best as a means of forcing up rents, perhaps providing incentives to cost efficiency as a side effect, as authorities strive to preserve services while minimizing rent increases. A further consequence of the notional HRA approach is that government is not constrained to ensure that management and maintenance allowances really reflect 'need to spend' in individual authorities, or that actual rents correspond to guidelines.

Like its predecessor, the new regime is driven by the Public Expenditure Survey Committee (PESC) system. This means that the starting point for deciding the annual increases in guideline rents and management and maintenance allowances is the determination of the amount for expenditure estimates. Ministers are also likely to take a view on what sort of rent increases they want to see. The point here is that the use of housing capital values in the new regime is merely as a device to distribute the aggregate increase determined by the public expenditure decision.

The same applies to management and maintenance allowances; these are not derived from an estimate of an authority's need to spend. The aggregate allowance for management and maintenance is determined once aggregate subsidy and rents are known (together with aggregate capital spend and receipts estimates); and targeting of management and maintenance allowances is only a means of distributing this total.

In the PESC process, government too is faced with a trade-off between rents and spending levels. A given total amount of subsidy can be distributed to local authorities by specifying relatively low rent guidelines and management and maintenance allowances or higher rent guidelines matched by higher management and maintenance allowances.

It was claimed in the 1987 White Paper that some local authorities tend to spend too little on repairing their stock, because they are politically biased towards low rents regardless of the consequences for repairs spending. This suggests that, in order to address this problem government ought to adopt relatively high management and maintenance allowances, and guideline rents to match. However, this choice has political and economic consequences. Although Conservative governments have not shown themselves unwilling to seek rent increases from local authorities, there is an upper limit to the increases that the Government wishes to be seen to be recommending, particularly in a system where rent guidelines vary with capital values and the highest capital values are in Conservative-controlled authorities in the South. Equally, projected local authority rent increases are fed into economic forecasting models, so that it may be necessary for the Government to limit rent increases in order to make plausible a projected fall in inflation. Thirdly, the terms of the subsidy trade-off for the Government are such that an increase in rent guidelines does not permit a pound-for-pound increase in management and maintenance allowances, since higher rents also mean that provision must be made for additional rent rebate subsidy.

These considerations have tended to bias annual subsidy determinations towards a relatively low rent-low management and maintenance pairing, particularly within the context of a substantial reduction in overall subsidy, despite the claimed long-term objective of higher repairs spending. The effects of this bias are in the experience of the first two years of the new regime – the majority

of authorities spent well above their allowances for management and maintenance, and financed this spending with rents substantially above government
guidelines. Paradoxically, therefore, the new regime has achieved the Government objective of higher spending financed by higher rents, despite the limitations of the notional HRA.

Conclusion

This chapter has looked at a clear example of a top-down exercise in policy
implementation, an unambiguous attempt to change local decisions and policy
outcomes: central government was aware that the 1980 system was not delivering its policy objectives, largely because the local authorities had regained
considerable autonomy over housing finance, and the Government's response
was, in a classic top-down way, to 'get a better grip on the situation' (Ham and
Hill 1984: 110). However, it is important to remember that the Government did
not seek to eliminate local discretion entirely, and the retention of the notional
HRA indicates a commitment to the maintenance of a role for local authorities
in setting actual rents and spending levels. On the other hand, it is clear that the
Government anticipated implementation problems and designed the new
financial regime with these in mind, leaving councils very little scope to resist the
centre's policy.

Examination of the new financial regime suggests that implementation is not
to be understood as simply a local level activity; this is not an example of central
government establishing legislation and leaving the local level to get on with
implementation. On the contrary, the DoE and the Welsh Office are actively
involved in implementation work on a continuing basis.

The new financial regime also raises questions for the bottom-up perspective.
In this case implementation is not appropriately understood in terms of the
negotiated activities of street-level bureaucrats, nor the mobilization of a multi-
tude of market motivated actors (Houlihan 1988). The key decisions made by
local authorities in responding to the new financial regime take place some
distance from the interface with the public, and are handled by officials who
rarely meet the public in the course of their everyday work.

References

ADC (1991) *Survey on Council House Rents, Housing Subsidy and Capital Expenditure
    1991–92*, London, Association of District Councils.
AMA (1991) *New Financial Regime Survey Report 1991–92*, London, Association of
    Metropolitan Authorities.
Barrett, S. and Fudge, C. (1981) *Policy and Action*, London, Methuen.
CIPFA (1991) *Housing Revenue Account Statistics 1991–92 Estimates*, London, CIPFA.
DoE (1988) *The New Financial Regime for Local Authority Housing in England and
    Wales*, London, DoE.
DoE (1991) *Annual Report 1991*, London, HMSO.
Forrest, R. and Murie, A. (1990) *Selling the Welfare State*, London, Routledge.

Garnett, D. Reid, B. and Reilly, H. (1991) *Housing Finance*, Harlow, Longman.

Gibb, K. and Munro, M. (1991) *Housing Finance in the UK: an Introduction*, Basingstoke, Macmillan.

Ham, C. and Hill, M. (1984) *The Policy Process in the Modern Capitalist State*, Brighton, Wheatsheaf.

Hills, J. (1991) *Unravelling Housing Finance*, Oxford, Clarendon Press.

Houlihan, B. (1988) *Housing Policy and Central–Local Government Relations*, Aldershot, Avebury.

Joseph Rowntree Foundation (1991) *Inquiry into British Housing, Second Report*, York, Joseph Rowntree Foundation.

Maclennan, D., Gibb, K. and More, A. (1991) *Fairer Subsidies, Faster Growth*, York, Joseph Rowntree Foundation.

Malpass, P. (1989) 'The road from Clay Cross', *Roof*, January–February.

Malpass, P. (1990) *Reshaping Housing Policy*, London, Routledge.

Malpass, P. (1991a) 'Cash till eternity', *Roof*, July–August.

Malpass, P. (1991b) 'The financing of council housing', in S. Lowe and D. Hughes (eds) *A New Century of Social Housing*, Leicester, Leicester University Press.

Malpass, P. and Murie, A. (1990) *Housing Policy and Practice*, 3rd edn, Basingstoke, Macmillan.

CHAPTER 8

Housing renewal in an era of mass home ownership

PHILIP LEATHER AND SHEILA MACKINTOSH

Introduction

Housing renewal policies for the private sector have been something of a sideshow in the housing debates of the 1980s and 1990s. The right to buy, the role of housing associations, the transfer of the housing stock, changes to the structure of housing management, the nature of housing subsidies, and the question of affordability have been key issues for academics and policymakers alike. As home ownership has grown, attention has focused on whether households could afford to buy, and whether home owners could sustain their mortgage payments, rather than on whether they could afford to pay for repairs, improvements and maintenance.

But public investment in private sector housing renewal has been substantial. Between 1969 and 1990, more than 2.5 million renovation grants were paid by local authorities to private home owners in England and Wales alone, accounting for expenditure of almost £6 billion. As in other areas, the period since 1979 has seen a significant re-orientation of policy, although the process of change began much earlier, in the late 1960s, when the post-War slum clearance programme, which had formed the main focus of private-sector housing renewal, came increasingly under question. In this chapter we shall chart the only partially successful attempts to re-orientate renewal policies away from dealing with a housing stock owned primarily by private landlords towards one which is predominantly owner occupied. This has required a shift away from policies and mechanisms geared to the compulsory acquisition and comprehensive redevelopment of substandard housing towards policies which rely primarily on incentives, persuasion, and the attitudes and investment decisions of individual home owners. Area renewal, although ostensibly the central element of policy since 1969, has never been pursued with the commitment and resources which it demanded except in a few local authorities, and there has been continuing concern that state aid has not been effectively targeted upon the poorest condition dwellings or on the people who needed it most. The new renovation policy framework established by the Local Government and Housing Act 1989 has for the first time established mechanisms for targeting grant aid to home owners, but in line with the Government's overall approach to welfare provision it seems likely that this has been designed to focus investment mainly on bringing dwellings up to the minimum standards and on helping only the very poorest households while containing overall expenditure at current levels. In the first part of this chapter we shall trace the development of these policy changes against the background of the continuing growth of home ownership. We shall then go on to examine the development of the new renovation policy framework in more detail and to look at how it has worked during the first two years of operation.

The growth of home ownership in the older housing stock

The proportion of dwellings in Britain which is owner occupied has increased throughout the post-War period. From less than one-third in the early 1950s, the home ownership rate rose to almost 50 per cent by 1971, to 56 per cent by 1981, and then more rapidly to over 67 per cent in 1990. Important regional and national differences remain, and in England and Wales in 1990 home ownership rates were 69 per cent and 72 per cent respectively while the equivalent figure for Scotland was only 51 per cent (Department of the Environment 1991). But overall, home ownership has become the dominant tenure throughout the country and it is unlikely that the recession in the housing market in the late 1980s and early 1990s will have any long-term impact on tenure patterns.

As a result of this growth, there is now great variety in the characteristics of home owners and much academic debate on the significance of increased home ownership is concerned with the exploration of this variation (Forrest *et al.* 1990). An important consequence of the growth in home ownership has been the increasing number of home owners on low incomes. More than one-third of all households with an income of less than £150 per week were owner occupiers (OPCS 1991). As Figure 8.1 shows, more than one-fifth of home owners in Britain in 1989 had an income of less than £150 a week and a further 8 per cent had an income of between £150 and £200 per week. One-quarter of the former, or in absolute terms some 800 000 households, were still repaying a house purchase loan. The remaining three-quarters owned their dwelling outright without an outstanding mortgage, but few of these could afford home ownership if they were now buying for the first time.

A significant number of low income home owners are older people. As Figure 8.2 shows, an increasing proportion of older people are entering retirement as owner occupiers at a point when their income often falls sharply. The majority are outright owners who purchased their dwelling at a point when their income was higher in relation to average house prices, but they may still face substantial

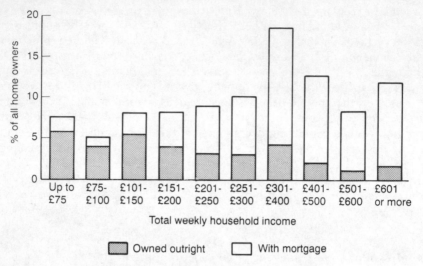

Figure 8.1   Household income of home owners, Great Britain, 1989
Source: OPCS (1991)

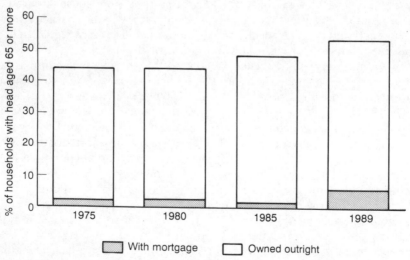

Figure 8.2   Home ownership amongst older households
Source: OPCS (1991)

repair, improvement and maintenance costs. Higher ownership rates amongst middle-aged households and long-term demographic changes suggest that the number of older home owners on low incomes will continue to increase in the future (Kirk and Leather 1991).

The growth in owner occupation has stemmed from four main sources: new construction, purchases of existing dwellings from private landlords, purchases from local authorities or new town development corporations, and losses as a result of slum clearance. These have varied considerably in relative importance over time (Holmans 1987). In the 1953–61 period, more than 1 million dwellings were transferred into owner occupation from the private rented sector, but from 1961–81, new building was the main source of growth. During the 1980s, transfers from the public sector under the right to buy also contributed substantially to the increase in home ownership. Figure 8.3 shows these changes.

The transfer of almost 4 million formerly privately rented dwellings into the owner-occupied sector has been of particular significance because the majority of these dwellings were built before 1919. By 1986, some 74 per cent of occupied pre-1919 dwellings in England were owner occupied and these dwellings made up almost one-third of all owner-occupied dwellings (Department of the Environment 1988). Many of these dwellings were in poor condition when they were transferred and because of their age most require higher levels of repair, improvement and maintenance expenditure than more recently constructed dwellings. Some 60 per cent of occupied poor condition dwellings in England in 1986 were owner occupied and 11 per cent of these required urgent repairs costing £1000 or more, one-quarter required total repairs costing more than £1100, and 10 per cent required total repairs costing more than £2500. In Wales the position was worse with 31 per cent of owner-occupied dwellings requiring

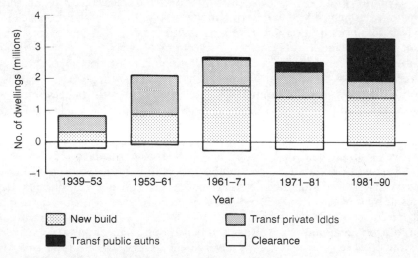

Figure 8.3   Components of the growth of home ownership
Source: Holmans (1987), DoE (1991)

repairs costing over £1000 (Welsh Office 1988), and in Northern Ireland a survey undertaken in the following year indicated that 22 per cent of owner-occupied dwellings required repairs costing £3000 or more (Northern Ireland Housing Executive 1988). Although there were significant house condition problems in the inter-War and post-War owner-occupied stock, some two-thirds of owner-occupied dwellings in poor condition in England in 1986, representing more than 1 million dwellings, were built before 1919. In addition, a further 420 000 pre-1919 dwellings in poor condition still remained in the privately rented sector.

Overall, the picture which this reveals is of a private-sector housing stock where poor conditions remain predominantly concentrated in dwellings built before 1919. These poor condition older dwellings are increasingly owner occupied rather than rented from private landlords. Although the private rented sector still has proportionately the worst conditions, the majority of dwellings requiring repair or improvement are owner occupied.

The evolution of renewal policy

Slum clearance

Although renovation grants to assist home owners had been available for many years, it was not until 1969 that renovation became a major focus of housing renewal policy. Throughout the post-War period, the majority of renewal investment had gone into the acquisition and clearance of poor condition housing, but as Figure 8.4 shows, the level of clearance in England and Wales fell rapidly from more than 50 000 dwellings in the mid-1970s to only just over 6000 in 1989/90. The majority of houses cleared during this period were in very poor condition and most of the households affected by clearance policies rented their house from a private landlord and many were happy to be rehoused into newer accommodation rented from a local authority.

But from the mid-1960s onwards, objections to clearance emerged from a number of sources. Despite the historically high rate of clearance, there was concern that areas of older housing outside planned clearance programmes were deteriorating towards the point where action to deal with them would soon become essential (Central Housing Advisory Committee 1966). The results of the first national house condition survey in 1967, covering England and Wales, also revealed that problems were far more extensive than local authorities had previously estimated, with 1. 8 million dwellings found to be unfit rather than the 0.8 million estimated by local authorities (Ministry of Housing and Local Government 1967) and a need for aggregate expenditure of £5 billion at 1967 prices. Economists such as Needleman argued that renovation was a more cost-effective way of dealing with the older housing stock than clearance and rebuilding (Needleman 1969). Against a background of economic crisis and the devaluation of sterling in 1967, the government decided to scale down clearance proposals and divert resources on a larger scale to the renovation of the housing stock (Gibson and Langstaff 1982).

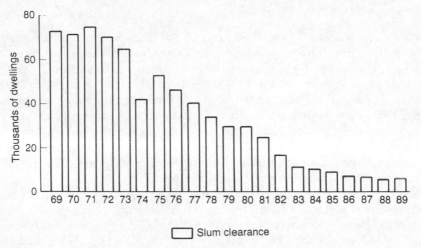

Figure 8.4   Dwellings demolished or closed, England and Wales 1969–89
(data for 1969–72 in calendar years, 1973–89 in financial years)
Source: Housing and Construction Statistics (various)

But opposition to clearance also came from those who were affected by it. The process of clearance and rehousing often took several years to complete and many households found it extremely stressful. But in addition, increasing numbers of people began to object to the loss of contacts with friends and community associated with rehousing, and to the unattractiveness of a move to a large local authority estate perhaps located on the periphery of a city with the associated problems of a long journey to work and an absence of shopping or social facilities. In some areas, there were long struggles by residents to resist the clearance process and to persuade the local authority to improve their houses instead (Davies 1972; Dennis 1970).

Underlying these changes was an important shift in the tenure pattern of housing in proposed and potential clearance areas. Since the end of the Second World War, the process of dwelling sales by private landlords to sitting tenants or others had been gathering momentum and the level of home ownership in clearance areas had been increasing. As clearance programmes progressed, the focus of effort also shifted from the very poorest stock to houses in better condition with higher ownership rates. For many home owners, the clearance and rehousing process was extremely unattractive (English *et al.* 1976). Apart from the inconvenience and disruption, compensation for a house which was declared unfit was at site value only, and the sole option for most of those affected was to become a local authority tenant. A grant to assist with rehabilitation seemed a better option to many home owners. A combination of financial constraints, inadequate overall progress by local authorities, and opposition from local communities therefore brought about the shift in policy.

Voluntary improvement

The resulting legislation, the Housing Act 1969, envisaged that area-based rehabilitation and clearance would proceed in parallel. The Act's main mechanisms were a new, high standard improvement grant, intended to provide properties with a minimum 30 year life, and the General Improvement Area (GIA) powers, which enabled local authorities to declare specific areas on which they would focus their improvement efforts. In these areas, residents would receive more generous grants and local authorities would receive subsidy to invest in environmental improvements with the aim of generating public confidence in the future of the area. Lack of long-term confidence was a real issue in many cities where clearance programmes were in operation.

But, from the outset, the desire to run clearance and improvement programmes in parallel was a naive aspiration and the number of properties closed or demolished fell sharply between 1969 and 1974. But the new improvement grants introduced by the 1969 Act also missed their target. After a very slow start (only 30 000 grants were provided in England and Wales in 1970) the number of grants was boosted by a temporary measure which increased the rate of grant in certain areas of the country where help with economic development was concentrated and almost 190 000 grants were paid in 1974 (Figure 8.5). This measure was very effective in increasing the level of grant-aided investment, but relatively little of this investment went into older, privately-owned housing. A third of grant approvals in the 1969–73 period were for local authority dwellings (Thomas 1986).

The number of GIAs declared by local authorities was very small and the number of grants awarded in these areas amounted to only 5 per cent of all grants paid, even in the best year 1973. By 1974, declared GIAs contained only 273 000 dwellings and improvement work had been completed on only 14 per cent of these dwellings. Finally, grants were also badly targeted at individual level, with many taken up by more affluent owners living in inter-War housing. In some areas, there was concern that builders and speculators were applying for grants and using them to refurbish formerly privately rented housing before selling it on for owner occupation (Hamnett and Williams 1979).

The results of the Housing Act 1969 demonstrated the problems of implementing renewal polices for the owner-occupied sector which were reliant upon a change in direction by local authorities and grant take-up by home owners themselves. The core of the Act's approach, the new GIAs, were unsuccessful because too few were declared by local authorities, and because owners living in the declared areas were slow to take-up grants. Many local authorities with large clearance programmes lacked the staff and financial resources to complement them with an improvement programme and some were also reluctant to wind their programmes down. It also took some time to develop experience with the implementation of the new area improvement mechanisms, even where local authorities were keen to do so, because they were reliant on voluntary improvement rather than compulsion.

The lack of demand from those living in declared areas stemmed from the

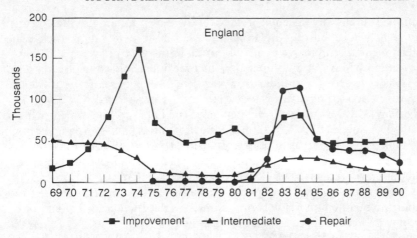

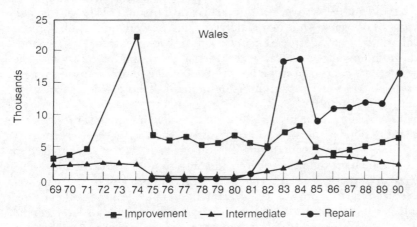

Figure 8.5   Grants paid by type 1969–90
Source: Housing and Construction Statistics (various)

inability of many to afford to meet their share of the costs. The bulk of the demand for grants came from the areas of the country where higher rates of grant were temporarily available, demonstrating the positive impact of higher rates on take-up, but there was criticism that the grants were not going to properties which were most in need of improvement. The difficulties of getting those living in the worst housing to voluntarily improve their properties were becoming apparent.

Improving the poorest housing

The response to these problems was further legislation. The Housing Act 1974 effectively recognized that the complementary approach to clearance and re-habilitation had failed, and as well as a number of powers designed to restrict exploitation of grants by speculators and individual households, the Act introduced a new mechanism, the Housing Action Area (HAA), which was designed to secure the improvement of housing in the very poorest condition.

In an attempt to improve take-up by low income households, the rate of grant aid in HAAs was set at a standard 75 per cent of eligible costs, with local authority discretion to increase this to 90 per cent in cases of hardship. The grant rate in GIAs was also increased to 60 per cent. The Labour Government which enacted the Housing Act 1974 recognized the difficulties of encouraging voluntary grant take-up in the areas of poorest housing, so local authorities were also encouraged to buy up houses in those areas for improvement if private landlords would not do so voluntarily. The Act also introduced more generous funding for housing associations to enable them to expand their involvement in area renewal. But the main emphasis was on voluntary sales by landlords, with only cumbersome powers to force reluctant owners to sell.

The implementation of the 1974 Act also ran quickly into difficulties. The rate of area declarations continued to be disappointing and most local authorities were cautious in their use of the new powers. In 1975, only 8 per cent of grants paid in England and Wales were within HAAs or GIAs and by 1978, this had only risen to 14 per cent. While many individual HAAs were successful, this was often achieved by the widespread acquisition of dwellings from private landlords and home owners by local authorities and housing associations. The majority of grants continued to be paid outside declared areas, but even here there were problems which made it difficult for many of those on low incomes to afford to take up a grant.

The first problem was the owner's contribution. Even with grant rates at 90 per cent, many poor owners could not afford to meet their share of costs. A further factor was that the actual contribution which an owner was required to make was often larger than the theoretical contribution because of cost limits which were applied by legislation and by local authority practice. This frequently reduced the true proportion of grant aid to much less than 90 per cent. As a result, grants were more likely to go to those who could afford to meet the additional costs rather than to those on the very lowest incomes.

Confirmation of the failure of policies to deal with the worst problems came from the 1981 national house condition surveys (Department of the Environment 1982, 1983). The number of dwellings with repair costs of more than £7000 at 1981 prices increased by about one-quarter over the 1976–81 period and there was no change in the number of unfit dwellings over the same period. Older people, those who had lived in their house for a long period, and those on low incomes were particularly likely to live in poor condition housing, but these groups could not afford to deal with house condition problems and they were least likely to obtain a grant. Households which took up a grant had higher incomes on average than those potential applicants who did not. Even in HAAs and GIAs, the proportion of dwellings unfit or in serious disrepair had remained more or less static. While the old policy of large scale clearance had come to an end in most areas, it had not been replaced by area improvement on a commensurate scale.

1979 and after

The 1981 house condition survey findings were not initially available to the Conservative Government elected in 1979 and the changes made to renewal policy in the Housing Act 1980 did not emerge from a fundamental review of renewal policy. The main changes were relaxations to the repayment conditions for grants as they related to owner occupiers (accepting that the 1974 changes had been something of an over-reaction to abuses) and more significantly, the extension of the availability of the repair grants introduced in 1974 in HAAs and GIAs to all dwellings built before 1919. The immediate impact of the 1980 Act in the housing renewal field was relatively minor and it was overshadowed by the right to buy and by the cuts in local authority capital expenditure imposed by the new Government (Leather and Murie 1986).

By 1982, however, the first results from the 1981 house condition survey became available and the Government responded by announcing an increase in the rate of grant payable for all repair and intermediate grants to 90 per cent, initially for a period of one year, but later extended until 1984. This led to a major surge in the demand for repair grants, paralleling that for improvement grants in the 1972–74 period. In 1981, only 6000 repair grants were paid in England and Wales but by 1984, this figure had increased to almost 140 000.

The repair grant boom was initially funded by an open-ended supplement to local authority capital allocations, but after 1984, the resources available for grants were again incorporated into the HIP system and levels of grant payments fell back rapidly. At local level, expenditure on the renovation of private-sector housing was often in competition with expenditure on the renovation of local authorities' own stock. Between 1984/85 and 1989/90 the level of expenditure on public-sector renovation rose while expenditure on private-sector renovation and clearance fell back substantially. Many local authorities still had large numbers of outstanding approvals to be met from their normal HIP allocations and this affected their capacity to provide other types of grant for some time afterwards. In addition, the higher rates of grant had generated large waiting lists in many areas and attempts to prioritize applicants often led to political controversy. The boom in demand also put pressure on local renewal strategies (Gibson 1986). Approvals were scattered throughout the pre-1919 housing stock and many local authorities were forced by political pressures to abandon or suspend area-based renewal policies.

There were also changes in the distribution of grants in terms of property type and the characteristics of grant applicants. An unpublished Department of the Environment survey of the distribution of grants showed that fewer grants went to unfit properties, or properties lacking amenities, and more grants were provided for semi-detached and detached houses than in the pre-1982 period (Department of the Environment, unpublished). There was also strong anecdotal evidence that more affluent households living in pre-1919 properties who could have afforded to carry out work without grant aid formed a substantial proportion of grant applicants because they were more capable of preparing an application and could readily afford the owner's contribution, whilst poorer households could still not afford to contribute, even at the higher rate.

The review of improvement policy

After the results of the 1981 house condition survey became fully available, the Government decided to undertake a more fundamental review of renewal policy. The results of this were published in a consultative Green Paper in 1985 (Cmnd. 9513). The Government's proposals for renewal policy were very much in line with its other policies for welfare benefits. In future, the primary responsibility for repairs and improvements would lie with individual home owners rather than the state. State aid would be concentrated on helping those who could not afford to help themselves and this help would be restricted to the provision of work to basic rather than higher standards. It was proposed that all grants to home owners should in future be means-tested and that aid would only be provided for work which would bring dwellings up to the standard of fitness for human habitation, rather than the higher 30-year life (or 10 point) standard which had formed the target for improvement grants. For work above the fitness standard, it was proposed that loans would be made available, secured by means of an equity share taken by local authorities in the grant recipient's property, repayable when the property was eventually sold. In order to assist owners to cope with the responsibility for housing improvement, the Green Paper also proposed that the private sector should do more to educate people about the need for investment in their houses. The private and voluntary sectors were urged to sponsor or establish home improvement agencies to provide more practical assistance to older people, disabled people, or those with low incomes. Area improvement, while still available as a renewal tool, was seen as less important because of the need to concentrate help on the worst properties, wherever they were to be found.

Not surprisingly, the Government's proposals were received with widespread hostility by local authorities and professional bodies concerned with home improvement. They represented a fundamental shift away from an emphasis on high standard area improvement towards a more residual function for grants. In practice, however, there was a great deal of underlying evidence to support the general direction of the Government's proposals. More than ten years of area improvement had met with only limited success, partly because few authorities had targeted their grants effectively into declared areas, and partly because the HIP allocation mechanism had never directed resources to the authorities with the greatest concentrations of poor condition housing. As a result, progress with declarations and improvement work in declared areas was always constrained. And finally, because grant aid since 1969 had been widely available for all older properties meeting broad eligibility criteria, it had rarely been sufficiently generous to enable the poorest households living in the worst condition properties to benefit. While the tales of exploitation by affluent households were probably exaggerated, the properties on which grants had been provided were often not the poorest, nor were they located in the areas where the poorest housing was concentrated, and in many cases households with incomes large enough to afford the owner's contribution were the main beneficiaries. Renewal policy had failed to confront the key problems because of a lack of targeting, either by area or by household.

But although the Government's diagnosis had much to commend it, the solutions proposed owed more to ideology than to analysis. There was no evidence to suggest that private-sector organizations such as the building societies or the building industry would be willing to play a major part in renewal policy. In addition, the unfitness standard above which no grants would be available was very low and many practitioners foresaw the rapid decline of many older houses leading to an increase in future levels of clearance. The equity-sharing proposals were also dismissed as impractical.

The reform of housing renewal

As a result of the adverse reactions to the Green Paper, proposals for reform were shelved until 1987, when a second consultation paper appeared (Department of the Environment and Welsh Office 1987), and new legislation did not reach the statute book until the end of 1989 as part of the Local Government and Housing Act 1989. Renewal policy issues continued to be of low priority in the Government's legislative plans. The Act itself only provided a framework for the new system and specific details were set out in a series of subsequent circulars. Despite the long period of review and consultation which preceded the legislation, a very tight deadline was set for the introduction of the new Act and many details were finalized in haste to enable the system to become operational in April 1990. In practice this timetable proved too tight and the bulk of the legislative changes were delayed until July. Even then it was several more months before most authorities were in a position to process the new grants effectively and this caused the new system to get off to a very slow start. As a result of the haste, some major problems soon emerged with some elements of the system and barely a year after its introduction the Department of the Environment undertook a formal review of its operation.

The main elements of the new system

The new system was, in principle, similar to that proposed by the 1985 Green Paper. The core of the system was the standard of dwelling fitness for human habitation. Although this was updated and broadened in scope, it did not take into account factors such as an adequate electrical wiring system, the provision of central heating, or the energy efficiency of a building which could be considered essential in housing in the 1990s. Under the new legislation a local authority must take action to deal with any properties which are found to be unfit.

Secondly, the new legislation included a revised set of grants for home owners. The principal grant was the renovation grant which replaces the former improvement and repair grants. Local authorities must provide a grant (i.e. the grant is mandatory) for any works required to bring a dwelling up to the fitness standard, the amount of the grant being determined by a test of the applicant's resources. For work required to bring a dwelling up to a higher target standard, grant aid is also available but at the discretion of the local authority. A renovation grant can be used for the improvement and repair of owner-occupied properties or for the conversion of buildings into flats for letting but there are also common parts grants and house in multiple occupation (HMO) grants for the improvement of buildings already converted into flats or bedsits. Help to disabled people to enable them to remain living in their own homes is provided by the disabled facilities grant which is mandatory if used to provide access into a property or to allow a disabled occupant to get around and use essential facilities.

All applicants for the above grants are subject to a means test, referred to in circulars as the test of resources. The test is based on that used to assess entitlement to housing benefit. Average weekly income (including a notional amount of income from savings above a threshold of £5000) is set against a needs allowance made up of various personal allowances and premiums. This takes no account of mortgage outgoings. If an applicant's assessed weekly income is less than their needs they do not have to contribute to the cost of work, but if there is excess income, this is used to calculate the size of a notional loan that the applicant could afford to take out over a specified period. This amount is then deducted from the cost of work and the grant payable is the remaining sum, if any. The resources test for the disabled facilities grant is the same as that for the renovation grant, although the premiums are higher for disabled applicants. Where the disabled person is not the owner of the dwelling in question, the test of resources applies both to them and to the owner(s), and this can serve to reduce the amount of grant payable quite considerably in some cases. There is also a separate test of resources for landlords but this is based on the notional increase in the rental income of the property following improvement rather than on personal resources.

A further new discretionary grant called minor works assistance was also introduced for work costing up to £1000. The main purpose of the grant is to fund works necessary to enable an older person to stay put in their own home. There is no test of resources for minor works assistance and eligibility is based on the receipt of income related benefits such as housing benefit, income support and family credit.

Finally, the 1989 Act also made changes to the framework for area renewal. As the Green Paper proposed, GIAs and HAAs have been replaced by Renewal Areas which may vary in size from 500 to 3000 properties. The legislation and subsequent official guidance proposes that local authorities should develop broader strategies for these areas which do not just include housing but also tackle economic, social and environmental problems. Before declaring a renewal area authorities must carry out an assessment of the economic, social and environmental costs of different options for the area including selective clearance.

Implementing the new legislation

The aims of the proposed changes to the system of housing renewal were to 'secure better targeting, streamline the system wherever possible and encourage take up by those who need assistance' (Department of the Environment and Welsh Office 1987). But it is clear that local authorities have been experiencing considerable problems with implementation which may mean that not all of these objectives will be achieved. The new system got off to a very slow start and in the first full year of operation only just over 31 000 grants were approved in England, less than one-third of the level of activity under the last full year of the old system (Department of the Environment 1992). It is becoming clear that the main constraint on grant activity under the new system is resource levels. The Local Government and Housing Act 1989 also revised the system of allocating capital resources to local authorities, placing greater limits on their capacity to supplement HIP allocations by the use of capital receipts and squeezing all capital expenditure programmes. Secondly, the subsidy paid to local authorities for renovation grant expenditure (which was not cash-limited) was replaced by an annual capital grant which indicates the maximum amount of Exchequer subsidy for renovation grant expenditure available to each local authority. Finally, controls on revenue expenditure are also restricting the capacity of local authorities to provide renovation grants because they cannot afford to meet their share of the costs. As a result, many experienced considerable resource pressures and claims for supplementary credit approvals were oversubscribed by £30 million (*Environmental Health News* 1992).

The main problem for authorities with a large number of poor condition dwellings has been the potential demand for mandatory grants. Before the new system came into operation, 12 local authorities were involved in a pilot study to determine the impact of the new fitness standard. One authority, Blackburn, estimated that 99 per cent of properties surveyed were unfit and would qualify for mandatory grants, while 43 per cent of owners were assessed as being eligible for 100 per cent grants. However Blackburn's resources were not increased in order to meet this potential demand (Turney 1992).

Many authorities have begun to develop ways of managing demand which may undermine the objectives of the new system. Firstly, few authorities have actively promoted the new grants, or publicized the right to a grant where a dwelling is unfit. Secondly, the fitness standard is being interpreted very strictly in some areas in order to reduce the number of properties declared unfit or to restrict grant-aided work to the minimum necessary to bring the property up to the basic fitness standard. Finally, there has been little provision of discretionary renovation grants. Local authority data returns show that, excluding minor works grants, over 90 per cent of grants in Northern authorities were mandatory and even in the Midlands and London only about 25 per cent were discretionary (Table 8.1). But despite these measures, many authorities already have a backlog of enquiries and the AMA has claimed that there is already a two-year waiting list for grants (*Environmental Health News* 1991).

Activity in the private rented sector has also fallen to an all-time low with only

Table 8.1   Regional variations in grant approvals July 1990–June 1991

	Number of grants*		Percentage mandatory
	Mandatory	*Discretionary*	
North	766	94	89
Yorkshire/Humberside	1846	77	96
E. Midlands	928	328	74
E. Anglia	466	103	82
Greater London	602	241	71
Rest of S.E.	1505	313	83
S.W.	1002	207	83
W. Midlands	778	331	70
N.W.	1500	122	92
Wales	955	183	84
Total	10348	1999	84 average

* Includes renovation grants, disabled facilities grants, HMO grants, and common parts grants, but excludes minor works assistance.
Source: Department of the Environment (1992)

127 HMO grants paid in the first year of the new system, and even fewer common parts grants. The lack of progress in this area is a cause for concern as some of the worst house condition problems are located in these types of properties. The test of resources for landlords has been criticized by local authority officers as being too generous (e.g. Samuel 1992), but if this is so landlords have not realized it as only 3 per cent of enquiries came from this source compared to 12 per cent in 1989/90 under the old system (Kirkham 1992). Tenants have also been discouraged as they formed only 5 per cent of applicants compared with 16 per cent under the old system. The enforcement powers of local authorities were also strengthened by the 1989 Act but there is no evidence that this has resulted in more action being taken against unfit dwellings (Campbell 1992).

The test of resources has substantially increased the workload of grant departments by requiring them to make a two-stage assessment covering both the means of the applicant and the condition of the property. Most local authorities have developed an initial screening test to determine likely eligibility before going through the lengthy process of determining the applicant's contribution (which is the key factor determining the likelihood that a client will proceed), and before investing staff resources in a survey of the property. Authorities have had to invest in new computer software. In many areas authorities have had to increase the numbers of administrative staff and to provide extensive training programmes on the test of resources and the new fitness standard. In some cases, the new system has precipitated departmental reorganizations which have added to the delays in introducing the new system.

The main successes of the new system in numerical terms have been the new disabled facilities grant and the minor works grant. Almost 12 000 disabled facilities grants were approved in the first year. Minor works grants, although discretionary, were provided by a high proportion of authorities, in part because they were introduced in April 1990, three months before the other new grants. In total almost 20 000 were approved in the first year of the new system. However, the administration of these grants has not been without problems. The disabled facilities grant requires co-ordination between the department providing the grant and the local social services authority, usually the county council, which is required to assess the adaptation work required. In many parts of the country, severe shortages of occupational therapists who carry out these assessments have caused delays. In addition, because of the strictness of the test of resources, some applicants are unable to take up a grant because they cannot afford to meet their assessed contribution to the cost of work. In these circumstances, the social services department still has a duty to help the applicant, but since the 1989 Act came into force many have cut back on the resources which they have available to provide this top-up finance (Morris 1991).

The system has also succeeded in targeting grants on the groups most in need of help. According to the Department of the Environment, over one-third of enquiries for grants (excluding minor works) came from people on benefit and just under one-third were older people. In comparison less than one-quarter of people identified as receiving grants in the 1986 English House Condition Survey were older people (Department of the Environment 1988). Incomes of grant applicants were low in comparison to the national average with more than one-quarter of potential applicants having an income of less than £60 per week and only 17 per cent having more than £200 per week (Kirkham 1992). The minor works grant has also helped to target assistance on older people with low incomes. However, some problems have also emerged with targeting. The test of resources excludes consideration of housing costs such as mortgage repayments and as a result younger people with average incomes which are absorbed by large mortgage commitments are assessed to be capable of making a large contribition when in practice they cannot. In the past these have been the people most likely to carry out substantial home improvements. There is thus a danger that the new system will deter younger people from buying and renovating older, inner-city properties.

A further problem with targeting is the failure to direct resources on the pockets of poorest housing. The emphasis on responding to applications from individuals for mandatory grants is continuing the pepper-potting of grant aid which occurred in many areas under the old grant system and undermining the ability of local authorities to develop renewal strategies. Local authorities have been deterred from declaring renewal areas because of the complexity of organizing area renewal and because there is no long-term guarantee of resources for implementation. So far the number of declarations has been quite small. The powers provided by the 1989 Act to replace the old block repair and enveloping programmes have also proved cumbersome to operate (Moore 1992).

A further feature of the 1989 Act was the introduction of powers to enable local authorities to fund or to operate home improvement agencies. These are projects which offer practical help to home owners in dealing with building problems (Leather and Mackintosh 1992a). Agencies first developed in the early 1980s but expansion was restricted by a lack of secure funding. At the end of 1986 the Government launched an experimental initiative to provide support with the running costs of almost 80 projects and the 1989 Act made these arrangements more permanent. By 1992, Exchequer funding was being provided for more than 100 agencies, and in a number of other areas projects were running without the Government's funding. In the context of the new grant system, agencies have an important role to play in helping vulnerable or priority client groups to take up grants, or in providing advice to those who are now ineligible for grant aid. However, the level of coverage is still only partial, with only about one-third of districts in Britain having an agency service at present.

Overall, therefore, the original objectives of the Government to target resources more directly, streamline the system and encourage take-up by those in need have so far been only partially achieved. Targeting has focused resources on specific groups such as those on low incomes, older people and disabled people but weaknesses in the test of resources have excluded some younger home owners with large mortgage commitments and some disabled people from the receipt of adequate grant aid. Targeting has clearly not yet worked in terms of directing resources at the areas which have greatest concentrations of poorer condition housing and there is a danger that there will be a return to the pepper-potting of investment which was a characteristic of the early 1980s. The changes in housing renewal have certainly not simplified the operation of the grant system, but local authorities do appear to be rationalizing the way renewal policy is handled and seeking to provide a more customer-oriented service in some areas through an agency service. The final objective of encouraging take-up amongst those in greatest need has been least successful. In many areas, local authorities are not encouraging people to come forward for help as they have been overwhelmed by the demand for mandatory grants.

The review of the new system

As we have indicated, the Department of the Environment has already undertaken a review of the operation of the new system. From 1993/94 it is likely that the national sum available for renovation grants will be earmarked with the amount allocated to each authority determined by separate needs indicators. This should direct more resources to authorities with a higher proportion of poor condition housing, as at present those with fewer problems spend relatively more (Leather and Mackintosh 1992b). The allocation will also depend on an assessment of local authority performance (*Environmental Health News* 1992). This change could help those authorities presently unable to meet the demand for mandatory grants, but it is unlikely to do so unless the overall amount provided for grants is increased. It may also mean that future grant expenditure work will be directed solely at dealing with unfitness rather than prevention of further disrepair. This, of course, would be very much in line with the Government's broader approach to the provision of state aid. Any other short-term changes to the system will affect the test of resources, including the allowances and premiums which apply to disabled people. It is not yet clear whether any account will be taken of mortgage commitments. Longer-term changes will require amendments to legislation.

The future for housing renewal

This chapter has shown that housing renewal policies over the last 20 years have failed to address the rise in the level of home ownership in the older housing stock. Lack of resources, ineffective targeting, and the need to rely primarily on voluntary participation by owners to secure the implementation of policies have led to pepper-potting of grant investment and the abandonment of local renewal strategies in most areas.

Reform of the housing renewal system was therefore long overdue but the new powers provided by the Local Government and Housing Act 1989 will not prove satisfactory in dealing with house condition problems in the private sector. The legislation appears to have been conceived in order to focus investment solely on bringing properties in the poorest condition up to a minimal fitness standard at the least expense to the public purse. Beyond this level the responsibility for repairs and improvements lies with the owners and the legislation shows little concern with the way they tackle these problems.

There are also some issues which the new legislation did not address. As Figure 8.4 showed, the level of clearance in England and Wales fell off sharply from the mid-1970s to reach a very low level by the 1990s. Guidance on renewal area implementation stresses that clearance should be considered as a viable option for the worst property. But resident opposition remains strong and, even with improved compensation levels, it is often impossible for affected households to remain as owner occupiers because they cannot afford to purchase a house elsewhere. In many inner city areas, close community ties also strengthen opposition to clearance by ethnic minority groups (Heywood and Naz 1990). If the level of clearance is to increase, new mechanisms are needed which recognize and seek to meet the objections of home owners, but these are bound to be expensive. With continuing constraints on HIP allocations there is little prospect that authorities will be able to afford more clearance in the foreseeable future.

The new grant system continues to rely on the injection of a large sum of money to stimulate improvement at one point in time and does nothing to address the problem of long-term maintenance. If the state is prepared to invest resources in 100 per cent grants to owners it is sensible to preserve the investment by ensuring that buildings are kept in good condition through the provision of a similar means-tested benefit for assistance with ongoing maintenance. It can be argued that owners should meet maintenance costs but it is unrealistic to expect low income households to give home maintenance any priority when there are more pressing demands on their scarce resources. In some Dutch cities grant aid has been made conditional on owners signing a long-term maintenance agreement, but income levels may not be as low as those which qualify for grant in England and Wales (Benko 1991). An experimental project in Walsall aims to encourage maintenance through the use of an in-surance scheme but it is too early to determine if low income households will take advantage of this scheme. Individual local authorities have also tried to encourage maintenance by issuing grant recipients and home owners with booklets describing the need for maintenance and the checks which they should periodically carry out. However, all these schemes are small in scale.

For those who fall outside the grant system, especially those on low incomes, it is important to obtain information on alternative sources of finance. Home improvement agencies have shown that they have an important role to play but so far the resources available for the expansion of this service have been inadequate. The national coverage is still far from complete, and where projects exist they can only cover small areas or help a restricted client group, mainly older people. Local authority agencies have developed but they are narrowly focused on grant recipients and do not offer the broader service which is required in an era of mass home ownership. It is possible that fee-paying services could develop for people in higher income groups but there is still a need for more public resources to fund agencies for those people falling outside the grant system who are on low incomes and living in older, poor condition housing.

Finally, there are new and emerging problems to be dealt with. The ageing of the home-owning population is leading to an increase in the numbers of low-income older home owners needing practical and financial help with repairs and maintenance. The inter-War stock is now beginning to require major investment in repairs, and properties bought under the right to buy will begin to need attention. The period of high house prices combined with the recession in the late 1980s means that many people will have deferred maintenance and repair expenditure exacerbating the problems of poor conditions in the future. Unless state funding for private-sector renovation is substantially increased, or new mechanisms such as equity-sharing loans or increased welfare benefits are found to enable low income home owners to fund work, we face the prospect of a continuing decline in the condition of the older housing stock.

References

Benko, A. (1991) *Home Maintenance Insurance Schemes: The Dutch Experience*, An-chor European Occasional Papers No.1, Oxford, Anchor Housing Trust.

Campbell, R. (1992) 'Houses in multiple occupation – the new regulations', *Housing*, December 1991/January 1992: 24–5.

Central Housing Advisory Committee (1966) *Our Older Homes: A Call for Action*, Report of the Sub-committee on Standards of Housing Fitness (the Denington Report), London, HMSO.

Davies, J. (1972) *The Evangelistic Bureaucrat*, London, Tavistock.

Dennis, N. (1970) *People and Planning*, London, Faber.

Department of the Environment (1982) *English House Condition Survey 1981, Part 1: Report of the Physical Condition Survey*, London, HMSO.

Department of the Environment (1983) *English House Condition Survey 1981, Part 2: Report of the Interview and Local Authority Survey*, London, HMSO.

Department of the Environment (1988) *English House Condition Survey 1986*, London, HMSO.

Department of the Environment (1992) *Housing and Construction Statistics Part 2, No. 46*, London, HMSO.

Department of the Environment, Scottish Development Department, Welsh Office (1991) *Housing and Construction Statistics 1980–1990, Great Britain*, London, HMSO.

Department of the Environment and Welsh Office (1987) *Home Improvement Policy: The Government's Proposals*, London, Department of the Environment.

Department of the Environment (unpublished), 'Distribution of Grant Enquiry', London, Department of the Environment.

English, J., Madigan, R. and Norman, P. (1976) *Slum Clearance*, London, Croom Helm.

Environmental Health News (1991) 'Confidential DoE report confirms grant shambles', August: 4.

Environmental Health News (1992) 'Grant resources to be allocated separately in HIP', February: 7.

Forrest, R., Murie, A. and Williams, P. (1990) *Home Ownership: Differentiation and Fragmentation*, London, Unwin Hyman.

Gibson, M. (1986) 'Housing Renewal: privatization and beyond', in P. Malpass (ed.) *The Housing Crisis*, London, Croom Helm.

Gibson, M. and Langstaff, M. (1982) *An Introduction to Urban Renewal*, London, Hutchinson.

Hamnett, C. and Williams, P. (1979), *Gentrification in London 1961–71*, Research Memo No. 71, Birmingham, Centre for Urban and Regional Studies, University of Birmingham.

Heywood, F. and Rashid Naz, M. (1990) *Clearance: The View from the Street*, Birmingham, Community Forum.

HMSO (1985) *Home Improvement – A New Approach*, Cmnd. 9513, London.

Holmans, A. (1987) *Housing Policy in Britain*, London, Croom Helm.

Kirk, H. and Leather, P. (1991) *Age File: The Facts*, Oxford, Anchor Housing Trust.

Kirkham, A. (1992) 'First results from the new system', in S. Mackintosh and P. Leather (eds) *Home Improvement Under the New Regime*, Occasional Paper 38, Bristol, School for Advanced Urban Studies.

Leather, P. and Mackintosh, S. (1992a) *Maintaining Home Ownership: The Agency Approach*, London, Longman/Institute of Housing.

Leather, P. and Mackintosh, S. (1992b) *A Profile of Activity Under the Old Grant System*, mimeo, Bristol, School for Advanced Urban Studies.

Leather, P. and Murie, A. (1986) 'The decline in public expenditure', in P. Malpass (ed.) *The Housing Crisis*, London, Croom Helm.

Ministry of Housing and Local Government (1967) 'House condition survey, England and Wales 1967', *Economic Trends*, No. 175, London, HMSO.

Moore, P. (1992) 'Renovation: is group repair the answer?' in S. Mackintosh and P. Leather (eds) *Home Improvement Under the New Regime*, Occasional Paper 38, Bristol, School for Advanced Urban Studies.

Morris, J. (1991) 'Adding injustice to disability', *Inside Housing*, October: 8–9.

Needleman, L. (1969) 'The comparative economics of improvement and new building', *Urban Studies*, Vol. 6, No. 2: 196–209.

Northern Ireland Housing Executive (1988) *1987 House Condition Survey*, Belfast, Northern Ireland Housing Executive, Housing and Planning Division.

Office of Population Census and Surveys (1991) *1989 General Household Survey*, London, HMSO.

Samuel, R. (1992) 'Implementing the new system: the local authority experience', in S. Mackintosh and P. Leather (eds) *Home Improvement Under the New Regime*, Occasional Paper 38, Bristol, School for Advanced Urban Studies.

Thomas, A. (1986) *Housing and Urban Renewal*, Urban and Regional Studies 12, London, Allen and Unwin.

Turney, J. (1992) 'Dealing with unfit properties', in S. Mackintosh and P. Leather (eds) *Home Improvement Under the New Regime*, Occasional Paper 38, Bristol, School for Advanced Urban Studies.

Welsh Office (1988) *1986 Welsh House Condition Survey*, Cardiff, Welsh Office Publications Unit.

CHAPTER 9

The enabling role for local housing authorities: a preliminary evaluation

GLEN BRAMLEY

Introduction

This chapter discusses the 'enabling role' of the local authority (LA) in housing, with particular reference to the provision of new social housing opportunities. This role has become a central element in the Conservative Government's view of the future institutional framework for housing policy in Britain, as developed since 1987 (Department of the Environment 1987, 1989), although it can be argued that many local authorities have tried to play such a role over at least a decade (Bramley *et al*. 1979). The chapter addresses six key questions:

- What is the *policy*?
- Is it *genuine*, or symbolic?
- Is enabling *sufficient*, in the sense of being potentially capable of delivering appropriate social housing?
- Is the enabling approach *performing* adequately in practice?
- Is a reliance on enabling *fair* in its outcomes?
- Do *organizational and professional* approaches matter?

The treatment is thus somewhat sceptical and questioning, applying some of the perspectives of policy analysis and implementation theory to this particular arena. Although some of the practical techniques of 'enabling' the provision of social housing are identified and briefly described, this chapter does not constitute a 'how-to-do-it' manual (examples of this include House Builders' Federation 1989, 1990; Clark and Dunmore 1990; Institute of Housing 1990; Bishop *et al*. 1991; Fraser 1991). Most references to specific aspects of policy and practice refer to England, although there are some limited references to Wales. And the emphasis is largely on enabling the provision of new or additional (e.g.

acquired) social housing provision, rather than upon the renovation of the housing stock or its management.

What is the policy?

How do we define 'enabling' here? A short definition would be to say that the LA's enabling role consists of that range of activities that makes possible, encourages or facilitates the provision of social housing opportunities by bodies other than the LA itself. In practice, the most important other type of body would be housing associations, but private developers, financial institutions and other bodies, for example local community trusts, could also be involved.

'Social housing' is defined here as rented or shared ownership housing provided at less than full market rents and managed by a socially responsible landlord conforming to a form of tenants' charter or guarantee. The terms 'low cost' or 'affordable' housing are often used rather loosely in this context; arguably, all social housing should be affordable and (relatively) low cost, but not all low cost or affordable housing, particularly schemes involving private developers and full owner occupation, constitutes social housing in the above sense.

Probably the nearest to an official government statement on what they had in mind by 'enabling' was contained in an appendix to a circular letter from the Department of the Environment (1989: 1–2) to the local authorities:

> Local authorities are ceasing to be the main providers of subsidized housing for rent; but they will remain responsible for ensuring, so far as resources permit, the needs for new housing in their areas are met, by the private sector alone where possible, with public sector subsidy where necessary. This will require some of them to take a broader view of their responsibilities than they have in the past, and to develop their information sources and monitoring arrangements accordingly. Much of the HIP [Housing Investment Programme] submission itself will be about expenditure needed to provide for people who cannot afford housing at market prices or cannot maintain their homes without public sector support. Need should be justified, however, by reference to the extent to which the private sector is able and willing to make provision for low cost housing and the steps that the authority is taking both to maximise the private sector contribution, and to make the best use of its own stock.

The first point to note is the rather disingenuous suggestion that the shift away from direct provision by local authorities was a wholly spontaneous, freely chosen outcome which had already happened. This contains a germ of truth, but local authorities had been strongly discouraged from new building by a number of features of the post-1979 regime (e.g. the Right to Buy, shortage of capital funds, and zero marginal subsidy in most cases; see Hills 1991), and the effective administrative discouragement since 1989 has been very strong. Secondly, it is clear that the private sector is seen as the primary provider of new housing, with publicly subsidized housing in a 'residual' role; furthermore, the private sector's role at the margin should be maximized, for example through low-cost sale schemes. Thirdly, assessment of need should have an explicit economic component, both in terms of what households can afford and in terms of what developers may be willing and able to provide.

However, this policy should not be interpreted as a simple case of privatization, since the existence of needs requiring publicly subsidized provision is acknowledged. In addition, the second sentence of the quotation actually urges local authorities to adopt a *wider* role than some have in the past, at least in relation to their assessment of need and monitoring functions. This echoes advice on the broader concept of local housing strategies going back at least to the introduction of HIPs in the 1970s (Department of the Environment 1977; Bramley *et al*. 1979) and arguably back to Cullingworth in 1969.

The 'strategic' role of the LA is something which is more strongly emphasized by some other organizations. The Association of District Councils (1990: para. 5.8) draws a distinction between the strategic and enabling roles as follows:

If the strategic role is about the district council 'holding the ring' amongst these players, acting as a catalyst and orchestrating their various contributions to the meeting of local need, the enabling role is the direct provision of help to these other agencies – particularly housing associations and builders/developers – within the overall housing strategic plan drawn up by the district council in conjunction with the other partners.

Apart from employing an interesting mixture of metaphors, this statement makes the important point that a potentially large number of other 'players' or 'partners' are involved; in addition to those already mentioned, other local authorities, health authorities, government departments, the Housing Corporation and voluntary organizations. The distinction between strategy and enabling is broadly helpful, although in practice some activities in the former category may simultaneously act to facilitate housing provision. For example, involving some key groups in general consultation may cause them to become supportive of some specific initiative. The ADC report (para. 5.6) also stresses the statutory planning function of the LA which overlaps strongly with much of the strategic housing role. This point is echoed by the Institute of Housing (1990: 106), who go on to add a number of other elements. These include promoting tenure diversity and choice, standard-setting, access to housing, homelessness, housing advice services, Housing Benefits, and liaison with health and social services.

Some more concrete examples of enabling activities can be identified within the DoE guidance. These include the following:

- ensuring adequate land supply for private housebuilding
- releasing land held by the authority, perhaps under licence, in partnership schemes providing low-cost sale and shared ownership
- land assembly, for housing associations or others
- nominating tenants to low-cost sale schemes or use of other incentives to encourage better-off tenants to move out of council housing

- achieving better utilization of the stock, reducing voids and underoccupation
- promoting private renting by appropriate land disposal and direct subsidy (permitted under the Local Government Act 1988)
- using powers to allocate LA capital resources to housing associations ('LA HAG') to extend the programmes of HAs, now the main providers of additional social housing;
- considering large-scale stock transfers to HAs.

This list could be described as something of a hotch-potch of various schemes or preoccupations currently favoured by the Government, and indeed the Institute of Housing (1990: 107) suggested that the key legislative Acts of 1988 and 1989 had 'a piecemeal character' with 'little that unifies them'. It is also fair to say that the Government's illustrative list of examples of enabling (a) put more emphasis on the importance of private, as opposed to housing association and voluntary sector, involvement, and (b) confirm a rather strong set of assumptions about the 'residual' role of council housing (Forrest and Murie 1983), compared with the picture obtained from the other organizations mentioned.

This chapter assumes that there is indeed a need for the provision of additional social housing, an issue which has been much discussed elsewhere (Bramley 1989, 1991a; Niner 1989; Wilcox 1990; Joseph Rowntree Foundation 1991; Audit Commission 1992). Another important assumption is that completely unfettered market systems do not in practice meet all such housing requirements (see Chapter 5; Le Grand and Robinson 1984; Muellbauer 1990).

Attention should also be drawn to one general feature of this policy, that distinguishes it from many other policies. The focus is on means, rather than upon ends in the conventional sense (housing outputs and outcomes). In fact, the emphasis is on institutional frameworks and styles of operation. It is much easier to come up with a negative definition of the policy, especially for the Conservative Government, namely that the most important characteristic of enabling is that it is *not local authority* provision.

The general implementation literature reviewed in Chapter 2 highlights the dependence of implementation on the co-operation of other agencies and the tendency of problems to mount with the number of other agencies involved. The enabling approach to social housing provision is inherently a high-risk approach for this very reason, because it relies by definition on outside agencies. Voluntary co-operation would seem to be much more likely to be achieved where there is a good deal of consensus about broad goals and a high level of trust. Continuing ideological discord, or even a recent history of such discord, may greatly undermine voluntary co-operation. So also would distrust arising from the latent competition between different agencies for key roles in the process. This may arise in this case, not just in the obvious case of the private and public sectors, but also in relation to local authorities and housing associations; it is noticeable that the leading professional body has seen the need positively to promote models of collaborative working for the 1990s (Fraser 1991).

The policy is, as already pointed out, mainly about institutions and about styles of working. It is not centrally about numbers, unlike many housing policies of the past (although some agencies are engaged in various numbers games, as discussed further below). It is not about achieving some clearly defined goals in terms of quantitative outcomes. After 1979 the Conservative Government resolutely refused to commit itself to any national assessment of housing need (House of Commons 1980), although this position has come increasingly to be questioned (Audit Commission 1992). It is easy to criticize crude numerical targets of the kind that characterized the 1950s and 1960s; such targets may neglect quality and discount diversity. But the lack of quantitative targets makes it much harder to judge how far the policy has been implemented.

This lack of quantification also implies that a LA could probably acquire the trappings of the enabling role – for example certain internal and external organizational structures, strategic documents identifying a number of programmes, and so forth – without necessarily doing very much or, crucially, spending very much. This can be linked to the point that it is local authorities, if anyone, who are supposed to assess need and develop strategies appropriate to local conditions. While some authorities might follow this through in a very comprehensive and ambitious way, coming up with a strategy that would indeed be hard to implement without far more resources, others (even in objectively similar housing markets) might produce estimates of need and strategies for action which were, in the quantitative sense, very modest. These local strategies are to some extent judged by the Department of the Environment, but through a process that could not easily be described as open and accountable.

If the LA is the key strategic agent in bringing about the provision of social housing, it might seem a little odd that it is not the main channel for public resources into the main provider agencies, the housing associations. This role is currently performed by the Housing Corporation. In theory, this separation could seriously weaken local authorities in their strategic enabling role. In practice, it can help to overcome the phenomenon alluded to above, of inactive local authorities where the Housing Corporation can and often does attempt to compensate.

At a more general level, there is a basic tension, if not contradiction, between enabling in the sense of loosening constraints (e.g. planning, regulation, bureaucracy) on other agencies, and enabling in the sense of enabling some outcome to happen by using certain powers or modes of influence to modify the behaviour of certain actors (e.g. use of compulsory purchase powers to complete assembly of a site). Enabling in the first sense may come very close to withdrawal from the field altogether. Enabling in the second sense probably becomes necessary because not all actors share all goals and there are some conflicts of interest.

One other obvious feature of the enabling policy which is relevant to implementation is that it is likely to be highly dependent upon market conditions. This is particularly so in the Conservative Government's vision, which places great stress on the private sector. As we shall see when this is discussed further below, it is actually not quite so clear how market conditions affect the ability of an enabling authority to achieve results.

Is the policy genuine, or symbolic?

This question is a natural extension of the discussion about the nature of the policy. Edelman (1971) coined the term 'symbolic policy' to describe situations where the symbolism created by statements and apparent action by Government is more important, in its impact on public opinion in the political marketplace, than the actual substantive achievements of the policy on the ground. This phenomenon seems rather commonplace, but perhaps this depends how stringently one defines it, for example in relation to the intentions of Government and the information and resources it has available. Many policies are well-intentioned but inadequately resourced, relative to the absolute size of the problems they address; other policies may be uncertain in their effectiveness, but this may be difficult to judge in advance; others again may start off 'symbolic' but become more substantial in response to continuing political pressure.

Is the enabling role of the LA in housing an exercise in symbolic politics, or a genuine policy? If we start with the case for regarding it as symbolic, we have to establish two things: that the policy is inherently unable or unlikely to deliver much substantial output; and that this was known (or assumed) by Government at the outset. The evidence on the first proposition is detailed in subsequent sections of this chapter, but the gist of the argument is that the policy, while flawed and incomplete, is not inherently doomed to failure. With regard to the second proposition, it is rather difficult to produce hard evidence about intentions or assumptions lying behind contemporary policies, because of the relatively closed nature of British central government and the general nature of politics. However, it is not difficult to speculate about the reasons that might lie behind the promotion of the enabling role as an essentially symbolic policy.

Firstly, this approach certainly saves public expenditure, something which all governments have to be concerned about, and particularly a government which gives priority to tax cuts. It is worth noting that the Local Government and Housing Act 1989 reformed the system of control over LA capital investment and finance in a way which reduced flexibility in the use of resources as well as the sheer volume of resources (Association of District Councils 1991). The majority of the large quantity of capital receipts accumulated by local authorities, mainly from council house sales under the Right to Buy, are treated as unavailable for reinvestment, and must be set aside to repay debt, thereby reducing the Public Sector Borrowing Requirement (PSBR) and the Government's subsidy bill.

Secondly, the Conservative Government of the 1980s was clearly engaged in a process of trying to reduce the role of the state and expectations about what the state can and should provide. A view that the LA's role is to enable others, particularly individuals or private enterprise, to provide housing rather than to provide it itself, fits naturally into this strategy. The whole concept of 'social housing' smacks of 'social engineering', something else which was also very much out of favour at this time. Some uneasiness about aspects of the enabling role, particularly in relation to new style social housing, may be related to a concern that this might constitute a new form of social engineering.

But one problem in particular has meant that the Government could not completely ignore the need for social housing: the problem of homelessness. The number of statutory homeless households accepted by local authorities in England rose from 53 000 in 1978 to 147 000 in 1990/91. In addition, problems of access to owner occupation (Bramley 1989, 1990a) at a time of house price boom, and subsequently affordability of mortgages in the face of record interest rates, have also been issues to which the Government felt compelled to make some response (Joseph Rowntree Foundation 1992). The enabling role could be said to allow the Government to be seen to be doing something about the provision of social housing. It also provides a good opportunity to deflect criticism for inadequate performance on to local authorities. The role of local government as a convenient scapegoat for policy failure has been noted in other contexts (Bramley 1990b).

Finally, it could be argued that the Government could quite easily have made a judgement about the likely extent of contribution of the private sector to the provision of social or low-cost housing. Essentially this is a matter of economics and the sums are not that difficult. In addition, the extent of actual or prospective participation in social or rented housing investment by major companies and financial institutions would not be difficult to establish, whether through published sources or informal personal contact.

While we can see some obvious reasons why the enabling role might be a symbolic exercise, we cannot clearly demonstrate that this was its intention. In fact, there are a number of tangible indications that it does have some substance.

Homelessness provides the first instance. Ministers appear to be genuinely concerned about this issue and to accept the responsibility for ensuring some action in response. Various special programmes have been developed to attempt to tackle the worst manifestations of the problem. More importantly, perhaps, the opportunity of a special review of the homelessness legislation (Department of the Environment 1988) was not used as an occasion to reduce significantly the scope of the LA's responsibilities to homeless families, and indeed the Code of Guidance was strengthened (Department of the Environment 1991b).

It is important to recognize that the enabling role gives local authorities legitimacy to operate in quite a wide-ranging fashion. Thus, they can try to influence the behaviour of many other organizations, public and private. They can effectively mobilize voluntary and community groups which may then become an additional source of pressure for action and resources. They are strongly encouraged, as for example in the planning context, to undertake special surveys of local housing need or provide better data on needs generally (Department of the Environment 1991a).

Thirdly, the range of powers open to local authorities has on balance been widened. The details are discussed further below, but the use of land use planning powers to secure the provision of social housing is a major development. On a more modest scale, modifications were made to the Local Government and Housing Act 1989 to enable certain types of LA land disposal for social housing not to create a major penalty or disincentive in terms of the capital controls rules. The Local Government Act 1988 made it possible for local authorities directly to subsidize private landlords or housing associations providing housing to rent. Contrary to many predictions, local authorities have retained the right to lend to housing associations and thereby commit part of the public capital grant known as HAG. The decision of the Government to give the lead responsibility in Community Care to local authorities, the major role of housing in this, and the likely move towards unitary local authorities together also provide another important example of how the scope of the LA role is in some respects expanding.

Ultimately, the proof of the pudding is whether some or most local authorities show that they can achieve substantial results through enabling. As discussed further below, there are indications that some at least can. It is also currently the policy of the Department of the Environment to use the allocation of general and specific capital resources to local authorities as a mechanism for rewarding efficiency and effectiveness of performance; in part this is concerned with housing management, but it is increasingly clear that active 'enabling' is also being rewarded.

So a case can be made either way on this issue. On the whole it would seem to be unfair to dismiss the whole enterprise as symbolic politics. Even if it is symbolic, it may provide a legitimate vehicle for ingenious and energetic local authorities to do a lot; even if it is genuine, it may easily coexist with inaction at the local level.

Is it sufficient?

The next question to address is whether the enabling role is sufficient to bring about a reasonable supply of social housing provision at affordable cost. The possibilities depend crucially on whether LAs have adequate *powers and resources*, at least in those critical situations where other agencies have to be induced to do something that they would probably not do otherwise. Chapter 2 argued that negotiation is a central process and concept in implementation, and negotiation is generally analyzed primarily in terms of the power and resources of the participants. Clearly enabling is very much about negotiation. What levers does a LA have beyond exhortation and persuasion?

Figure 9.1 attempts to summarize the main levers that are potentially available. These fall into four main categories: finance; land ownership; land use planning; and clients/communities. The first three are perhaps more obvious and tangible than the fourth, but there are interesting ways in which this aspect of the LA role can be used in the enabling context. Figure 9.1 lists some of the specific powers or resources under each heading. The figure also illustrates the point that many schemes involve combinations of these elements, so they are not mutually exclusive alternatives. Some very interesting examples illustrating this point are to be found in Fraser (1991), and it would take too long to describe such schemes in detail here.

To provide social housing requires finance in two forms, capital to finance the development and a subsidy to lower the cost for lower-income occupiers to an

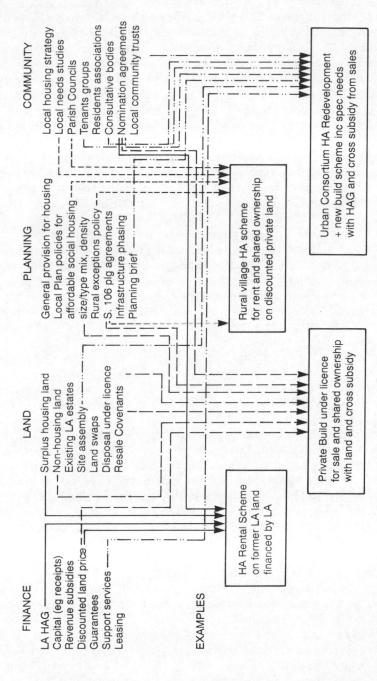

Figure 9.1 Enabling powers and resources

FINANCE

LA HAG
Capital (eg receipts)
Revenue subsidies
Discounted land price
Guarantees
Support services
Leasing

LAND

Surplus housing land
Non-housing land
Existing LA estates
Site assembly
Land swaps
Disposal under licence
Resale Covenants

PLANNING

General provision for housing
Local Plan policies for
affordable social housing
size/type mix, density
Rural exceptions policy
S. 106 plg agreements
Infrastructure phasing
Planning brief

COMMUNITY

Local housing strategy
Local needs studies
Parish Councils
Tenants groups
Residents associations
Consultative bodies
Nomination agreements
Local community trusts

EXAMPLES

HA Rental Scheme
on former LA land
financed by LA

Private Build under licence
for sale and shared ownership
with land and cross subsidy

Rural village HA scheme
for rent and shared ownership
on discounted private land

Urban Consortium HA Redevelopment
+ new build scheme inc spec needs
with HAG and cross subsidy from sales

affordable level. The main issues on the capital side are risk and the 'front-loading' of financing costs (Hills 1991). In the past local authorities borrowed to finance housing, and as public bodies with independent tax raising powers they could borrow on virtually the same terms as government. As their housing stocks grew they increasingly took advantage of the ability to pool debts and rents. Now, relatively small housing associations and other bodies have to borrow against their limited assets on a market which is unfamiliar with them, without government guarantee. Currently British Treasury rules treat any guarantee given to a lender by central or local government or their agencies as public expenditure to the full value of the loan; this rule is particularly unhelpful in the housing field. Opinions differ, but it would appear that broadly finance is available, at least to the larger associations, but at a price (Couttie 1991; Pryke and Whitehead 1991). In effect, though, this availability of private finance assumes that subsidy will be available in substantial measure through some route or other.

While the Conservative Government wishes to see maximal involvement of the private sector, those close to the scene realize that social housing still requires subsidy in some form. There is indeed implicit acceptance that there is a need for general subsidy on new investment, sometimes called 'bricks and mortar subsidy', as well as the individual means tested subsidy to renters provided by HB; although it could be argued that a reformed HB system together with better capital financing and pooling arrangements might lessen the need for external general subsidy (see, for example, Bramley 1990c; Hills 1991; Joseph Rowntree Foundation 1991). The most direct form of subsidy is the Housing Association Grant (HAG) paid at a rate of around 60–70 per cent on new capital schemes, mainly by the Housing Corporation but in some cases by the LAs themselves. For a LA to provide HAG it must use some of its scarce allocation of capital spending/borrowing permission or the limited (25 per cent in most cases) share of capital receipts from the sale of council houses and other assets. LA HAG currently represents £250 million per year or about 12 per cent of the overall HA programme. Where LA stock is transferred wholesale to a HA, there is usually an expectation that some at least of the usable capital receipt would be re-applied to new social housing investment through this mechanism.

Much of enabling activity by LAs is about trying to get more of a given budget for public subsidy (i.e. HAG) spent in its area, although there is currently a good deal of attention given to 'HAG-stretching', a sort of co-financing arrangement where the LA throws in some subsidy by another mechanism, most often cheap land. Apart from this, it is difficult for LAs to control in a positive way the resource allocation decisions of the Housing Corporation, although it has some negative power in some situations insofar as the Corporation rarely supports a scheme actively opposed by the LA.

Local authorities have had since 1988 a general power to subsidize housing provision by private landlords as well as HAs but so far only limited use has been made of this power, partly because of the tight situation of most LAs on their general revenue funds. As Care in the Community develops, LAs may increasingly find themselves spending on intensive management and support arrangements associated with the housing of people with social care needs, and this may become one of the main channels of revenue subsidy to social housing at the local level.

The most important source of subsidy other than HAG is land value, or rather discounts on land value, although 'cross-subsidy' within mixed developments is also potentially quite important. The cheap land may be local authority or other public land; if so, the rules define this as public subsidy too, which has several specific implications. Firstly, if there is a cheap land subsidy, HAG will be reduced accordingly; thus, the subsidy cannot be used to produce lower rents than the levels implicit in the HAG formula. The LA's options are limited here to trying to get more units built, and do not include trying to pursue a low rent policy based on a different view about affordability from the Government. Secondly, if any public subsidy (including cheap public land) goes into a shared ownership scheme, the occupier must have the right to 'staircase' to full owner-ship (except in small rural settlements). This means that the unit may well not be available as social housing in the future, an issue of great concern to many LAs. Indeed, this issue has led many LAs to be less eager to support low-cost sale schemes because of the same longer-term outcome, together with the excess capital gain enjoyed by the first occupier. The staircasing rule has actually encouraged a more innovative approach to enabling, involving private rather than publicly owned land. Thirdly, discounting the land could be disadvan-tageous for the LA under the capital expenditure and receipts rules. But late modifications to the Local Government and Housing Act 1989 and associated regulations make it possible to make such a subsidy, in exchange for nomination rights and undertakings (e.g. through covenants) about future occupancy and resale, without having to set aside non-existent notional receipts to pay off debt.

Some LAs have at times been unclear what powers they still had to provide land at a discount. The general power to dispose of land requires the authority to get the best price, and some auditors have questioned certain practices in relation to low cost housing. Another example of confusion was the case of 'in-and-out' or 'swap' schemes, which some LAs used in the 1980s, whereby land was bought and sold almost immediately, or swapped, in a way which created no longer-term increase in public liabilities; the Government moved to disallow these in 1989. These interrelated points about the financial aspects of discounted land illustrate a general theme in implementation. Sometimes Government policies overlap and to a degree conflict. This is certainly true here: the Government wanted to control capital spending and the proliferation of loopholes in the control system, and it wanted to maximize its public spend-ing/PSBR savings; at the same time it wanted LAs to switch to an enabling role in housing. What emerged, after some zigzags and lobbying, was something of a compromise. But the process itself was confusing and left many LAs uncertain and consequently probably less active. And the rules as they now exist are not exactly simple and transparent, which rather discourages a free-floating, inno-vative approach at local level, and encourages a somewhat legalistic obsession with the rules.

LAs can use HAG or other subsidy, where available, and their ownership of development sites, to exercise considerable influence over what social housing is produced. As landowner the LA has much more influence over who does the development, when and on what terms, than in cases where some other agency owns the land. Covenants can be used to restrict future occupancy, tenure and prices. LAs can and do invite HAs to compete in putting forward schemes for particular sites, with a view to choosing that which maximizes the achievement of the LA's objectives and priorities.

The third main lever open to LAs is particularly relevant to development on land not owned by the LA, including that held by private developers. This is the use of Town and Country Planning powers to specify that part or all of certain developments should be affordable social housing. Use of the land use planning system in this way, for social housing purposes, is largely a new departure, although there were some attempts to use planning powers to restrict housing to 'local needs' in some areas (e.g. the Lake District) and some use of planning agreements to secure housing within commercial developments (Barlow and Chambers 1991). Current official policy is set out in DoE *Circular 7/91* (Department of the Environment 1991a) and *Planning Policy Guidance Note 3* (Department of the Environment 1992), while the underlying issues are discussed in Bishop and Hooper (1991).

There are two versions of this mechanism. The first is the rural 'exceptions sites' case, whereby small sites typically on the edge of villages in rural areas of planning restraint, which were not previously designated for housing use, may be released for affordable social housing to meet identified local needs. Mixed private/social schemes are discouraged so that generally cross-subsidy is not available, only the subsidy from the land being made available at a low price by its (normally) private owner. The second version is potentially the more important, and arises on medium-large developments seeking planning permission, where the LA may require a certain proportion of the development to be affordable social housing. This proportion must not be a 'rigid quota' regardless of circumstances, and must be justified by evidence of needs and local plan policies. In both cases the implementation of the agreed social housing package is ensured through the use of planning agreements under Section 106 (formerly 52) of the Planning Act as well as covenants and the involvement of HAs (or possibly other bodies like local trusts).

The evolution of this mechanism sheds interesting light on the policy process. Firstly, it represents a significant break with established Government policy on the nature of the planning system, which had previously been to try to restrict it to a narrower agenda of physical land use and environmental issues and to discourage its use for 'social engineering' purposes. Secondly, the first break, the thin end of the wedge as it were, occurred in respect of the rural exceptions element. The rural lobby were relatively successful in persuading the Conservative Government that there was a problem that called for some response. Thirdly, the policy process, as with other aspects of enabling, had quite a strong 'bottom-up' character. The attempted use of planning powers in this way was pioneered by a number of individual LAs (e.g. New Forest district) before central government eventually responded by legitimizing and indeed promoting certain aspects.

The fourth lever the LA has in the enabling arena is the influence it can command over and through the representative organs of the local community. This power is less concrete in the legal sense but may be very important in reality. The LA is uniquely well placed in this regard because it is the only general purpose elected local body with wide-ranging powers and a general competence to act in the best interests of the locality. Many leading figures in the community are or have been elected councillors or are connected through local party networks. Most local voluntary and community groups depend in different ways upon their relationship with the LA. The LA's activities are heavily reported in the local media.

The significance of this is that any particular agency seeking to undertake a development will need to involve certain other groups or agencies and secure their support or at any rate acquiescence. For example, a private developer trying to build on a former hospital site will have to get the co-operation of the health authority, statutory infrastructure providers, and hopefully local residents. The LA has ongoing relationships with these other parties and may well be able to orchestrate the views of some of them, either in favour if the scheme fits in with its enabling strategy or against if it does not.

A more particular aspect of the LA's legitimacy and role in respect of the local community is its involvement with housing needs and the potential clients of social housing. The LA is the body officially charged with assessing local housing needs and ensuring, so far as possible, that these are met, particularly in the most serious cases including homelessness and unfitness. In some ways, the current policy thrust strengthens this aspect of the LA role, although in the particular case of voluntary stock transfers the future is less clear insofar as LAs seem to be confined to the statutory homeless in whom they can nominate to HAs. Although subject to caveats, the LA can be seen as the intermediary client representative in the emerging 'quasi-market' for social housing (Le Grand 1990). A HA which did not satisfy the LA that it was meeting priority local needs, for example, would find it difficult to expand in that area.

The question was posed as to whether the enabling approach was sufficient to deliver the requisite range of social housing outputs. So far, we have concentrated on the powers and resources potentially available to LAs to secure their goals. In this qualitative sense, the picture is quite positive. LAs have four important types of levers which they can use in negotiations: finance, land, planning and communities/clients. But experience of policy implementation in all areas shows that it is also necessary to have a quantitative sense of the adequacy of the levers and the activities they affect, to see whether potential is actually realized.

Is enabling performing?

It is quite difficult to appraise the quantitative performance of the enabling approach at the present time. Certain aspects can be identified, but others are difficult to separate out, and others again are not monitored systematically. For example, there seems to be no systematic monitoring of HA developments not funded by public subsidy; this could be because such activity is trivial in scale, or because it is assumed to be, or because 'the powers that be' are not actually very interested in the outcomes of enabling. What it probably does indicate is a strong tendency for monitoring to follow public expenditure accountability lines. Whether such traditional approaches to policy monitoring are adequate to an era of regulatory intervention rather than direct provision is obviously questionable.

The negative aspect of the enabling policy has already been commented upon: that LAs should withdraw from direct provision. This is happening in some respects, but not in others. The level of new building by LAs is falling from its generally low level in the 1980s towards zero; it is clear that the DoE is exerting strong pressure via the HIP allocation process to bring this about. In the 1987 General Election the headline-grabbing policies were 'Tenants' Choice' and 'Housing Action Trusts'; in the event, neither of these have resulted in significant numbers of LA tenants changing landlord and so reducing the direct provision role. More significant in practice have been voluntary stock transfers by LAs to HAs, normally ones specially created for the purpose (see Chapter 11). By the end of 1991, 16 such transfers involving 75 000 dwellings had taken place, and more were in the pipeline. Such transfers are clearly approved of by the Conservative Government and currently have financial attractions to some LAs, relative to the alternative of operating under the post-1990 financial regime for LA housing. Voluntary transfers ought to signal a clear shift to an enabling role; whether in practice the transfer authorities perform impressively as enablers remains to be seen, but there are some doubts mentioned below.

While LA provision declines, the HA programme increases in size substantially. The major part funded by the Housing Corporation is planned to rise from 22 000 completions in 1990/91 to 52 000 in 1994/95. These figures include some items which might be questionable as additions to social housing provision (e.g. portable discounts for existing tenants wishing to buy), and there are some grounds for scepticism about whether such a steep rise can be achieved. It requires certain new or currently low performing programmes in the shared ownership field to take off on a large scale, and also assumes that the kinds of programme management difficulties experienced by the Corporation in 1989–91 can be avoided. LA direct funding of HAG accounts for a further 4000 units a year at present. LAs are also clearly contributing a good deal in the way of free or cheap land subsidy to HA schemes; this is sometimes referred to as 'HAG-stretching', in the sense that the HAG on the particular scheme is reduced pound for pound, so releasing resources within the overall budget to build more units. It is clear that current pressure from DoE on LAs is to do this wherever possible; this was seen as the most tangible aspect of approved enabling activity in a recent ADC survey. This in turn indicates some anxiety on the part of central government that the whole strategy should be seen to be performing.

LA land disposals for partnership schemes involving the private sector in low-cost sale and shared ownership schemes have been quite common since the late 1970s and averaged 2000 units per year in the period 1985–90 (House Builders' Federation 1990: 2); this was actually a fall on performance in the early 1980s. Given lags in reporting data it is too early to assess performance in the 1990s, but in general LAs have less surplus land to spare and are more cautious about the low-cost sale approach. Suitable data are difficult to obtain but it is likely that a high proportion of HA output is on former LA land. It is difficult to assess the impact of discounts on the price of such land, because the recession is pushing market values and construction costs down, but it is clear that currently (early 1992) the HA programme is benefiting from a fall in unit costs (Department of the Environment 1992: 80–3).

Shared ownership has been on the British scene since the late 1970s but it is fair to say that it has so far not taken off on a massive scale. There are a number of probable reasons for this: the tenure is relatively unfamiliar to consumers; it is less attractive financially than either buying outright, if you can afford it and especially if given a discount, or traditional LA renting at relatively low rent with the future possibility of a Right to Buy at very substantial discount; the occupier is responsible for repairs and maintenance; there may be some difficulties in future mobility. Bramley (1991a; 1991b) shows that the segment of households who can afford shared ownership but not outright purchase may be narrow, especially in regions with lower prices, and this segment is narrowed further by any tendency of costs of procurement to exceed prices at the lower end of the market. From the point of view of the LA or HA providing shared ownership, there are uncertainties about marketability, as for example with leasehold schemes for elderly people, which have been particularly sensitive to the general state of confidence in the market. In addition, LAs and HAs would often have taken the view that rental provision for the poorest section of the population, including the homeless, remained their highest priority.

However, in the circumstances of the 1990s, shared ownership may take on a new importance. Firstly, renting is less cheap under the new financial regimes. Secondly, outright owner occupation has lost some of its appeal in the wake of a significant fall in prices and record levels of repossessions; many of the mortgage rescue schemes now being developed involve shared ownership (Joseph Rowntree Foundation 1992). Thirdly, the Government is promoting this tenure, including use of the flexible Do it Yourself Shared Ownership (DYSO) scheme. Fourthly, approaches to enabling based on planning agreements, private land and cross-subsidy lend themselves to mixed tenure approaches including shared ownership, and avoid the perceived problem (from the LA viewpoint) of 'staircasing'. Early evidence on new style planning agreements suggests that two-fifths of the affordable housing resulting will be shared ownership (Barlow and Chambers 1992). Finally, the growing importance of owner occupation among the elderly potential clients of social housing suggests that a mechanism that can flexibly tap into some of their housing equity will be increasingly used.

The use of the planning system and planning agreements to secure affordable social housing is becoming moderately important and could become more important later in the decade. Barlow and Chambers (1991) estimate that relatively few units (3000) were provided in this way in the 1980s, mainly as a byproduct of commercial developments in cities. Under the new regime there is widespread interest and many individual schemes. The rural exceptions policy has been widely adopted, but since the average scheme size is a handful of dwellings and the time taken to complete the development is often long, aggregate numbers are less impressive. Clark and Dunmore (1990) showed that annual social housing output in predominantly rural districts might rise from 2–3000 in the late 1980s to 6400 in the early 1990s, of which perhaps one-third might be represented by the exceptions planning policy.

The exact extent to which LAs can require particular percentages of land or units on larger private sites to be affordable social housing has not been fully tested through the appeals system. Many developers are actually offering social housing content unilaterally within their planning applications, and may be quite willing to co-operate in the current very flat market conditions where the social housing units may have a more certain market than the private ones. Barlow and Chambers (1992) estimate that planning agreements might generate 1500–2000 units of social housing per year in the early 1990s, with an average 'quota' of around 25 per cent. Some of these may also attract HAG, so we should be wary of double-counting. Three-quarters of LAs had had discussions about the possibility of using planning agreements, while 18 per cent had been directly involved in larger-scale schemes.

Clearly, this approach does not give the LA much leverage over sites which already have planning permission, and in many areas these account for five or more years' worth of development (as required in DoE guidance on land availability). A new set of district-wide local plans are now in preparation, providing an opportunity for affordable housing policies to be given more legitimacy. For these reasons we should expect the approach to yield significantly more social output in the late 1990s. At this time the market may have revived and the size of the implicit subsidy obtainable out of land value will be higher than under current conditions. However, because of this, developers and landowners may be less willing to co-operate and the powers of the LA may be more tested at appeal. Under an optimistic scenario, 20 per cent of 'private' output in higher demand regions might be affordable social housing, perhaps amounting to 15 000 units per year.

Nominations of households in need by LAs to HAs are increasingly important. The HA movement has responded to criticism that in the 1980s the overall level of nominations and, more especially, the number of homeless families nominated fell short of what should have been achieved (Fraser 1991: chapter 8).

Indications are that the scale of activity on enabling is building up from rather a low point at the end of the 1980s. At the moment, there is little indication that the whole of the gap between recent levels of social housing provision and the widely quoted estimates of need (of the order of 100 000 units per annum) can be bridged by output stimulated by enabling in all its forms. At the same time, a great deal is happening on the ground in many areas and the emphasis on enabling has begun to be reflected in a substantial shift in the orientation of many local housing strategies. One of the commonly voiced concerns about this approach is that it takes a great deal of officer time and energy to negotiate schemes and that this effort is sometimes out of proportion with the rather modest number of units produced.

Is it fair?

A part of any evaluation of the impact of a policy should address questions of equity or fairness. In this case we can consider fairness between areas (sometimes called 'territorial justice'), as well as some aspects of fairness between different types of household. In terms of territorial justice, for example, the Barlow and Chambers (1992) study shows a dramatic North–South divide in the likely use of planning agreements; few significant schemes are shown in the northern half of England. This is easily explicable. House prices and hence land values are much higher in the South, where growth pressures are stronger at the same time as planning control is tighter. Planning only delivers subsidized housing if there is significant positive land value over and above existing or alternative use value, allowing for infrastructure and site costs. Land values in general are much lower in the North. Also, urban sites often do not offer the potential for land value subsidy because of the cost of making sites usable and the higher use value, and more northern sites are urban. The whole rural exceptions policy is of course of no direct help to urban areas. The same factors affect the possibility for cross-subsidy as for land subsidy, since cross-subsidy essentially comes from the residual land value on the units sold in the market or any commercial content in the scheme. They also affect the significance of subsidy delivered through discounted LA land. Northern LAs may well face relatively little developer interest in competing for opportunities to develop mixed schemes.

Another North–South imbalance is in the availability of capital receipts from the sale of council housing, land and other assets. These have accrued disproportionately to southern shire and suburban districts, and only since 1990 has some partial offset to this been made in the allocation of new borrowing (HIP) approvals. Shared ownership plays a significant role in many of the kinds of initiatives coming under the enabling role. Yet the potential demand for shared ownership has been shown to be much more limited in northern regions characterized by low house prices and income poverty (Bramley 1991a). In northern districts, the predominant housing problems are more likely to be poor physical housing conditions. There are enabling approaches to tackling some of these problems, including run-down council estates, but on the whole more public subsidy is likely to be needed. The voluntary transfer option, which is in part a form of re-mortgaging the stock to raise money for backlogs of repairs, has so far only taken off in the South; presumably, many northern LAs would have either negative stock values, allowing for disrepair and rent potential, or values which fall well short of outstanding debt.

Thus, there is a systematic North–South inequity in the potential of the whole enabling approach, insofar as this is defined as producing social housing with little or no extra public subsidy. This implies that the public resource allocation system may have to target more of the subsidy-carrying resources to northern regions and urban areas, relative to the distribution of need. This would actually be a reversal of recent trends. In addition, it should be noted that the most recent development in resource allocation by central government has been a shift from a criterion of equity to one of efficiency/effectiveness (see Bramley 1990b). The DoE judges the performance of LAs on various (not very explicit) criteria, of which 'enabling' is one, so that the more active and effective enablers get more public money as well. While understandable as an incentive mechanism, this could reinforce inequalities between different LAs in the ability to meet housing needs.

Some questions can also be posed about equity aspects of enabling approaches at the individual or household level. Greater reliance on HAs for re-housing of those in need means that responsibility is split between a number of agencies, some of whom do not have the same degree of public accountability as LAs. Not all cases will be channelled through LA nominations (typically nominations represent 50–75 per cent of net lettings), and in the case of voluntary transfer only homeless households may be nominated. This poses questions as to the openness, comprehensiveness and fairness of the operation of HA waiting lists. This in turn requires a significant change from past practices, where such lists have often been closed for much of the time, or only open to certain restricted categories. Many HAs are specialized and there is some danger that certain types of household might fall through the gaps in coverage. It should be said, on the other side, that LA practice in their own management of waiting lists has been variable (see, for example, Bramley and Paice 1987; Prescott-Clarke et al. 1988). There is currently considerable interest in unified common waiting lists linking LAs and all active HAs operating in a particular area, especially in some of the larger cities.

An enabling strategy tends to put greater emphasis on housing provision on the boundaries of the mainstream social and private sector tenures, namely low-cost sale and shared ownership. This has the positive aspect of lessening polarization in some ways, and of widening choice, especially where the existing supply of rented lettings is large. But part of the reason for these intermediate tenures being encouraged is that they economize on public subsidy and provide a vehicle for private-sector participation. Such an emphasis, especially if it becomes dominant in the programme, can be criticized as a diversion of resources and attention from groups who ought to be the highest priority, namely homeless people and other potential clients of rented housing who are on very low incomes.

Rural affordable housing initiatives may be particular examples of this tension. There is an added complication here, which is that the whole basis for both the planning system and local communities sanctioning developments, in villages with tight planning constraints, is that *local* needs are being met. Although it is difficult to pin down hard evidence, it has been alleged that in some cases conflict has arisen between housing local potential households (e.g. young couples from the village who cannot afford to buy) and homeless families nominated by the LA who might currently be in bed-and-breakfast accommodation in the nearby town and only have a more tenuous connection with the village. Sensitive and sensible rules about defining local connections would seem to be part of the answer here, but there is still the potential for conflict between equity for the homeless and the very localist conception of need implicit in the rural initiatives.

One of the problems with relying on a large scale upon HAs for rehousing is that there may be large discrepancies in rents. This is a particular problem for households whose income is just above the level where Housing Benefit would be payable, such as lower paid working households. Traditionally, in most areas HA rents were above LA rents. The post-1988 financial regimes are pushing up rents in both sectors, but HA rents are in general still far ahead of LA rents. The continuance of the present regime could lead to different patterns of relativities, rather than convergence, with market-related LA rents higher in the South East while so-called 'affordable' HA rents are higher in the North.

There are then some grounds for concern about equity between both areas and individuals in the new style enabling housing strategy. However, there is professional and policy awareness of these issues, and one should not idealize the previous, LA-dominated system. It is well known that the policies, practices, performances and rents of LAs varied enormously, and so also did the chances of households with given objective needs being helped.

Do organizational and professional approaches matter?

The arguments developed in the early part of this chapter suggest that the extent to which individual LAs achieve their full potential in the enabling role depends a great deal on the behaviour of key officers (and members). Is the political will there to use resources and powers for social housing, to strive to achieve targets, and to act proactively, innovatively, even entrepreneurially? Even if the politicians are willing, how will the LA officer structure rise to this new kind of challenge?

Casual observation of the differences in behaviour between different LAs, both similar and different authorities, suggests that the extent and success of enabling activity does vary enormously. In part, these differences can be linked to different political approaches to housing, but some of these differences are at the subtler level of individuals or local styles rather than formal party labels. Overall, though, it seems that it is at officer level that enabling succeeds or fails.

Clearly, if the new land use planning levers are to be used effectively, the housing department has to work closely with the planning department; often they have not in the recent past. The creative use of planning briefs, on schemes where the LA is disposing of land, assembling a site, or orchestrating a consortium approach, is potentially very important (Bishop *et al.* 1991). Where land disposal and potential capital receipts are involved housing must also work closely with treasurers and estates departments, and secure their support for a course of action which might appear to conflict with those departments' normal operating goals (maximizing the price or capital receipt). The setting up of complicated consortium arrangements may involve not just difficult site assembly but also the creation of special institutional vehicles (charitable and non-charitable) to act as channels for cross-subsidy, to hold leases, and so on (see Fraser 1991), which require sophisticated legal expertise.

In short, enabling puts a premium on corporate working. Interdepartmental teamwork is not a new requirement in housing programmes; what is new is the emphasis on partnership with outside agencies, financial/commercial awareness, flexibility and entrepreneurship. Corporate working has a chequered history in local government. It is perhaps when traditional ways of delivering services are under challenge that the need for a corporate response is widely perceived. The outcome of corporate working depends, though, on the nature of the political steer given to the system and the relative strength of different professional/organizational power structures. Housing has tended to have a strong political priority in some LAs (typically urban, Labour-controlled ones) but very often a weak position in the professional power stakes. If enabling fails, in many areas, one could look internally as well as externally for explanations. Housing might not have had the clout to direct the corporate machine in such a way as to give priority to the requirements of an enabling strategy. Some housing managers might well not have had the skills or style to run with the enabling style of operation. One major question, or contradiction, is that housing is less likely to have much organizational clout where the direct provision role is small and being reduced. The extreme case of this is the large-scale voluntary transfer (Institute of Housing 1990); from a distance, the impression gained from the early transfer LAs is that many of these are not very active as enablers, and that the residual housing function is very residual indeed. At the other end of the scale, there are the large urban authorities in which housing has enormous political and organizational strength; yet for these authorities enabling may be (a) unattractive as a priority or style of working, and (b) much less promising in financial and performance terms than it would be in a southern shire district.

Enabling, with its complexity, diversity, and uncertainty, is contrasted with traditional mechanisms of social housing provision, which operated on a large scale according very standardized rules and procedures which could be and were clearly set out in procedure manuals. The traditional style could be implemented by a traditional kind of bureaucracy of the kind which British central and local government well exemplify. The move away from this style of organization is a very widespread phenomenon (Hoggett 1990). For housing, enabling is one pressure for change; others include decentralization and pressures for more consumer (tenant) control and accountability. This change of emphasis has implications for training, recruitment and careers in housing.

Will the housing associations become the main body in which the key skills lie and which take the main initiative? If so, then housing will come to resemble other services like health where the 'providers' tend to dominate the 'purchasers'. However, it could be argued that LAs which pursue active enabling policies will provide interesting and challenging jobs which offer more scope for achievement and a wider variety of activities; such positions in such authorities could be seen as the peak of the profession.

Just as with HAs, will many private developers be able to compete/operate in this arena? While HAs might be seen as having the decisive advantage in housing management, private developers might be expected to have particular skills in operating the development process. Especially as this moves into a climate of risk and uncertainty, where interactions with private finance and property markets is important, such skills could be adapted to the particular task of enabling social housing through partnership deals of various kinds. Private developers also, paradoxically, have more practical experience with the planning system than orthodox housing managers.

One type of formally private organization which has played a very important role in the transformation of social housing in Britain since the late 1980s is the consultancy firm, both large management consultants with specialist housing/public-sector divisions and a small number of specialist housing consultants, both largely employing former public/social sector staff. This feature has a number of implications for the locus and accountability of key policy implementation decisions, as well as for professional career structures and networks.

Conclusion

This chapter has argued that the shift from a direct provision to an enabling role for LAs in social housing is a rather profound shift. It is a genuine, not just a symbolic, policy. There is a positive role for an enabling authority; it is not just a polite word for privatization and withdrawal from the field. Enabling is a policy that raises many interesting implementation issues. Some of these stem from the conflicts and tensions of which the policy was born and from the inherent difficulty of the task, which is to get social housing produced by other people and without using too much public money.

Four major levers were identified by which the LA can seek to get its housing strategy implemented by others: finance, land, planning and the local community. Although the rules governing LA action are far from transparent, and quite restrictive in some respects, they do allow a considerable amount of scope for enabling in a number of different ways. It is too early to assess the overall quantitative performance of the enabling approach, which seems to be producing some expansion of output from a low base but not one commensurate, yet, with the overall need. There are a number of grounds for concern about greater inequities in access to social housing that may result from a reliance on enabling. And it is also clear that enabling requires a major change in the professional and organizational approaches used in the provision of social housing; success will depend as much on successful adaptation in this respect as upon material and environmental factors.

References

Association of District Councils (1990) *Affordable Housing, Planning and Land: The Enabling Role of the District Council*, Discussion Paper prepared for the Housing, Planning, Environment and Transport Assembly, 14 November, London, ADC.

Association of District Councils (1991) *ADC Survey of Council House Rents, Housing Subsidy and Capital Expenditure 1991/2*, London, ADC.

Audit Commission (1992) *Developing Local Housing Strategies*, London, HMSO.

Barlow, J. and Chambers, D. (1991) 'The impact of planning agreements on the provision of affordable housing', *Housing Research Findings*, No. 40, York, Joseph Rowntree Foundation.

Barlow, J. and Chambers, D. (1992) *Planning Agreements and Social Housing Quotas*, York, Joseph Rowntree Foundation.

Bishop, J., Davison, I. and Oliver, S. (1991) *Development Briefing: Stage Two Report*, Report produced for the Housing Research Foundation, London, HRF.

Bishop, K. and Hooper, A. (1991) *Planning for Social Housing*, Report prepared for the National Housing Forum, London, Association of District Councils.

Bramley, G. (1989) *Meeting Housing Needs*, London, Association of District Councils.

Bramley, G. (1990a) *Bridging the Affordability Gap: Report of Research on Access to a Range of Housing Options*, Birmingham, BEC Publications.

Bramley, G. (1990b) 'Explaining the puzzles in policy change; local finance reform in Britain', *Journal of Public Policy*, Vol. 10, No. 1: 45–65.

Bramley, G. (1990c) *Public Sector Housing Rents and Subsidies*, Working Paper 92, Bristol, School for Advanced Urban Studies.

Bramley, G. (1991a) *Bridging the Affordability Gap in 1990: Update of Research on Housing Access and Affordability*, Birmingham, BEC Publications.

Bramley, G. (1991b) *Bridging the Affordability Gap in Wales: A Report of Research on Housing Access and Affordability*, Cardiff, House Builders' Federation, in association with the Council of Welsh Districts.

Bramley, G. and Paice, D. (1987) *Housing Needs in Non-Metropolitan Areas*, London, Association of District Councils.

Bramley, G., Leather, P. and Murie, A. (1979) *Housing Strategies and Investment Programmes*, SAUS Working Paper 7, Bristol, University of Bristol, School for Advanced Urban Studies.

Clark, D. and Dunmore, K. (1990) *Involving the Private Sector in Rural Social Housing*, Cirencester, ACRE (Action for Communities in Rural England).

Couttie, D. (1991) *Institutional Investment in Rented Housing*, York, Joseph Rowntree Foundation.

Department of the Environment (1977) *Housing Policy: A Consultative Document*, Cmnd. 6851, London, HMSO.

Department of the Environment (1987) *Housing: the Government's Proposals*, Cm. 214, London, HMSO.

Department of the Environment (1988) *The Government's Review of the Homelessness Legislation*, London, HMSO.

Department of the Environment (1989) *Local Authorities Housing Role; 1989 HIP Round*, Appendix to letter from Department to Local Authorities inviting annual submission of Housing Strategy and Investment Programme, London, Department of the Environment.

Department of the Environment (1991a) *Circular 7/91: Planning and Affordable Housing*.

Department of the Environment (1991b) *Homelessness: Code of Guidance for Local Authorities*, London, HMSO.

Department of the Environment (1992) *Planning Policy Guidance Note 3*, London, Department of the Environment.

Edelman, M. (1971) *Politics as Symbolic Action*, Chicago, Markham.

Forrest, R. and Murie, A. (1983) 'Residualization and council housing: aspects of the changing social relations of housing tenure', *Journal of Social Policy*, Vol. 12, No. 4, 453–68.

Fraser, R. (1991) *Working Together in the 1990s: A Guide for Local Authorities and Housing Associations*, Coventry, Institute of Housing.

Hills, J. (1991) *Unravelling Housing Finance: Subsidies, Benefits and Taxation*, Oxford, Clarendon Press.

Hoggett, P. (1990) *Modernisation, Political Strategy and the Welfare State: An Organisational Perspective*, DQM No. 2, Bristol, School for Advanced Urban Studies.

House Builders' Federation (1989) *Meeting Community Housing Need: The New Challenge*, Birmingham, BEC Publications.

House Builders' Federation (1990) *Partnership Housing and the '89 Local Government and Housing Act*, prepared by the Social Housing Unit of the HBF, Birmingham, BEC Publications.

House of Commons Select Committee for the Environment (1980) *Enquiry into the Implications of Government's Expenditure Plans 1980–81 to 1983–84 for the Housing Policies of the Department of the Environment*, First Report from the Environment Committee, Session 1979–80, HC 714, London, HMSO.

Institute of Housing (1990) *Social Housing in the 1990s: Challenges, Choices and Change*, Coventry, Institute of Housing.

Joseph Rowntree Foundation (1991) *Inquiry into British Housing: Second Report June 1991*, York, Joseph Rowntree Foundation.

Joseph Rowntree Foundation (1992) 'Pros and cons of mortgage rescue' and 'The story so far', *Innovations in Social Housing*, No. 2, York, Joseph Rowntree Foundation.

Le Grand, J. (1990) *Quasi-Markets and Social Policy*, DQM No. 1, Bristol, School for Advanced Urban Studies.

Le Grand, J. and Robinson, R. (1984) *The Economics of Social Problems*, London, Macmillan.

Muellbauer, J. (1990) 'The great British housing disaster', *Roof*, May–June: 16–18.

Niner, P. (1989) *Housing Needs in the 1990s*, London, National Housing Forum.

Prescott-Clarke, P., Allen, P. and Morrissey, C. (1988) *Queuing for Housing: A Study of Council Housing Waiting Lists*. London: HMSO.

Pryke, M. and Whitehead, C. (1991) *Private Finance for Social Housing: Enabling or Transforming?*, Monograph 23, Cambridge, Department of Land Economy.

Wilcox, S. (1990) *The Need for Social Housing in the 1990s*, London, Institute of Housing.

CHAPTER 10

The decentralization of housing services

IAN COLE

Introduction

As Chapter 3 indicated, housing has been at the forefront of the Conservative Government's policy since 1979, through a series of measures designed to assert the superiority of market mechanisms and marginalize the public sector. In the first two terms of the Thatcher Government this strategy was pursued by the relentless preference for expanding owner-occupation at all costs, at the expense of other tenures, particularly council housing. At the 1986 Conservative Party Conference, a change of emphasis in policy became apparent. The then Minister for Housing, John Patten, launched the 'Right to Rent' as a parallel objective to the 'Right to Buy'. After the election victory the following year, legislation focused on the need to retain, but restructure, rented housing provision. The Housing Act 1988 and the Local Government and Housing Act 1989 resulted, with the objective, *inter alia*, of ending local authorities' role as direct housing providers, and supplanting it with an ill-defined 'enabling' function.

Some of these policy initiatives had a decisive impact on the housing market – the Right to Buy being the most obvious example. In other cases, the initial clamour about ambitious measures was followed by an embarrassed silence, as achievements fell well short of intentions – one thinks of the Right to Repair, the first wave of Housing Action Trusts, or Tenants' Choice. Whatever the outcome of these various proposals, it has been clear that the Conservative Government has held the initiative, set the agenda and pushed ahead with a long-term political project through its housing policy in a uniquely determined manner. The balance of control shifted decisively towards central government during the 1980s, as local authority autonomy was eroded through a combination of financial controls, expenditure reductions, subsidies towards privatized alternatives and other inducements to tenants to opt out of council landlordism. The political success of Right to Buy, the further marginalization of council housing, and the extension of working-class home ownership cast a shadow over attempts by other political parties to develop a fully articulated housing strategy as an alternative to the forthright privatization of the Conservative governments.

However, it would be misleading to conclude that local housing authorities during the 1980s were simply the hapless receptacles for the latest enthusiasms emanating from Westminster or Marsham Street (the Department of the Environment), only offering resistance by attempting to thwart Government controls rather than offering a more positive vision for public-sector housing. This turbulent period in fact witnessed the development of many ideas, initiatives and projects by local authorities which sought to establish the continuing relevance of their role as housing providers, reacting creatively, rather than defensively, to Government policy. In the face of growing central control, it was inevitable that these initiatives were partial and incoherent, but they offered a glimpse of the potential for council housing to be more than a marginal operation mopping up the most severe casualties of the housing market.

Decentralization was central to many of these local authority strategies. During the 1980s, it was heralded as the final hope for council housing to respond to the hostile onslaught of central government, and to emerge from the process as a more popular and accessible housing tenure. Decentralization rapidly became a familiar feature of organizational change in many local housing authorities across the country.

The purpose of this chapter is to consider why decentralization was initiated by local authorities during the 1980s, to show how the original ambitious aims of going local were modified by the sober realities of implementation and to evaluate the responses from different actors in the policy process – senior officers, front-line housing staff and elected members. The account then moves on to consider which aspects of decentralization are likely to endure as key policy concerns for social housing agencies during the 1990s.

At the most basic level, decentralization involves the establishment of area or neighbourhood offices to provide certain local authority services. This administrative reform may be accompanied by a parallel change in decision-making structures, through the creation or strengthening of area or neighbourhood committees with delimited responsibilities, and perhaps control over a specific budget. It may involve a single local authority service, or involve a number of departments and other agencies, such as the health service, police, probation and voluntary sector. Decentralization may involve a restructuring of the entire department and a reshaping of centralized systems and control – alternatively it may simply extend the tentacles of service provision with little disturbance to structures and procedures based in the Town Hall.

This rather bald description does not really convey the sense in which the policy of decentralization became an emblem of more grandiose visions for a new system of local government in general, and council housing in particular. In the early 1980s, decentralization was full of promise – as a harbinger of radical reform, as a critique of the prevailing political and managerial culture in local government, as a riposte to Thatcherite ideology and as a vehicle to win public support for services under increasing financial and political attack.

Decentralization sagged under the weight of divergent, or even contradictory, aspirations, which gradually unravelled when the idea was put to the test by local authorities across the country. By the early 1990s, programmes of service decentralization had become commonplace – but they had lost much of their aura as a means of salvaging local government and securing the future of council housing. A more modest view of its potential to transform services had taken hold (Cole *et al.* 1991).

In this account, the implementation of decentralization proposals by local authorities will be highlighted to show how different policy factors influenced the form and character of the organizational changes which eventually transpired. However, the origins of decentralization related less to these influences than the growing tensions between central and local government which emerged during the early 1980s.

Decentralization in the context of central–local relations

Chapter 2 has charted the growing hostility in central–local relations during the past decade, and the defence strategies devised by Labour-controlled councils to combat the assault of central government on service provision and expenditure. Decentralization initiatives often formed part of such programmes, as a way of closing the gap between service providers and consumers so that more people would rally round and support local authorities under external threat. The key point is that the impetus behind decentralization was primarily *reactive* rather than pro-active. It was a response to failings in decision-making systems and services provided by local authorities rather than a coherent forward programme in its own right. As a consequence, it was easier to discuss the lofty aims of decentralization than to specify how such aims might be achieved in practice. One of the key lessons from the experience of decentralization in the past ten years is that the process of implementation, and the difficulties encountered in the early schemes, began to change the objectives aligned to later initiatives, when a more modest, managerially inclined perspective held sway.

Like many policy innovations, decentralization was less a new idea than a distinctive distillation of existing initiatives and trends. The neighbourhood focus had been prominent in various schemes such as area management trials, community development projects and public participation experiments during the 1970s (Hambleton and Hoggett 1987). Many of those active in community organizations at that time had subsequently joined local authorities as officers or elected members, and carried their ideas with them.

Decentralization also entailed both a political and an administrative critique of the prevailing mode of local authority service provision (Stoker 1987). The election of the Thatcher Government in 1979 suggested that criticisms about the high cost and poor quality of public services had struck a popular chord. Local government could be portrayed as little more than a rest home for the benighted welfare professionals, incompetent bureaucrats and self-regarding councillors, thus paving the way for cuts in expenditure in the interests of more efficient management. As many Labour councils came under the control of the 'New

Urban Left' (Gyford 1985), decentralization rapidly took on the mantle of a gesture of political defiance – as a way of demonstrating the continuing vitality and activism of many working-class neighbourhoods and the positive contribution which could be made by local government.

The political significance of decentralization was not only as a riposte to Thatcherism – it carried a resonance for internal debates in the Labour Party about the nature of state provision and socialist practice. The ossified organizational structures and forms of representation typical of local government in the 1970s were linked to Fabian socialist principles of top-down service delivery – the mechanistic model of municipal socialism which had guided the post-War expansion of welfare provision (Lee and Raban 1988). Advocates of decentralization could hark back to an alternative, guild socialist tradition in the Labour Party, which emphasized localized and open forms of management and decision-making. According to this model, consumers should be seen as active participants in the development of local services rather than as passive, and humbly grateful, recipients of public resources (Wright 1984; Beuret and Stoker 1986).

While the Left embraced decentralization as a means of regenerating local authorities as effective and popular forms of government – and a bulwark against central government control – the radical Right's enthusiasm for the project acquired a different emphasis. The breakdown of a centralized bureaucracy for service delivery into neighbourhood units was viewed as a transitional stage in the wider restructuring of local government. It paved the way for the eventual removal of key services from local authority control, either through the creation of independent trusts at area level, or the devolution of direct responsibility to community groups (Henney 1985). For the Right, decentralization was therefore a strategy to abolish local political intervention in service provision, rather than a means of extending its influence.

The original policy objectives of decentralization were therefore framed as much as political statements as strategies for administrative reform. Jeremy Seabrook's judgement on Walsall's decentralization programme expressed this clearly enough – 'a project that bases itself on the reality of neighbourhood in the 1980s is actually engaged in one of the great ideological battles of our time' (Seabrook 1984: 5). Nevertheless, the ideological battle was accompanied by managerial skirmishes too, especially with the consequences of local government reorganization which had taken place in 1974.

The managerial critique for decentralization centred on the damage caused by reorganization – through the creation of larger units of administration, the growth of arid professionalism and the eclipse of democratic political representation by technocratic forms of decision-making and control. Furthermore, the passing enthusiasm for corporate management had tended to 'emphasize leadership and hierarchy and centralize power into the hands of a small group of leading councillors and officers' (Dearlove 1979: 183). Decentralization was advocated as a means of prising open these enclosed systems.

At the heart of many decentralization initiatives was a commitment to extending the influence of middle managers, front-line staff and service users. This

trend meshed with emergent thinking about 'post-Fordist' organizational structures and processes in the private sector, which stressed team working, flatter
hierarchies, flexibility and consumer choice (Rustin 1989). The task was to
develop, through decentralization, a 'listening' organization which placed the
customer first and developed a genuine 'public service orientation' (Peters and
Waterman 1982; Clarke and Stewart 1987). The physical relocation of services
into the neighbourhood, it was envisaged, would promote accessibility and
responsive forms of local provision. The bureaucratic paternalism of post-1974
local government (Hambleton and Hoggett 1987) would be superseded by a
more open, user-friendly version.

In theory, the defence strategy of decentralization was applicable to all local
government services. In practice, local authority housing services were often
singled out for attention, and many councils introduced neighbourhood housing
offices without involving other departments. There were several reasons for this.
First, the nature of housing departments had been particularly affected by local
government reorganization. The average size of housing stock controlled by
local councils increased threefold in 1974 (Power 1987). The anxieties about
officers and councillors 'losing touch' with their tenants therefore carried particular weight. Second, the determination of appropriate boundaries for neighbourhoods in an area often took its cue from the location of large council estates
– and council houses were often refurbished as neighbourhood offices. Third,
decentralization often implied a weakening of professional specialism and control in favour of more generic responsibilities – a task easier to achieve in a
weakly professionalized area such as housing management than in social work,
for example, where the advocates of neighbourhood working touched many
raw nerves in the profession. Fourth, councillors were prominent in devising
many of the early strategies for decentralization; and there is a unique tradition
of councillor involvement in service delivery in housing departments –
over repairs inspections or allocations, for example – which does not extend
so readily to other areas of local government activity (Cole and Furbey
1993).

However, the main reason why council housing was at the forefront of
decentralization initiatives relates to growing tensions in central–local relations
during this period. If decentralization was a strategy for survival, local authority
housing was clearly the public service under the most direct threat in the early
1980s. State housing was the first target in the Thatcher Government's programme to restructure welfare provision. The sharp reduction in public housing
investment, the removal of subsidies for local authorities, the overwhelming
political preference for the private market, and the growing impact of the Right
to Buy, all constituted a direct challenge to council housing, as the most
vulnerable element of local government provision. As local authorities came
under attack, it was clear that council housing was in the front line. Going local
was thus a vital necessity for many urban Housing Departments if the service
was to be retained. The prospects for the future of other local authority services
were less apocalyptic, and the need for transformation less pressing.

The four phases of decentralization

It is helpful to distinguish different stages in the varied pattern of decentralization initiatives undertaken by local authorities during the past ten years, because, as Robin Hambleton has claimed: 'Decentralization can mean very different things to different people. Policy confusion, rather than policy ambiguity, characterises the scene'. (Hambleton 1988: 132). The first wave of projects were shaped by a commitment to *comprehensive political and managerial change*. The unlikely starting point for this revolution was in the West Midlands. In 1981, Walsall MBC introduced a network of 31 neighbourhood housing offices within six months, and literally emptied the housing department offices in the Town Hall. A 'flat' organizational structure, an imaginative approach to staff recruitment and training, committed leadership from the controlling Labour Group and forthright managerial direction characterized the Walsall approach (for an assessment, see Mainwaring 1988). Other councils were quick to follow suit with ambitious strategies for going local, especially in Labour-controlled London boroughs. Many of these programmes promised far more than they achieved, particularly as a result of poor planning, staffing disputes, financial problems, difficulties with information technology and inter-service rivalries. The blueprints (or 'redprints') for change were usually more impressive than tangible outcomes in improved service delivery.

However, there were exceptions. Islington Borough Council, for example, opened 24 offices from 1983 to 1986, including 16 purpose-built units, complete with 'Pizza Hut' facades and open plan internal designs, at a capital cost of around £10 million (Islington Borough Council 1987). The Islington programme went further than Walsall's by incorporating multi-service local provision and structures for local decision-making. Each neighbourhood office consisted of staff from the Housing Department, Social Services Department, Environmental Health Department and Building Works Department, with administrative and community development support provided by the Chief Executive's Department. Neighbourhood Forums were established, with a budget for environmental improvements, and community representation in policy deliberations and service provision. The Islington scheme was implemented in the face of difficulties over the introduction of new technology, training programmes and tensions evident in inter-service collaboration at the local level (Burns and Williams 1989). Nevertheless, it stood as a testimony to decentralization as a means of achieving sweeping administrative and political reforms in local authority structures and processes.

Other local authorities embarked on fundamental restructuring through decentralization. Liberal-controlled Tower Hamlets, for example, devolved significant responsibilities to seven Area Committees across the borough, with parallel demarcation of managerial structures (Morphet 1987). Basildon also established a system of seven neighbourhoods, involving housing, environmental health, welfare rights, recreation and planning, with Area Committees as the main areas for decision-making under different forms of local political control (Burns and Williams 1989). Local authorities such as Harlow and North

East Derbyshire have developed comprehensive neighbourhood schemes for housing provision, whereas councils such as Rochdale have opted for multi-service programmes (Decentralization Research and Information Centre 1991). Nevertheless, there is growing evidence that the promotion of decentralization as a means of wholesale organizational restructuring is now on the wane.

A second stage in decentralization initiatives involved a more modest view about its potential, in which the strategy emerged as a result of *incremental reform*. In these cases, local authorities built on the foundations of existing area-based structures. These programmes originated from two sources. In some cases, local authorities developed programmes following the introduction of specific neighbourhood initiatives on estates, through Priority Estates Projects (PEPs), Estate Action or similar schemes. In research into housing decentralization initiatives undertaken by councils in the North of England, it was found that over half the authority-wide proposals had been derived following the example of single estate projects (Cole and Windle 1992).

In other cases, decentralization involved the extension of the neighbourhood focus from earlier area-based structures: as the next step in moving services closer to local communities rather than as a 'big bang' transformation of centralized services. This piecemeal approach meant that new relationships and networks could be grafted on to existing systems more readily. On the other hand, the fundamental changes often linked to decentralization could be more readily thwarted by the reassertion of traditional practices.

In Leeds City Council, for example, housing services have been based on an area-based system for over 40 years. The original decision to introduce ten local housing offices was taken as long ago as April 1947, with many of the objectives echoing the intentions of local councils in more recent times (*Leeds Weekly Citizen*, 6 October 1950):

> In an attempt to overcome what was felt to be a distant control of the estates, the Housing Committee ... decided on a policy of decentralisation. This means that each estate or small group of estates has an office situated in a convenient spot to enable tenants to make easy contact with the management staff ... There is the advantage that tenants do get to know the manager of the estate they have chosen and of course the manager becomes fairly well acquainted with the problems of the tenant ... There is a better feeling arising between the tenants and the managers: the personal link is always far better than correspondence which invariably is written in formal fashion by both sides.

The system was extended during the 1950s in response to mounting demands so that 15 Estate Offices were managing the stock of 30 000 council properties by 1954 (Leeds City Council 1954). By 1974, however, the council stock had increased to 65 000, so that each local office now served an average of 4300 properties, compared with 1700 at the inception of the programme.

The structure of the housing service was subsequently changed at the time of local government reorganization, and again in 1982, under the direction of the controlling Labour Group. The number of offices was increased to 38, and boundaries redrawn, often following ward boundaries. The 1982 reorganization was explicitly seen as an extension of service provision rather than an attempt to move to more participatory forms of decision-making. The influence of local councillors remained paramount. The council stated that 'any changes proposed will be within the context of decentralised housing management and will not fundamentally change our approach to the task for providing a sensitive and responsive service' (Almond 1986: 46).

The proposals reiterated two key themes in the original reorganization: the maintenance of a comprehensive housing service and the move towards more generic forms of estate management. Overall, the staffing implications were modest. The local authority was further reorganized in 1989–90, again at the behest of leading councillors, though the basic framework of local housing offices was retained. Significant organizational change had been achieved, only in stages rather than as a dramatic transformation. Decentralization had never been invested with heady aspirations about the political regeneration of local government, in contrast to those councils eagerly following the Islington model (Cole, *et al.* 1989).

Newcastle City Council offers a more typical example of decentralization by incremental change. On local government reorganization in 1974, the public housing stock was 51 000 and the previously central department was divided into eight areas, with specialist staff. In the late 1970s, an experimental PEP was introduced on the Cowgate estate, and three further local estate projects were set up in other areas of housing stress. However, the schemes existed outside the mainstream of the Housing Department – as special initiatives. These experiments in local management laid the foundations for the wholesale reorganization of the Department from its highly specialist functions to a more generic pattern of neighbourhood provision. Reorganization in 1982 and 1983 resulted in the establishment of six housing areas, each with its own Area Committee with councillor representation. Neighbourhood offices were then introduced under the ambit of area offices, so that, by 1988, 23 neighbourhood teams were operational.

The Newcastle example gives an illustration of the factors behind many decentralization schemes, which were less dramatic in their impact, and arrived at decentralization in stages, rather than as a complete overhaul of service provision

This model is more typical than the 'big bang' approach in characterizing the decentralization initiatives introduced by larger local authorities during the 1980s, in which a managerial orientation, a gradualist approach and a multi-tiered organizational structure were the keynotes. Even here the changes in structure were often restricted – multi-service forms of going local have remained a rarity, and attention has been focused on the vertical layers and channels of communication in the housing department, rather than its lateral responsibilities. Decentralization seems to have had little effect, for example, on the span of functions located in the housing department itself. It did not result in a more 'comprehensive' service and in many cases only a limited range of functions – rent collection, repairs inspection and estate management – were decentralized. Much remained in the centre.

So what was to be gained from going local? Improved service performance, and better staff-customer relations, were at the nub of decentralization initiatives, reflecting the managerialist emphasis of the 'second wave' of these schemes. Research evidence suggests that this enthusiasm was not misplaced – decentralization has often improved performance on factors such as reducing the level of rent arrears and the number of empty properties on estates, speeding up the process of allocations and monitoring repairs more effectively (Cole *et al*. 1988b). However, this evidence should be interpreted with caution. Most local authorities have only introduced consistent performance monitoring in the past year, and these measures are rarely sensitive enough to chart trends on a neighbourhood basis. The determination of any cause–effect relationship between management performance and decentralization is fraught with difficulty. In practice, the impact of decentralization is often based on little more than the intuitions of the Director of Housing, at a safe distance from the estates, and reliant on unduly positive messages from area managers eager to promote an aura of success. Additional complexities of interpretation arise if one tries to disentangle changes resulting from the introduction of a new organizational structure from those which have occurred as a consequence of other council policies, or factors outside the local authority's control. To take an obvious example, levels of unemployment, or changing housing benefit requirements, may have a greater effect on rent arrears than whether management is neighbourhood-based or centralized.

The Glasgow University research study into the effectiveness of housing management in England reinforced the view that decentralization fell well short of being a panacea, although it often led to better performance, as a result of 'being closer to the consumer'. It concluded: 'Performance is largely a function of managerial conduct, rather than industrial structure. As this report suggests that no single organizational structure is overwhelmingly superior, then policies should emphasize the attainment of performance' (Department of the Environment 1989: 130). This message directed attention towards channels of communication, performance review techniques and managerial competence rather than organizational form, and ushered in the era of 'customer care'. Decentralization could assist in this process, but was not of itself sufficient.

If the advantages of decentralization were less pronounced than initially proclaimed, the costs of going local became increasingly evident as schemes were implemented. Decentralization entailed capital costs, through the provision of local offices and the installation of new technology, and revenue costs, through increased staffing, regradings, and higher demands for services. Again, the precise costs of decentralization are impossible to evaluate, given the absence of clear 'before–after' comparisons, and the generally poor quality of financial information in housing departments, let alone disaggregated to the neighbourhood level (Building Use Studies 1986: 1987). The Glasgow University survey of housing management suggested that large local authorities which had decentralized provided a more effective service than centralized departments and that costs were not above the average. The research could not determine, however, whether costs in any one authority had in fact increased, as a result of decentralization, from a previously low base.

The ironical aspect to the growing costs of decentralizing, however they might be estimated, is that local councils risked being the victims of their own success. The price of a more accessible service was, ultimately, a higher rent for tenants – as the only way of paying for an expanded management and maintenance service to meet increased demands. The convenience of a neighbourhood office usually prompted tenants to ask for more repairs, or complain more often about delays or poor standards – and these increased demands were rarely contained through efficiency gains alone. If consumer expectations were not to be disappointed, it had to be acknowledged that decentralization would cost money.

Many local authorities had been nervous from the outset about both the start-up costs and the ongoing expenses of decentralization. The new vocabulary of efficiency and value for money did not always fit easily with the pressures to respond readily to tenant demands through a more accessible service. The financing of organizational change was also rendered more difficult as a result of growing central control over local authority expenditure. These concerns gathered pace with the introduction of a more competitive environment for social rented housing under the Housing Act 1988, and the new capital and revenue finance regime for local authorities in the Local Government and Housing Act 1989. These measures reduced local housing departments' room for manoeuvre in attempting to increase the costs of service provision while limiting rent increases for tenants.

The third phase of initiatives behind local housing management schemes might be termed, therefore, *cost-conscious and customer-conscious decentralization*. In planning organizational restructuring, ambitious objectives for decentralization were now being replaced by balance sheet calculations in the art of the possible. There were cautionary lessons. Manchester City Council, for example, had embarked on a grandiose strategy of neighbourhood provision, having undertaken extensive public consultation over community boundaries, office type and location, service functions and modes of participation. A budget crisis in the local authority resulted in the scheme being abandoned, with only six of the proposed 48 neighbourhood offices opened.

Local authorities considering the option of decentralization therefore sought ways of enhancing accessibility without introducing a full network of expensive offices, without employing vast numbers of additional staff and without overloading public expectations through consultation. Mansfield District Council offers an example of a local authority which sought to improve its housing service without a dramatic increase in costs. The housing department was reorganized in several stages during the 1980s. Initially, three divisional teams were established to service the district, but they were subsequently replaced by 'patch' workers undertaking generic housing functions for a set number of properties. The staff all operated from the Civic Centre, rather than from specific neighbourhood offices, although they also use existing community rooms in sheltered housing schemes as an informal basis, to hold 'surgery' sessions covering a wide range of problems. The idea has been to develop a personalized, accessible service without the additional expense of a local office network.

The Mansfield scheme is merely one example of how local authorities began to adapt the principles of decentralization to their own circumstances and traditions, despite tight financial restrictions. As the experience of neighbourhood-based services became more widespread, the emphasis of schemes varied from one council to the next, as it was recognized that decentralization was not a blanket remedy for a poor quality housing service. In Mansfield, for example, the compact nature of the area, the distribution of the public-sector housing stock and the dominant managerial and political culture made it possible for staff to be based at the Civic Centre, while still offering a more personalized service. The council relied more on existing resources (such as its current staff) rather than undertake massive additional expenditure through opening new offices or recruiting new staff. This strategy of course entailed its own costs, through the introduction of an extensive retraining programme to prepare staff for a wider range of responsibilities, and heavier workload, under the new regime. The neighbourhood housing officer, rather than the neighbourhood office, was the local service point for tenants.

It is unlikely that a scheme like Mansfield's would have been implemented in local housing departments where trade union activity was more developed. The apparent virtues of flexible working, generic practice and open-ended job descriptions might have been viewed more critically elsewhere. The Mansfield programme 'put the customer first', by highlighting the importance of staff/tenant interaction, and sought to retain consumer loyalty in the face of competition, without spending money on a network of neighbourhood offices, or being unduly concerned about multi-service provision or collective involvement. Yet the strategy essentially relied on extending the capacity and expertise of existing housing officers, in order to 'get more from the same'. In such a fashion, value for money and efficiency criteria entered debates about how a more responsive housing service could be established under adverse financial conditions.

The fourth, and probably final, phase of decentralization in council housing services is only just taking shape. It applies to two quite different types of local authority. In the first category are those local authorities which have bucked the trend of the past ten years and remained doggedly centralized in their operations. They will be coming under increasing pressure to reduce their stock and hand over management functions to other bodies. The second group comprises those councils with mature decentralized housing services which might be entering a new phase of local autonomy and control.

We can refer to this trend as *decentralization through contract management*, in which the localization of housing functions and budgets makes it easier to develop satellite agency-style services for particular housing estates and neighbourhoods, often under a management agreement with the local authority. Many of the larger authorities with centralized services have so far retained much of their stock, due to relatively low rates of Right to Buy and the failure of Tenants' Choice and the original version of Housing Action Trusts. However, the voluntary transfer of the housing stock to another organization may now begin to look more attractive, if it is politically acceptable to the council. Prior to the 1992 election, voluntary transfer was mainly confined to smaller district councils in the South of England. The average size of stock for the first 16 local authorities to undertake voluntary transfer was under 5000 (Gardiner *et al*. 1991). For local authorities with larger housing stocks, the viability of immediate wholesale transfer is open to question. It might test the resources of any housing association(s) involved, and be ruled out by central government anxious to avoid recreating mass landlordism through another sector: numerical limits will be maintained on such transfers (Conservative Party 1992).

The decentralization of housing functions could thereby be a prelude to the eventual *phased* transfer of stock to other agencies. This process could, of course, be implemented more readily in the second group of councils entering this phase – those local authorities which have moved farthest down the road of promoting neighbourhood autonomy, and freedom from central direction or control. Local authorities such as Tower Hamlets have been developing their area offices as free-standing cost centres, with considerable control over budgets, priorities and performance standards. Councils with a firm commitment to independence and self-determination for local offices may be particularly susceptible to the replacement of the local housing department by more diverse management and maintenance arrangements – especially with the introduction of compulsory competitive tendering. Decentralization may thus become a vehicle to hasten the break-up of local authority housing management and the expansion of other options, such as Estate Management Boards, full-blown tenant co-operatives, housing associations, private organizations or arm's length agencies from the council itself. In this manner, decentralization may indeed usher in a new era for social housing in Britain – but in a rather different way than that orginally envisaged in the first phase of decentralization schemes in the early 1980s.

Over the past ten years, decentralization has therefore been a chameleon concept, changing its appearance as the environment for regenerating council housing has become more hostile. The policy objectives of decentralization have been revised and redefined to ease the process of implementation. Local authorities have moulded these aims to suit their own political cultures, organizational styles and administrative networks. The changing emphasis of decentralization programmes in fact owes more to the growing visibility of external constraints – financial restriction, central government control and the prospects for diversification and privatization in socially rented housing.

To what extent can decentralization be consigned to a list of policy 'failures', in which the outcomes have fallen short of anticipated intentions? It was fanciful to have ever assumed that opening a clutch of neighbourhood offices would somehow turn the tide of history and reverse the residualization of council housing in Britain. But there is, perhaps, a sense of disappointment by policy-makers about the impact of decentralization within the local authority itself: it has not transformed the organizational culture of housing departments in the way that was originally envisaged. In order to account for this, we need to look more closely at the process of negotiation and interaction between those devising the policy and those charged with implementing it – between senior officers, front-line staff and elected members. Decentralization often brought to the surface underlying tensions between the interests and values of these groups.

The dynamics of implementation

It has been suggested above that the focus of decentralization initiatives gradually shifted during the 1980s from an attempt to change systems of representative democracy and collective involvement in local government to a narrower concern with improving performance where it mattered – on the 'front line'. It became a truism among senior managers that the success or failure of decentralization was ultimately dependent on gaining the support and commitment of those housing officers in regular contact with tenants. However, the realities of implementation have often belied the rhetorical flourishes about the value of front-line staff in the housing department. Although many councils have undertaken consultation exercises with tenants over their plans to decentralize, the views and interests of existing staff were often neglected or sidelined. They tended to be excluded from a process of organizational change which affected their working practices and conditions in fundamental ways. Lucy Gaster, for example, has described how front-line staff became disenchanted with departmental priorities when Birmingham City Council introduced neighbourhood-based services: in consequence, they developed an oppositional alliance with consumers of the housing service (Gaster 1990). The plans of several London boroughs also met with resistance from staff wishing to negotiate changes with senior management through their trade unions – as a defensive response to the imposition of new working practices (Heery 1987).

It was often stated that the locus of power in decentralized housing departments would shift towards officers based in neighbourhood offices, but a more complex process unfolded. Decentralization was proclaimed as a 'bottom-up' initiative – but it was usually developed and implemented in a very 'top-down' manner. Schemes were hatched by a coterie of senior officers and members and then 'delivered' to other staff and tenants. This strategy encouraged the view that neighbourhood provision was simply an optional extra, to be grafted on to a basically stable organization, rather than a means of transforming intra-departmental patterns of communication and control (Hoggett 1987). In the early phases, many local authorities recruited new staff to positions of responsibility in the area offices – a decision carrying an implicit judgement on the capabilities of existing housing officers. The introduction of decentralization often served to demoralize front-line staff, rather than empower them, and to marginalize them rather than extend their involvement in forming a new culture for the organization.

It is valuable here to distinguish between operational functions, which were selectively decentralized, and strategic control, which was concentrated in the centre. Hoggett (1990) characterizes the trend in post-Fordist private organizations in which the 'core' retains a tight grip on the essential features of organizational values, culture and strategy, while the 'periphery' carries out the functions. Decentralization of production is thus accompanied by centralization of command. This model applies to the internal restructuring of many housing departments, in which user-friendly localization has been undertaken alongside more assertive and directive management control from the centre.

Recent Government legislation has tended to intensify this process of organizational change. Strategic financial control over capital and revenue expenditure has been tightened, even while day-to-day spending is being relocated to neighbourhood cost centres. The introduction of performance indicators following the Local Government and Housing Act 1989 enhanced the potential for competition between different area or neighbourhood offices striving to attain 'good scores', while those at the centre sat in judgement. This process could well be taken further with the introduction of compulsory competitive tendering for housing management. Decentralized housing departments may then be governed by one of the oldest control strategies of all: divide and rule.

The distinction between strategic and operational management was blurred in the centralized bureaucratic housing departments of the past – 25 years hard labour as a rent collector was often seen as an essential precondition of becoming a middle manager. The paths have now diverged, and this distinction is reflected physically in the decentralized housing service. Senior officers in the centre devote time to forward strategy and planning, and fostering a corporate image or culture – issuing the name badges so that their staff out in estate offices can be more easily insulted by frustrated tenants.

Decentralization has nevertheless brought positive benefits to front-line staff in many local authorities. Neighbourhood working often requires the introduction of more generic forms of housing management, which can open up new opportunities for skill development and broaden promotion and career prospects. Front-line officers may gain more control over working methods and enjoy greater job satisfaction from the variety of tasks (Cole and Windle 1992). They may take on supervision responsibilities for other staff, such as wardens, community workers and estate caretakers. They may have more responsibility for administering local budgets, or estate-based allocations, or the enforcement of tenancy conditions. In a vibrant and active neighbourhood office, staff may feel part of a team, and build up a sense of commitment and service to the local community which is simply not possible when working in a Town Hall setting.

The greater flexibility engendered by neighbourhood housing work is, however, a two-edged sword. The position of front-line officers may become more vulnerable, without the protection of bureaucratic control and a specialized division of labour. Staff may feel isolated from their peers, and exposed to continual demands from line managers, active ward councillors or angry tenants. Team building exercises, even regular staff meetings, may become dispensable luxuries in hard-pressed neighbourhood offices. Very few decentralized housing departments have invested sufficiently in preparing staff through training in work planning, time management or monitoring effectiveness. Above all, front-line officers are faced daily with the dilemma of rationing between the increasing demands arising out of a more convenient service, and the decreasing resources available to respond. This sense of frustration is intensified by the lack of control exercised by neighbourhood housing officers over one of the critical elements of a local service – the effectiveness of the repairs process. In local authority housing departments in the 1990s, the 'gatekeeper' function is more of a poisoned chalice than ever – and it was precisely this role which was devolved most readily to the front line.

Decentralization placed too much faith in organizational shape and structure as a determinant of the quality of a housing service, and gave insufficient attention to intra-organizational processes of communication and patterns of influence (Clapham 1991). Staff morale and motivation was often undermined at the very time that their role was being extended or enhanced through neighbourhood working. Housing departments have begun to develop staff care codes to set aside their customer care programmes, in belated recognition of this dimension (Passmore 1990).

Elected members were often closely involved in the formulation of proposals to decentralize services. However, their role at the stage of implementation has received little research attention. This is surprising, given the questions raised by decentralization about forms of representation, participation and service delivery. It is even more surprising when one considers that many councillors take a close interest in council housing management (especially allocations and repairs). In practice, decentralization may disrupt relationships between councillors, by driving a wedge between ward-oriented members and the policy élite, even within the same party. It also prompts different forms of officer-member contact and communication.

Research evidence suggests that elected members have been generally positive about the effects of service decentralization (Cole et al. 1988a). This does not necessarily stem from careful scrutiny of comparative management performance at local housing offices. Instead, decentralization is more an article of faith. The virtues of a neighbourhood presence are self-evident: a sign that the council is providing for 'their' community rather than merely serving the interests of Town Hall bureaucrats. It is open to interpretation whether this commitment symbolizes a welcome advance for community politics in local government, or a retreat to the bad old days of petty parochialism.

Local councillors generally adhere to a 'consumerist' view of decentralization, which is stronger on qualities such as convenience and accessibility than on tenant empowerment or control. Elected members have rarely been too eager to establish neighbourhood committees alongside local offices – the Tower Hamlets model is the exception rather than the rule. Councillors tend to place greater emphasis on directing resources to the point of service delivery and developing flatter organizational structures. Generic forms of housing practice are also favoured, possibly prompted by councillors' suspicions about professional specialization and control. Ward-based members tend to look at the housing department from the 'outside in', rather than as a series of tiers emanating from the centre: this encourages them to take a view that decentralization is a way of putting the money 'where it counts' rather than feathering the nests of middle managers. Tenant activists are often inclined to the same view.

Officer–member interaction may change significantly in a decentralized housing service. In particular, the relationship between ward members and the Area/Neighbourhood Manager can become pivotal, although its character may develop in different ways. Some councillors tend to adopt a *tribune* role, protecting (and supervising) the Area Manager from central, line management control in the department. Such councillors feel they should exercise strategic influence over management priorities at the neighbourhood level. The area-based housing staff, on the other hand, may be faced with contradictory advice from senior officers, on one side, and local members, on the other.

Alternatively, the local councillor may act as an *ally* to the Area Manager. Such an approach emphasizes a ward-centred, problem-solving orientation, and the need for constant contact with housing officers. If the local office is being used extensively by councillors, this provides positive signals for tenants as well, making them less likely to bypass the Area Manager and 'go to the top' to have enquiries sorted out. On the other hand, too close an alliance may lead to a complete blurring of the respective responsibilities of officers and members. There is often a fine distinction between councillors' legitimate concern with standards of service in their ward, and undue interference in management tasks, and this balance may be struck differently in each neighbourhood across a local authority.

Thirdly, the ward member may act as an *interrogator* of local management performance. Such councillors will preserve a constitutional distance from housing officers, acting as advocates for local residents. This separation of responsibilities may provoke mutual trust between area-based staff and ward members, or lead to a situation where officers feel consistently threatened or under pressure. In this way, the relationship between officers and councillors often becomes more turbulent in a decentralized housing service, as the organization departs from the constitutional fiction of a twin pyramidal structure, with the sole point of contact arising between the director of the housing department and the chair of the housing committee. In the neighbourhood office, housing staff view this new element of member involvement in expected ways: it is valuable as an antidote to intrusive control from the centre; and it is resented if staff feel undermined or confused by councillors becoming too closely involved in the operation of the housing service.

Conclusion

It has been suggested here that the aims of decentralization have been down-scaled in the face of difficulties in implementation, internal tensions in housing departments, limitations on expenditure and growing external pressures on the service. Decentralization has been a useful means to achieving a more responsive and customer-oriented housing service: but changing the shape of the organization has only been a first step, rather than the last word, in this process.

What does the future hold? If voluntary transfer and compulsory competitive tendering come to the fore, the centrifugal tendencies on organizing housing management might be intensified, with multiple locally-based providers being established. However, fragmentation would be a more appropriate term than decentralization to describe such a process. The residual housing functions for local authorities are more likely to be recentralized, and comprise activities such as forward strategy, co-ordination and arbitration between competing landlord interests. There is hardly a compelling case to have such responsibilities located in different areas or neighbourhoods rather than at the centre. This trend is already evident in smaller housing authorities (with a stock of less than 6000 properties) where rationalization of functions has taken precedence over responsiveness to neighbourhood housing needs (Windle *et al.* 1988).

Decentralization has emphasized structural change as a way of improving local authority housing departments. However, it is now quite possible that a free-standing housing service in local government will become obsolescent. If unitary local authorities are established, one is likely to witness growing interest in relocating housing functions to other council departments. In the future, structural change may focus on lateral relationships – in terms of organizational responsibility for housing services – rather than the vertical relationships at the heart of decentralization initiatives. In such a scenario, the strategic housing function might be subsumed by the Planning Department, the 'welfare' function (including homelessness and community care) by the Social Services Department and private-sector regulation by the Environmental Health Department.

At the local level, one can imagine the use of neighbourhood offices being transferred to Estate Management Boards, or housing associations. Those neighbourhood offices which remain under local authority control will become isolated outposts of a housing service under siege – a tangible reminder of an era when the regeneration of council housing management through decentralization was a more promising prospect than it is today.

References

Almond, R. (1986) 'Housing Decentralization in Leeds', Postgraduate Diploma Dissertation, Sheffield City Polytechnic, School of Urban and Regional Studies.

Beuret, K. and Stoker, G. (1986) 'The Labour Party and neighbourhood decentralization: flirtation or commitment?'. *Critical Social Policy*, No. 17: 4–21.

Building Use Studies (1986) *Improved Information Systems for Decentralized Housing Management by Coventry City Council*, Royal Institute of Public Administration.

Building Use Studies (1987) *Monitoring the Cost of Local Housing Management*, Royal Institute of Public Administration.

Burns, D. and Williams, M. (1989) *Neighbourhood Working: A New Approach to Housing Provision*, University of Bristol, School for Advanced Urban Studies.

Clapham, D. (1991) 'Organising effective housing management' in D. Donnison and D. MacLennan *The Housing Service of the Future*, Harlow, Longman.

Clarke, M. and Stewart, J. (1987) 'P.S.O. – Developing the approach', *Local Government Policy Making*, Vol. 13, No. 4: 23–42.

Cole, I. and Windle, K. (1992) 'Decentralization', in C. Davies, *Housing For Life*, London, Spon.

Cole, I. and Furbey, R. (1993) *The Eclipse of Council Housing: Housing and the Welfare State*, London, Routledge.

Cole, I., Arnold, P. and Windle, K. (1988a) *Decentralization – The Views of Elected Members*, Housing Decentralization Research Project Working Paper 4, Joseph Rowntree Foundation.

Cole, I., Windle, K. and Arnold, P. (1988b) *The Impact of Decentralization*, Housing Decentralization Research Project Working Paper 3, Joseph Rowntree Foundation.

Cole, I., Windle, K. and Arnold, P. (1989) *Localised Housing Services in Leeds – Decentralization By Political Mandate*, Housing Decentralization Research Project Working Paper 8, Joseph Rowntree Foundation.

Cole, I., Arnold, P. and Windle, K. (1991) 'Decentralized housing services – back to the future', in D. Donnison and D. MacLennan (eds) *The Housing Service of the Future*, Harlow, Longman.

Conservative Party (1992) *The Best Future for Britain: Conservative Manifesto 1992*, Conservative Central Office.

Dearlove, J. (1979) *The Reorganization of British Local Government*, Cambridge, Cambridge University Press.

Decentralization Research and Information Centre (1991) *Going Local*, No. 17, Spring, DRIC.

Department of Environment (1989) *The Nature and Effectiveness of Housing Management in England*, London, HMSO.

Gardiner, K., Hills, J. and Kleinman, M. (1991) *Putting A Price On Council Housing: Valuing Voluntary Transfers*, Suntory Toyota International Centre for Economics and Related Disciplines, London School of Economics.

Gaster, L. (1990) *Quality At The Front Line*, University of Bristol, School for Advanced Urban Studies.

Gyford, J. (1985) *The Politics of Local Socialism*, London, Allen and Unwin.

Hambleton, R. (1987) 'Developments, objectives and criteria', in P. Willmott (ed.) *Local Government Decentralization and Community*, London, Policy Studies Institute.

Hambleton, R. (1988) 'Consumerism, decentralization, democracy', *Public Administration*, Vol. 66, Summer.

Hambleton, R. and Hoggett, P. (1987) 'Beyond bureaucratic paternalism', in P. Hoggett and R. Hambleton (eds) *Decentralization and Democracy*, Occasional Paper 28, University of Bristol, School for Advanced Urban Studies.

Heery, E. (1987) 'A common Labour Movement? Left Labour councils and the trade unions', in P. Hoggett and R. Hambleton (eds) *Decentralization and Democracy*, Occasional Paper 28, University of Bristol, School for Advanced Urban Studies.

Henney, A. (1985) *Trust the Tenant: Devolving Municipal Housing*, London, Centre for Policy Studies.

Hoggett, P. (1987) 'A farewell to mass production? Decentralization as an emergent private and public sector paradigm', in P. Hoggett and R. Hambleton (eds) *Decentralization and Democracy*, Occasional Paper 28, University of Bristol, School for Advanced Urban Studies.

Hoggett, P. (1990) *Modernisation, Political Strategy and the Welfare State: An Organisational Perspective*, SAUS Studies in Decentralization and Quasi-Markets No. 2, University of Bristol, School for Advanced Urban Studies.

Islington Borough Council (1987) *Going Local: Decentralization in Practice*, Islington Council Press.

Lee, P. and Raban, C. (1988) *Welfare Theory and Social Policy*, London, Sage.

Leeds City Council (1954) *Annual Report to Housing Committee 1953–4*, Leeds City Council.

Mainwaring, R. (1988) *The Walsall Experience*, London, HMSO.

Morphet, J. (1987) 'Local authority decentralization – Tower Hamlets', *Policy and Politics*, Vol. 15, No. 2: 119–26.

Passmore, J. (1990) 'Customer care – cultural change at Welwyn Hatfield', *Local Government Studies*, September–October: 1–8.

Peters, T. and Waterman, R. (1982) *In Search of Excellence*, New York, Harper and Row.

Power, A. (1987) *Property Before People*, London, Allen and Unwin.

Rustin, M. (1989) 'The politics of post-Fordism or the trouble with "New Times"', *New Left Review*, May–June, Vol. 175: 57–78.

Seabrook, J. (1984) *The Idea of Neighbourhood*, London, Pluto.

Stoker, G. (1987) 'Decentralization and the restructuring of local government in Britain', *Local Government Policy Making*, Vol. 14, No. 2: 3–11.

Windle, K., Cole, I. and Arnold, P. (1988) *Organizing Housing Services on a Small Scale*, Housing Decentralisation Research Project Working Paper No. 1, Joseph Rowntree Foundation.

Wright, A. (1984) 'The Labour Party and decentralisation', in A. Wright, J. Stewart and N. Deakin, *Socialism and Decentralisation*, Fabian Tract 496.

CHAPTER 11

Large-scale voluntary transfers*

DAVID MULLINS, PAT NINER AND MOYRA RISEBOROUGH

Introduction

Between 1988 and 1991, 16 local authorities voluntarily divested themselves of their entire rented housing stocks. While the 77 000 tenancies transferred represented under 2 per cent of all council tenancies in England, voluntary transfers were already providing a major contribution to the Government's privatization drive in housing. Speculation abounded that a further hundred or more authorities were 'waiting in the wings' considering stock transfer once the housing policies of the next Government became clear.

This chapter is informed by research undertaken by the authors into the implementation of voluntary transfer decisions by the earliest authorities to take this course. It locates voluntary transfers as local responses to national housing policies, and identifies the types of authority involved, before proceeding to consider local implementation processes. The role of local key actors with specific interests, and of local consultation and bargaining processes in each area are seen to have played their part in mediating the national determinants of this reactive policy. The relevance of these early case studies for the future is considered.

* This research was part of 'Evaluation of Large Scale Voluntary Transfers', a longitudinal study commissioned by the Department of the Environment. However, the interpretation, views and analysis presented are those of the authors alone, and do not necessarily represent the views of the Department of the Environment. An interim report of the project was due to be published by HMSO in 1992 (Mullins *et al.* forthcoming).

Voluntary transfers – background

Legislative background

Voluntary transfers have occurred on the initiative of individual local authorities using the powers established under sections 32–34 and 43 of the Housing Act 1985 which allow disposals of land and dwellings subject to the Secretary of State's consent. Requirements to consult with tenants before applying for Secretary of State consent were first set out in the Housing and Planning Act 1986, and extended to all forms of transfer in the Housing Act 1988. The 1988 Act also elaborated on the considerations the Secretary of State would look to in considering applications for disposals.

Interestingly, the statutory powers for disposal in the 1985 Act were not introduced with voluntary transfers in mind, and those provisions of the 1988 Act which were orientated to voluntary transfers can best be seen as a response to local government initiatives already underway. The first completed transfer in Chiltern in December 1988 actually predated the implementation of the 1988 Act. The legislation has been supplemented by guidance produced by the Department of the Environment and the Housing Corporation setting out expectations on such matters as independence of the new landlord from the local authority, protection of tenants' interests and the terms of sale (e.g. Housing Corporation 1989a). However, the early transfers involved considerable negotiation with both the Department of the Environment and the Housing Corporation to clarify the many grey areas. It is clear that for the pioneer authorities the full implications of transfer could not have been known at the outset. Certain key issues such as the calculation of catch up repairs in stock valuations were only resolved as these transfers proceeded.

As a local response to the national policy agenda

The 1987 White Paper 'Housing – The Government's Proposals' (Department of Environment 1987), set out its principal policy aims. As well as continuing to encourage the growth of home ownership, the Government wished to give council tenants the right to transfer to other landlords if they chose to do so.

Tenants' Choice and Housing Action Trusts formed the main new vehicles for transferring stock away from local authorities proposed in the 1987 Housing White Paper and enacted in the Housing Act 1988. By the end of 1991 neither of these had directly resulted in a single property moving away from local authority control. Instead, voluntary transfers initiated by local authorities had become an important component of privatization. The 77 000 dwellings transferred in the first 16 transfers more than made up for the decline in right to buy sales after 1988/89.

Nevertheless, voluntary transfer decisions cannot be understood in isolation from the national policy agenda. Interviews in case study authorities generally located the main impetus to voluntary transfers in reactions to the Government's housing policies. In a number of areas the process started with officer assessments of the implications of the 1987 White Paper for their authorities' future housing role. While implementation decisions were local, their context was clearly the relationship between central and local government, and the various threats which national policy was perceived to constitute to local housing services.

Main stimuli to transfer

In some cases, the main rationale for transfer was to maintain a stock of rented housing for letting to those in housing need and unable to gain access to other sectors of the local housing market. Some authorities had already lost over one-third of their rented stock during the 1980s under the Right to Buy, and were experiencing substantial reductions to re-lets, particularly of larger properties needed to meet homelessness duties. Transfer of housing to a new landlord was seen by some as an effective means of excluding new tenancies from the Right to Buy, and maintaining the capacity to develop new homes, and thereby stemming the rate of depletion of the rented stock.

For a time, the main impetus to voluntary transfers seems to have been to counter the threat of Tenants' Choice transfers of parts of an authority's stock to other landlords. Some authorities believed that they were vulnerable to Tenants' Choice applications by 'predatory landlords', and stood to lose their best estates. These fears were reported in the media; for example an article in *Roof* in January/February 1989 (p. 17) stated that 'Hertfordshire's proximity to London together with its excellent road and rail links make its council housing stocks . . . particularly attractive to "pick a tenant" speculators'. There was a significant time-lag between the original presentation of the idea of Tenants' Choice in the 1987 White Paper and the clarification of procedures to be followed, including criteria for approval of landlords. Furthermore, it was not until the 1988 Act had been in operation for a few years that the limited impact of Tenants' Choice became generally recognized, and fears of speculative or predatory activity were dispelled. During this period a number of authorities made plans for voluntary transfer in order to preserve their remaining rented stock intact.

No sooner had the perceived threat of Tenants' Choice declined than a new and greater challenge to continued housing provision by local authorities emerged as the main stimulus to consideration of voluntary transfers. The new financial regime introduced by the Local Government and Housing Act 1989 was widely perceived as spelling the end to new council building through its further controls on re-investing capital receipts. It also created new incentives for moving social housing away from the housing revenue account (through bringing rent rebates into subsidy calculations, upward pressures on rents and to a lesser extent ring fencing the HRA). For some authorities this new regime was the last straw, particularly for those who had been partly insulated from HIP cuts by a high level of capital receipts from sales, some of which they had re-invested in the housing service. Voluntary transfer packages were seen as providing an enhanced ability to build new homes, to protect new tenancies from the Right to Buy and to keep the rents down for existing tenants.

Thus, transfer decisions were made on the basis of perceptions of the local impact of national housing policies. Interestingly, with hindsight it is possible to see that some of these perceptions were inaccurate. Nevertheless, the overall constraints presented to local authorities by national housing policy were sufficient to ensure that as one perceived stimulus declined, another emerged to take its place. Moreover, the more favourable treatment of housing associations provided a constant incentive to consider transfer.

Impact of successful transfers on the national agenda

However, the relationship between the national policy agenda and local initiatives has not been one-way. Successful voluntary transfers have also played their part in shaping the Government's perception of the most effective modes of implementation to achieve its housing policy objectives.

As has already been noted, voluntary transfers were not among the mechanisms identified in the White Paper and following legislation to extend housing choice to council tenants. Indeed there may have been a perception that early voluntary transfers were actually attempts to subvert the Government's objectives and preserve local authority control over rented housing stocks. The Department of the Environment's first written guidance in relation to voluntary transfers (DoE 1988a) made it clear that consent would only be given to transfers to bodies independent of their local authorities. Criteria used to assess independence included a 20 per cent ceiling on local authority representation on the purchasing body (Department of Environment 1988b), a ban on the provision of services by the council (e.g. payroll, computers etc.) after a transitional period, and on the automatic redeployment of council staff to the new organization.

While the preamble to the guidance commented that 'in principle the Government welcomes these moves to transfer council housing into alternative ownership', it was some time before the 'rules of the game' became relatively clear to interested authorities. The Department of the Environment's initial approach was fairly neutral, seeing voluntary transfers as local authority initiatives which they were free to pursue if they wished. Guidance could only be developed as ideas were tried out and both the Department and authorities learned from the experience. Even after two-and-a-half years no written guidance was available on many matters. Repeated contacts were required with the Department to obtain verbal guidance, and there was a feeling of constantly 'shifting goalposts' as the experience of each transfer was assimilated. This was a cause of considerable frustration for some authorities. Nevertheless, there was also praise for the commitment of the Departmental officials involved, and a recognition that intense scrutiny was essential given the magnitude and 'once and for all' nature of the transfer decision.

By the end of 1991, with a number of examples of succesful transfers, more unequivocal Government support for transfers became apparent. In answer to a parliamentary question by the Conservative MP, Mr Moate on 6 November 1991, the Environment Minister Tim Yeo stated (*Hansard* vol. 198, p. 442):

My Hon. Friend rightly draws attention to the enormous benefits that accrue from such large scale voluntary transfers. There are benefits to the tenants in the form of improved stock condition, better repairs services and guarantees on rents. The research that we have carried out on the early transfers shows that tenants feel that their landlords are taking a closer interest in them.

The national pattern

Prior to the 1992 election, a relatively small number of authorities had actively pursued voluntary transfers. By the end of 1991, 16 transfers were actually completed and a further 47 local authorities had seriously progressed a transfer:

Transfer completed	16
Vote in favour: not yet transferred	2
Actively pursuing transfer	12
Rejected by tenants at ballot	12
Dropped prior to ballot	21

Thus, 63 of the 365 housing authorities in England had been involved. An analysis of some characteristics of these authorities suggests a rather narrow range, and the limited applicability of their experience to the larger numbers of authorities reported to be 'waiting in the wings'.

Location, political control and housing profile

The four Department of the Environment regions, South East, South West, Eastern and Greater London include just over half of English authorities, but 87 per cent of authorities who had actively considered transfer, and 94 per cent of those had completed transfers by the end of 1991 (Table 11.1). Significantly, no metropolitan authorities nor any inner London boroughs had actively considered transfer. Transfers were concentrated in resort areas, growth areas and suburban residential areas, principally in a ring around Greater London.

Interest was greatest amongst authorities under Conservative control, who comprised over two-thirds of authorities who had actively considered transfer, and 13 of the 16 completed transfers. However, the temptation to see this as a politically-led movement in tune with the Government's privatization policies provides an incomplete explanation of policy implementation as we shall see below (see section on Local Actors and Agendas).

The housing profile of interested authorities was also quite distinctive. Nine out of ten of authorities actively considering transfer, and all of those completing it, had council stocks below the English average of 11 300. Similarly, in virtually all cases, council housing formed a lower proportion of the local housing stock than the average (21 per cent) for English authorities. This may have reflected DoE guidance on the maximum size of stock to be transferred to a single landlord, but more likely was simply a correlate of the types of authorities involved in the first wave of voluntary transfers.

Transfer areas do not seem to have experienced high levels of homelessness

Table 11.1 Characteristics of local authorities who had actively considered voluntary transfer by the end of 1991

Local authority	All authorities considering transfer		Completed transfers	
	No.	Percentage	No.	Percentage
1 Location (DoE region)				
South East	21	33	8	50
South West	14	22	2	13
Eastern	14	22	5	31
Greater London	6	10	–	–
East Midlands	3	5	–	–
Yorks and Humberside	3	5	1	6
North West	2	3	–	–
North	–	–	–	–
2 Type of area				
Resort	13	21	5	31
Growth	16	25	3	19
Suburban/residential	13	21	4	25
Rural	9	14	2	13
Outer London	6	10	–	–
Traditional industrial	4	6	2	13
Regional service centre	2	3	–	–
Metropolitan	–	–	–	–
Inner London	–	–	–	–
3 Political control				
Conservative	42	67	13	81
No overall control	11	17	2	13
Independent	7	11	1	6
Liberal Democrats	2	3	–	–
Labour	1	2	–	–
4 Housing profile				
Council stock:				
under 6000	34	54	10	63
6000–11999	23	36	6	37
12000 and over	6	10	–	–
Council as percentage of all housing:				
Under 10%	13	21	5	31
10% but under 15%	24	38	7	44
15% but under 20%	22	35	4	25
20% and over	4	6	–	–

Source: Department of the Environment database

demand compared to their regional averages, but did generally have lower than average proportions of social rented housing to meet homelessness demand. Moreover, they were concentrated in the areas with high house and land values, which also produced higher indicator rents under the new council rent regime. They were likely to have enjoyed relatively high levels of capital receipts through buoyant right to buy sales, and thus to have been particularly adversely affected by the new capital expenditure rules introduced by the 1989 Act.

Types of Transfer

The term 'large-scale voluntary transfers' is used for authorities who have voluntarily disposed of their entire rented stocks to an alternative landlord. Other types of transfer such as of certain properties as they become available for letting ('trickle transfers') and newly-built dwellings only, are not considered here. Neither are the various housing management initiatives such as estate management boards, local management agreements and tenant management co-operatives which were amongst the other options being implemented as local responses to the same national policy agenda.

All but three of the 30 proposals which proceeded to ballot stage involved new housing associations set up by local authorities to receive their housing stock. These have become known as local community housing associations. Although early transfers involved relatively small council stocks, local community housing associations are already constituting an important and influential new group within the housing association movement, with stock sizes well above those of the majority of existing registered housing associations. Some local community housing associations are already developing on a significant scale outside of their original local authority areas.

Some alternatives to the local community housing association model have been attempted. In one successful transfer, Rochester on Medway, the new body did not register with the Housing Corporation. Two transfers to existing registered housing associations were attempted, Torbay and North Kesteven, but neither proceeded beyond the ballot stage.

Voluntary transfers – implementation

What is involved?

Implementing a voluntary transfer is a major undertaking for housing authorities. A typical transfer process can take two years, cost almost £2 million in consultants' fees and transaction costs, and involve enormous amounts of (largely unpaid) staff overtime. In a not untypical case study, seven different firms of consultants had been appointed to act on behalf of either the council or the association during the transfer process. In another, the transfer contract documents were said to stand four feet high. Voluntary transfer is likely to have been the most substantial housing undertaking to date for each of the authorities involved.

Four main stages are involved in the transfer process. First, the authority decides in principle to pursue the transfer option subject to tenant support and all the necessary approvals. Next, preparatory work is undertaken on developing the transfer package. In most cases this has involved establishing a local community housing association, drawing up a business plan, and a draft 'heads of agreement' for the transfer contract. The third stage involves consulting tenants on the draft package and obtaining their views in a ballot. Where the ballot results in adequate support for transfer, a fourth stage is required to finalize negotiations, agree a transfer contract, obtain funding for the transfer and the new association's business plan and secure Secretary of State approval. Needless to say, all this cannot be achieved without enormous commitment by those involved.

Local actors and agendas

So far in this chapter, voluntary transfers have been described as a major contribution to the Government's housing privatization objectives between 1988 and 1991. This description may be justified in terms of the numbers of dwellings transferred to local community housing associations, and the private finance regime of these associations. Most transfers were entirely financed by private sector loans, usually arranged by banks or building societies, sometimes on a syndicated basis. Tenants' rent and security are dependent upon the success of business plans drawn up with advice from private consultants. The potential for new development is governed by the borrowing collateral and asset base of the associations rather than by the Government's public expenditure plans. The process has aptly been described as a shift from political risk to market risk (Gardiner *et al*. 1991).

Yet few of the key actors involved in these transfers would recognize their local initiatives as part of someone else's privatization package. It would be difficult to fully understand the implementation process without reference to the perceptions of the local actors involved. The research conducted by the University of Birmingham included interviews with key actors in each case study authority in order to gain a clear picture of the local implementation process, including negotiations between the parties involved in the transfer contract and consultation with tenants. The consultation and negotiation processes are dealt with later in this section on implementation. First we review more general views of the transfer idea.

General perceptions

While there was some variation between authorities, one striking feature was how often the transfer idea was introduced and the implementation process led by officers rather than politicians. This challenges the notion of transfers being introduced for ideological reasons by local Conservative groups sympathetic to the Government's privatization agenda. There were a few examples of politically led transfer proposals, but virtually none of these resulted in a successful transfer.

The most common route to the transfer idea being explored was an initial officer committee paper reviewing the implications of the Government's Housing White Paper and prospective legislation for the continued provision of a local housing service. As we have seen above, the specific threats identified shifted from Right to Buy, through Tenants' Choice to the new financial regime; but reaction to central government policies was always a prominent theme. Consultants were usually employed to advise on the options available to the authority to respond to these threats, and provide a basis for committee decisions to proceed with transfer. Tenants were rarely involved at this stage of option appraisal.

While reaction to the national policy agenda was always present, there were frequently clear local agendas influencing those advancing the transfer idea. Often it was felt that a single purpose housing organization would be better able to deliver a good quality service than a council department.

Sometimes there were concerns that the housing department received poor value for money from centrally recharged services. In one authority, council housing had been part of the Environmental Health Department, and the most senior housing manager had not been part of the authority's corporate management team. It was felt that strategic decisions were made without adequate consideration of implications for council housing. The transfer was seen as a route to a higher profile housing service.

The common preference for transfer to a local community housing association may be seen as a reflection of key actors' interests. Not only would such a body achieve the objective of retaining the stock under one locally based organization, it also provided opportunities for existing housing staff to be appointed to posts in the new organization. Most local community housing associations were initially headed by an officer from the local authority.

Local councillors were keen to be represented on the governing bodies of the new landlords, and have generally taken up the maximum number of places under the '20 per cent rule'. In several cases the exception allowing councillors to chair the new organization for the first year has been used. However, we found no council attempts to control new associations. The Housing Corporation was generally satisfied with evidence of rapid moves towards independence by local community housing associations.

The negotiation process

The pattern of negotiation of voluntary transfers was rarely as simple as a property transaction in an established market. In the first place, there were considerable variations in the extent to which the local authority and the community housing association saw themselves as and acted as separate parties engaged in a bargaining process. Secondly, the considerations involved went beyond the definition and pricing of the assets to be transferred and were as much concerned with the future framework for housing provision in the locality. Thirdly, there is no established market for tenanted council properties and the structure of negotiations often seemed to be influenced more by the regulation of the Department of the Environment than by the different interests of the local parties.

Definition of interests

While the housing association required a sensible valuation in order to meet its business plan objectives and deliver the rent and repairs promises made to tenants, the local authority's interest was usually less clearly defined. It became clear from the case studies that the early transferring authorities initiated the process without any clear expectations of a capital receipt in excess of their outstanding loan debt. Indeed there was no evidence of transfer proposals being initiated simply because of the prospect of a significant capital receipt for the authority.

Analysis of negotiations suggests that a variety of approaches were adopted. In some cases a consensual approach was followed in which both parties worked together to achieve the transfer with little recognition of the different interests involved. This was particularly the case in the earliest transfers when the 'rules of the game' were far from clear. In others a more adversarial relationship prevailed between two sides, and there was a keenly contested struggle over the valuation and other matters such as the price and service standards for transitional services provided by the council during the first year of transfer, and the extent to which the new association should be favoured in any local authority housing association grant (LAHAG) investment financed from the capital receipt.

There were also differences in the extent to which officers acting for the association were precluded from continuing to advise the council. The timing of secondments to the new association was a difficult issue given the need to continue providing a housing service throughout the process. However scrupulous and professional officers were, their expectation of posts with the new association if transfer occurred, inevitably gave them a vested interest. Similarly there were potential conflicts of interest for councillors who were both members of the council's Housing Committee and of the new association. These conflicts were much more clearly recognized and provided for in some authorities than others. One unsuccessful transfer involved the early secondment of some senior personnel to the new association to develop and present the package, while their former colleagues 'minded the shop'. In this case the association appeared to be making all of the running and transfer was opposed by tenants who felt that the association was trying to take the council's housing against its will. Clearer expectations of independence have since been laid down by the Housing Corporation (1989b).

Consultants acting for both the local authority and the housing association played a key role in defining interests and influencing the negotiations. Sometimes there were perceptions that consultants were inadequately monitored. Where a shared understanding existed between consultants acting for the two parties, they may have played a more significant role than either party in determining the outcome of negotiations. The common practice of engaging the consultant, who initially advised on the options available, to then draw up the new association's business plan suggests that there may be a vested interest in promoting transfers.

Wider scope of negotiations

Transferring authorities were usually committed to the idea of transfer as the best way of continuing to meet the housing needs of the area. This concern was reflected in the scope of transfer negotiations. There was at least as much attention given to aspects of the transfer contract concerning future housing management arrangements as to those concerning the valuation. A key aspect of most transfer contracts was the arrangements for meeting the authority's homelessness reponsibilities through nominations to the new association. There was usually a political commitment to keeping rents at an affordable level; indeed in one authority the ballot procedure was delayed until politicians were satisfied that rent promises made in the earlier consultation campaign could be delivered.

Involvement of regulatory bodies

Another distinctive feature of the negotiations was the extensive involvement of the Department of the Environment and the Housing Corporation throughout the process. This made negotiations quite unlike those to be expected in a free market. In some cases it appeared that the council and housing association were united in seeing the Department of the Environment as the main 'enemy', and worked together to achieve a package agreeable to the Secretary of State. In one case both parties had wished to see the lowest possible rent increases for tenants, but had been persuaded to compromise after consultation with the Department of the Environment on what the Secretary of State would be likely to approve.

Working with the rather skimpy guidelines available in the early stages it was inevitable that the Department of the Environment and the Housing Corporation would themselves constitute key parties in transfer negotiations. One issue where this became particularly apparent was in the provision for major repairs to be made in the valuation process. One transfer was held up for a number of months whilst agreement was reached between the two bodies on this issue (Department of Environment 1990). Another matter resolved at an early date between the two was the interaction of voluntary transfers with Tenants' Choice (Department of the Environment and Housing Corporation 1989).

Other researchers (Gardiner et al. 1991) have suggested a tendency towards increasing valuations after April 1990, reflecting the influence of the Department of the Environment in seeking larger capital receipts for transferring authorities and higher rents for tenants. However, with the exception of the relatively low valuations in the first few transfers the figures in Table 11.2 do not indicate a clear pattern.

Consultation with tenants

Before transfers can obtain the consent of the Secretary of State, authorities must demonstrate that they have consulted with tenants. The statutory requirements, set out in Circular 6/88 (Department of Environment 1988c), include the provision of clear, even-handed information on the Council's proposals, the consideration of tenant responses, and a formal test of tenant opinion. The latter requirement has been met by a ballot of tenants in all cases; however, there have

Table 11.2 Transfers completed by December 1991 – Valuations and price per dwelling

Authority	Transfer date	Valuation (£m.)	Price per dwelling (£)
Chiltern	12/88	33	6900
Sevenoaks	3/89	64	10000
Newbury	11/89	47	6600
Swale	4/90	55	7500
Broadland	4/90	25	6700
North Beds	6/90	64	8600
South Wight	7/90	22	10600
Medina	7/90	28	10000
Rochester	7/90	77	9600
Mid Sussex	11/90	44	10000
East Dorset	12/90	22	9600
Tonbridge and Malling	1/91	54	8500
Ryedale	2/91	28	8300
Christchurch	3/91	14	9100
South Bucks	4/91	35	10300
Suffolk Coastal	4/91	34	6300

Source: Gardiner *et al.* (1991)

been some variations in the voting rules applied with a few early authorities using the widely criticized 'negative voting' system devised for Tenants' Choice ballots.

Role of tenants in transfer process

One finding of the research was the very limited involvement allowed to tenants in the transfer process. Tenants were consulted, but were not actively involved in the decision process about the future ownership of their homes. In only two of our early case studies was independent advice made available to tenants from a body other than the transferring council or new landlord. Many important decisions were taken in meetings from which the public were excluded. Aside from tenant representatives on the management committees of the new associations, tenants played virtually no part in either the initial decision to progress the transfer option or the final negotiations over the terms of transfer which followed positive ballots. The tenant consultation and ballot process often formed a relatively brief span within the overall transfer process.

This may have partly reflected the character of the authorities in which the early transfers took place. In many areas there were few if any organized tenant groups prior to the transfer, and consultation on the transfer was often the first serious attempt at tenant consultation on any aspect of housing policy. The research also reflects the earliest transfers, before the funding of independent advisers for tenants' groups became an accepted part of the transfer process.

Different position of existing tenants and new tenants

Nevertheless, existing tenants did have a considerable influence on the nature of the transfer packages. In order to achieve positive ballot results, the transfer proposals had to be presented in a way which was as attractive as possible to existing tenants. This was usually tackled by offering rent guarantees at a few percentage points above inflation for existing tenants, together with a package of service improvements particularly in relation to repairs and maintenance. Also, tenancy agreements were used to restore on a contractual basis some of the statutory rights which would have been lost in the move from secure to assured tenancies.

Rent guarantees after transfer were usually contrasted with high projected increases for council tenants under the new financial regime. However, an equally significant contrast, illustrating the influence of existing tenants on the package, was the considerably higher rents to be paid by new tenants in order to finance the business plans of the new associations.

Ballot results

By the end of 1991, 30 local authorities had balloted their tenants on voluntary transfer. Ballot turnouts were almost uniformly high, in comparison for example with local election turnouts. Only in Torbay was turnout under 70 per cent, while in over half of the ballots it exceeded 80 per cent. There was a wide variety of ballot outcomes ranging from 8 per cent to 91 per cent of those voting being in favour of transfer. Just over half of the ballots had resulted in a sufficient proportion of votes in favour for transfer to proceed (see Table 11.3). In most cases the result was fairly clear cut. One authority, Swale, achieved a very narrow majority (54 per cent of voters were in favour and 46 per cent against) but the transfer proceeded.

A number of factors seem to have influenced ballot results. The presence of a strong local campaign opposing the transfer was often an important factor in ballot defeats. However, not all opposition campaigns were successful, and some of those studied suffered from lack of tenant involvement, limited financial resources in comparison with the transfer campaign and unimpressive publicity material.

The factors which seem to have been most important in gaining a 'Yes' vote were a simple and clearly expressed case for transfer, and a good and trusting relationship between tenants and housing staff. Interestingly, several transfers were sold to tenants as the 'least change option' under which they would retain the same housing staff, and enjoy a similar but better service for a reasonable rent. Without a transfer this maintenance of the status quo would no longer be possible. The success of this 'least change' approach can be understood by considering the age and length of tenancy of many council tenants.

Local community housing associations – the future for council housing?

Three key questions concerning the impact of large-scale voluntary transfers remain unanswered.

Table 11.3   Voluntary transfer ballot results 1988–91

Local authority	No. of dwellings	Date of ballot	Ballot turnout	Percentage of vote in favour	Transfer date
Chiltern DC	4750	9/88	71	84	12/88
Torbay BC	4150	10/88	59	26	
Rochford DC	2450	11/88	87	8	
Salisbury BC	7900	12/88	77	25	
Sevenoaks DC	6350	12/88	80	85	3/89
Arun DC	4900	1/89	81	23	
Three Rivers DC	5750	3/89	86	24	
Newbury DC	7100	4/89	87	81	11/89
Broadland DC	3700	4/89	84	53	4/90
South Wight BC	2100	6/89	89	91	7/90
Medina BC	2800	7/89	84	68	7/90
Rochester CC	8050	7/89	76	60	7/90
Swale BC	7350	10/89	80	54	4/90
North Beds BC	7450	10/89	73	72	6/90
Canterbury CC	6550	11/89	79	25	
Brentwood DC	3400	11/89	88	19	
Redbridge LB	10200	12/89	73	31	
Mid Sussex DC	4450	12/89	80	77	11/90
East Dorset DC	2250	1/90	85	84	12/90
Bournemouth BC	6050	1/90	84	32	
Wokingham DC	3450	4/90	75	30	
South Holland DC	5050	7/90	80	37	
Tonbridge and Malling BC	6400	7/90	76	75	1/91
South Bucks DC	3400	7/90	82	75	4/91
Ryedale DC	3350	8/90	83	82	2/91
Christchurch DC	1550	11/90	76	54	
Suffolk Coastal DC	5350	11/90	78	57	4/91
North Kesteven DC	4900	12/90	85	45	
Tunbridge Wells	5500	6/91	81	52	
Bromley	12400	10/91	76	55	

Source: Department of the Environment database

- Do local community housing associations represent the future for local authority housing?
- How different a future would this be?
- How relevant is the experience of early transfers to this future?

The demise of council housing?

Do local community housing associations spell the end of council housing? Death by a self-administered suicide pill rather than through the various external assaults from Right to Buy to Tenants' Choice and Housing Action

Trusts? Implementation of transfers is clearly supported by a number of power-ful factors, but could yet be stemmed by changes in the Government's policy.

The consideration of the voluntary transfer option by more and more auth-orities was undoubtedly a response to the unfavourable treatment of local authorities compared with housing associations, particularly in relation to the ability to invest in new rented housing to meet growing housing needs. This general stimulus was supplemented in some areas by a set of local interests favouring transfer. The creation of single purpose housing organizations, inde-pendent of other local services and council organization was actively pursued in some cases. More generally, transfers to housing associations provided housing officers with an opportunity to transform their role and status. It is also difficult to ignore the vested interests of housing consultants in developing a significant new market advising all parties in the transfer transaction.

Nevertheless, it was questionable whether the transfer option would retain its attraction if the underlying stimulus of central government policy were to change. Most authorities were content to wait for the outcome of the 1992 General Election before committing themselves to this once and for all option. Even before the election, the idea of releasing controls on expenditure of capital receipts was reportedly being canvassed in Government circles as a way out of recession.

How different a future?

The motivation to retain the housing stock under one landlord was frequently the main motivation affecting the type of transfer adopted. Transfer was often sold to tenants as the 'least change option', retaining their friendly housing staff. Local community housing associations usually enjoy a similar local monopoly position in the provision of affordable rented housing to local authorities. Most transfers to date have occurred in areas with very small housing association stocks. The Department of the Environment's decision to approve transfers of more than 10 000 homes to a single new landlord in Bromley and Hillingdon will create significant new local near monopolies. Similarly, the decision of some transferring authorities to concentrate their LAHAG programmes on the new association rather than promoting local competition has served to strengthen local monopolies.

Nevertheless, both the Department of the Environment and the Housing Corporation have been keen to foster the independence of local community housing associations from their authorities. Many of the new associations have keenly embraced a rather more entrepreneurial culture. The appointment of a Finance Manager with housing association experience has sometimes been a key stimulus to change. Some associations, particularly those favoured by low stock valuations have quickly sought to become major developers both in their original areas and further afield. The 'Evaluation of Large Scale Voluntary Transfers' project will seek to identify the extent of organizational change over a period of years.

Relevance of early transfers

There are good reasons to question the relevance of the experience of these early transfers to any more general moves to privatize council housing. In the first place they represent a rather narrow band of types of authorities, both geographically, politically and in particular in the size of their housing stock and types of areas served.

Secondly, it has been widely recognized that any general move towards this option would have major implications for access to funding through the financial institutions. In late 1991 it was estimated that an additional 20 transfers a year would require an additional £1.1 billion annual funding, twice the amount that established housing associations need to attract to finance the private elements of programmed Housing Corporation schemes. There were suspicions that even if private-sector funding became available on the scale required, there would be significant Treasury concern about the diversion of investment on this scale simply to transfer housing away from local authorities to other social landlords.

Finally, it is likely that any significant increase would see changes in the rules applied by the regulatory bodies. The interventionist and advisory approach adopted by both the Department of the Environment and the Housing Corporation would need to be replaced by standard guidelines. Favourable treatment such as the availability of subsidy on local authority LAHAG schemes might be called into question if transfer receipts produced large increases in programmes.

References

Department of Environment (1987) *Housing. The Government's Proposals*, London, HMSO.

Department of Environment (1988a) *Large Scale Voluntary Transfers of Local Authority Housing Stock to Private Bodies*.

Department of Environment (1988b) *Councillor Representation on the Purchasing Body. Working note for voluntary transfer authorities*.

Department of Environment (1988c) *Consultation with Secure Tenants before Disposal to Private Sector Landlord: Commencement of Section 6 of Housing and Planning Act 1986*.

Department of Environment (1990) *Large Scale Transfers of Council Housing to Private Bodies. Use of Receipts*.

Department of Environment and Housing Corporation (1989) *Arrangements for Interaction between Tenants' Choice and Other Powers for Transferring Public Sector Housing*.

Gardiner, K., Hills, J. and Kleinman, M. (1991) *Putting a Price on Council Housing: Valuing Voluntary Transfers*. London School of Economics Discussion Paper WSP/62.

Housing Corporation (1989a) *Criteria for Landlord Approval*.

Housing Corporation (1989b) *Registration of Local Community Housing Associations*.

Mullins, D., Niner, P. and Riseborough, M. (1992) *Evaluating Large Scale Voluntary Transfers. An Interim Report*, London, HMSO.

CHAPTER 12

The politics of implementation

PETER MALPASS
AND ROBIN MEANS

Introduction

This final chapter will assess the strengths and weaknesses of the implementation strategies of Conservative governments since 1979, and goes on to reflect on the implementation challenge generated by the fragmented governance of housing in this country. It seems certain that the dominant housing objectives will continue to be the maximization of owner occupation and the further reduction in the role of local authorities in the provision of socially rented housing. These broad objectives, and their subsequent detailed policy manifestations, will set much of the implementation agenda in the next few years, and this is reflected in the overall focus of this chapter. First, however, it is necessary to make some rather more general points about the politics of implementation.

The challenge of change

Radical Conservative governments have faced, and will continue to face, numerous implementation challenges, but this is true of all governments. The Conservatives continue to face the task of how to make owner occupation affordable and attractive to those on low incomes as well as the need to revitalize private renting and to reduce the role of council housing. But a Labour government would have faced an even more daunting implementation challenge. There would have been the need to not only decide which policy innovations of the 1980s to keep and which to scrap, but also the need to develop strategies to ensure this happened. How can council housing be made attractive again? Should the growth of housing associations be restricted and their funding mechanisms changed? What restrictions should be placed on Conservative-

be pondering what an aspiration to achieve subsidy fairness across tenure should mean in terms of politically and administratively realistic policies. How best could a balance be drawn between ideology and pragmatism? There is much to be learnt from the policy implementation literature and from the implementation experiences of post-1979 Conservative governments which is of relevance to those of all political and ideological persuasions.

However, the emerging policy implementation agenda of the mid-1990s will be shaped by the ideological views about owner occupation and council housing of the Conservative rather than the Labour Party. But there would have been no simple return to the local authority housing departments of the 1970s, even if a Labour government with a clear majority had been elected on 9 April 1992. This is not just because of the complicated problems of policy reversal (Wilding 1992) which have to be faced, but also because of the changing views about management and organizational structures outlined in Chapter 2. The pressure for radical organizational change is deeply embedded in certain structural as well as political pressures. The continued search for what Hoggett (1991) calls the post-bureaucratic organizational form will ensure that housing managers have no alternative but to try and 'thrive on chaos', in the famous words of Peters (1987). Chapter 10 on decentralization underlines this point, since this shows the extent to which local authorities are willing to experiment with new organizational forms even when not forced to do so by central government. The inevitability of continued radical change is, also, underlined in Chapter 4 on housing associations, which predicts that smaller associations may be squeezed to the advantage of larger associations. But most of these larger associations lack the simple geographical boundaries of local authorities, and hence the model of the traditional bureaucratic housing department is not an appropriate one to even consider as they grow to a point where organizational overhaul becomes inevitable.

These new organizational forms generate their own regulation challenges. Chapter 9 quite correctly emphasizes that to be successful as an enabling authority, the local authority needs not only adequate resources but senior officers need to have the skills to develop partnerships with other agencies. Chapter 11 on voluntary transfer, Chapter 10 on decentralization and Chapter 6 on Housing Action Trusts (HATs) illustrate how local stakeholders can attempt to block policy initiatives. However, such opposition does not always melt away even when the new organizational form is established and this is especially the case where the former staff are redeployed within the new arrangements. It may be harder for a local authority to monitor its commitment to equal opportunities and non-discrimination when services are controlled increasingly through a network of decentralized officers with considerable policy and budgetary autonomy (see also Lowndes and Stoker 1992). The implications for housing of this trend towards more complex organizational forms is further discussed in the section on the fragmented governance of housing.

Assessing policy implementation

This next section is not an attempt to pass judgement on 13 years of Conservative housing policy. Rather than focusing on policy outcomes, it is concerned with the assessment of implementation as a process. It is about the importance of implementation in the determination of whether policy outcomes can be regarded as successful or unsuccessful. Measuring policy success or failure is inherently difficult, given the unreliability of political rhetoric as a guide to what governments (both central and local) really want to achieve. A policy which makes little or no impact in terms of houses built or people rehoused should not be lightly dismissed as a failure, because its purpose may have been symbolic, rhetorical or political, rather than substantive. Earlier chapters (for example Chapters 7 and 9) have referred to the importance of symbolic policies. Conservative governments routinely express support for the revival of the private rented sector, but as has been shown in Chapter 5, their policies have an element of the symbolic. It is as if Conservative governments must be seen to take some action to support private renting, but that they do so in the knowledge that there is neither sufficient popular support nor enough economic logic to justify action on the scale necessary to produce significant growth in the market for private renting. Other examples of symbolic or tokenistic policies would include the Government's response in December 1989 to the growing problem of visible homelessness, particularly in London, and their December 1991 response to the rapid escalation of mortgage arrears and repossessions. It is surely no co-incidence that both these responses occurred in the few weeks before Christmas, a traditionally good time for homelessness campaigns.

A focus on implementation can cast light on the Government's commitment to particular objectives and whether they actually believe that their policies can work; the financial resources and the political and administrative effort devoted to making policies work may be taken as a measure of the Government's commitment. Assessment of implementation would also involve consideration of factors such as the extent of policymakers' understanding of the causes of the problems on which they wished to make some impact, the clarity of their objectives and the degree of anticipation of implementation problems. The analysis of housing policy presented in preceding chapters suggests that it is necessary to look at the extent to which the ground was prepared before the implementation process began. Success in achieving policy objectives is dependent on preparation of public opinion as well as the adoption of effective instruments and the existence of political commitment. There are also questions about when is the right time to assess the way that a policy has been implemented. As Chapter 9 suggests it may at present be too early to assess the enabling role of local authorities. Policy responses may be slow to gather pace and success may be contingent upon certain political and economic conditions being met; for instance, the pace at which large-scale voluntary transfers of council housing go ahead is widely understood to depend on the outcome of the 1992 General Election, and it may be the case that Tenants' Choice and the deregulation of private renting will have much more impact when the property market and the economy as a whole recover from the recession of the early 1990s.

Any assessment of the implementation of housing policy in the past 13 years must take into account the impact of wider economic factors, and the consistent priority given to economic management. Thus, policies to encourage home ownership have been hampered by the use of high interest rates and high unemployment as tools of economic management; housing policy and economic policy have often been working against one another, and at times, such as in late 1988, the Government deliberately used the interest rate weapon to raise mortgage costs and to slow down consumer demand in the economy as a whole.

Looking at the implementation of housing policy in recent times it is clear that within the overall commitment to the private market and the concomitant decline of the public sector, the Conservative governments encountered different degrees of success. The new financial regime for local authority housing, for instance, may be seen as highly successful from the point of view of a government which was concerned to regain control of capital spending by councils and to drive up rents faster than the rate of inflation. An interesting feature of the new financial regime is that it can be seen as a Mark III policy, benefiting from the experience of implementation problems generated by the 1972 and 1980 Acts. Both these earlier attempts to reform rents and subsidies policies had been undermined by local resistance at the implementation stage. They had also contained significant loopholes which were exploited by councils. The 1989 Act, therefore, was designed to take account of anticipated implementation problems, such as the struggle over the ownership and control of HRA surpluses, and to eliminate any loopholes. Indeed, it may be said of the new financial regime that priority appears to have been given to the elimination of such problems, rather than to the production of a system capable of delivering the stated objectives.

In the case of HATs and Tenants' Choice, on the other hand, the Government was working with Mark I policies, untried in the context of British public housing. Moreover, they were brand new ideas which only emerged during the 1987 General Election campaign, just months before being written into the White Paper (HMSO 1987) which preceded the Housing Act 1988. There is an interesting contrast here with the lead up to the introduction of the right to buy in 1980; the sale of council houses had a long history and sales was a policy on which the Conservatives in Opposition in the 1970s had spent several years preparing public opinion before the legislation was passed. It is perhaps less surprising, then, that Tenants' Choice and HATs encountered implementation problems and marked lack of success. The Government clearly misjudged the attitude of council tenants, who were assumed to be eager to escape from the public sector. The Government also misjudged the enthusiasm of private-sector institutions, which were assumed to be keen to take over ownership of significant amounts of council stock.

In the case of Tenants' Choice, successful implementation relied on tenants voting for a change of landlord (although the prescribed form of ballot was rigged in favour of a change – a fact which backfired and helped to discredit the whole idea). It is noticeable that Tenants' Choice included no positive inducements or incentives (in contrast to the Right to Buy), which lends support to the conclusion that key aspects of implementation had not been fully thought out in advance.

The Government's misjudgement over HATs took a different form. Here the Government initially took an aggressively centralist view, taking no account of local opposition as a form of implementation problem. The implicit assumption was that any such opposition could be ignored or over-ridden – a good sign of an under-researched, Mark I policy. It was proposed that tenants should have no say at all in the declaration of a HAT, although, as has been pointed out in Chapter 6, once the principle of a tenants' vote had been conceded it became clear that the policy could fail.

Other policy areas discussed in preceding chapters contain further examples of failure to foresee implementation problems. The new financial regime for housing associations, for instance, got off to a very difficult start because of the failure to plan for the changed rate at which associations claimed grant from the Housing Corporation from the beginning of 1989.

To conclude this section, it can be said that the Conservatives in government during the 1980s and early 1990s showed themselves to be bold innovators in terms of policy instruments, often prepared to break out of established ways of thinking and working. However, the radicalism of their approach exposed them to unforeseen implementation problems. The record shows a mixture of well-prepared policies, designed with implementation problems in mind, and other policies which ran into severe difficulties because such problems had not been anticipated and taken into account. A feature of the Government's policy in general during this period was the determination to press ahead with change at almost breakneck pace, with obviously heightened danger of unforeseen implementation difficulties. The evidence indicates that even a government of deep ideological commitment and with a solid Parliamentary majority cannot be confident that it can bulldoze its policies through to successful outcomes. A degree of consent is necessary, and as policies become more complicated a higher premium is placed on collaborative working throughout the spectrum of actors and agencies involved in the policy process.

There is a tendency for policy action to generate a reaction, to the extent that local authorities, seeking to retain a degree of autonomy and discretion, look for ways to avoid or exploit government measures, thereby stimulating further central government action. This iterative process was accentuated in the 1980s under the abrasive conviction politics of Margaret Thatcher, but there is also an important sense in which her governments' determination to move more of housing policy implementation out of local government multiplied the uncertainties of policy action. The struggle between central and local government over the control and use of Housing Revenue Account surpluses during the 1980s illustrates the iterative nature of policy, and the problems of the supply of affordable housing in recent years highlight the consequences of relying on non-municipal suppliers.

The fragmented governance of housing

There is a sense in which the governance of housing always was fragmented: although local authorities were the lead agencies for policy implementation, housing has always been a responsibility of the lowest tier of local government, thereby maximizing the numbers involved, and historically councils enjoyed considerable freedom to reinterpret, avoid or even ignore central government policies (Bowley 1945: 258). In recent years much has happened to change that situation. Two related themes which have been discussed are that recent governments have attacked and undermined local authorities as providers of housing, and that they have sought to pursue housing policy objectives via other agencies, both commercial and not-for-profit. At the same time there have been changes in the management of organizations, with a widespread trend towards decentralization in housing organizations, as discussed in Chapter 10. This has implications for relations between top and bottom, or centre and periphery, which go beyond conventional debates about central–local government relations. As a result housing policy has become much more complicated, in terms of both the range of actors and institutions involved (together with their different motivations) and the web of relationships amongst them.

Part of the attack on local government has involved the centre becoming much more interventionist; reference has been made in Chapter 7 to the way in which the centre has been drawn into attempts to control local authority housing revenue accounts, and there is much more to be said about the tight control of capital spending. The increased use of 'top-slicing' and the introduction in 1991 of a competition system for the setting of housing capital allocations is evidence of the determination of the centre to specify not just the size of the capital programme in each area but also how it is spent.

The more general point to be made here is that whereas conventional top-down perspectives imply that implementation is an activity of the bottom or periphery, the evidence referred to here has drawn attention to the way that the top is also directly and closely involved in implementation, just as the bottom is involved in policymaking. Thus implementation needs to be analysed at both central and local levels. In relation to any policy there are separate questions about how the centre seeks to implement its objectives and about how the localities seek to implement their own policies or to impose their interpretation of policy received from above.

Local democracy and the autonomy of local government are rightly regarded as important principles in their own right. It should be stressed here, however, that there is a case for local autonomy which derives from efficiency arguments. A government which has little regard for the importance of local democracy may nonetheless be persuaded that central control is more costly and less efficient than local autonomy in relation to specific services. The concept of implementation almost by definition involves flexibility in the application of general policy principles to specific situations. The centre never has complete information and therefore cannot anticipate all the circumstances in which its policies will be implemented. When outcomes fail to match expectations it may be difficult to decide, even in principle, whether it is the policy or its implementation which has failed.

These observations suggest that the appropriate response to implementation problems is not necessarily to tighten control from the top. If the top cannot anticipate the full range of situations in which its policies will be implemented, tighter control from the top does not prevent policy failure but merely denies the implementers the flexibility needed to respond to the unanticipated. Further, the top finds it much more difficult to blame the failures on those responsible for implementation. The poll tax is a good example of this problem. Central government was able in the first half of the 1980s successfully to blame local authorities for excessive rate increases, even though the withdrawal of rate support grant was a major cause. With the introduction of the poll tax and unified business rate, however, coupled with widespread capping of local authorities, the restriction of local discretion became such that the widespread perception was that central government rather than local government was primarily responsible for the level of the tax.

Under Margaret Thatcher in the 1980s central hostility to local government reached unprecedented intensity, leading to a determination to work through private and non-municipal agencies wherever possible. It was suggested in Chapter 3 that this represented the private implementation of public policy, and that it had implications which needed to be drawn out. Of particular interest is the shift from elected councils to non-elected housing associations as the main providers of new social rented housing, and in some areas, of course, associations have completely replaced the local authorities as landlords. This raises questions not only about accountability within social housing, but also about key aspects of implementation.

First, there is the issue of how central government can achieve its objectives through organizations which do not necessarily share its political philosophy, which have their own agendas and which increasingly have to respond to market forces. The fragmentation of the governance of housing has implications for the kinds of policy instruments deployed and for the sorts of implementation problems likely to arise. A greater reliance on incentives is typical of approaches relying on non-governmental agencies, as demonstrated in Chapter 9. Enabling is an approach which involves setting up frameworks within which other agencies are encouraged to act in accordance with policy goals. From the point of view of central government the implementation problems associated with enabling are to do with the need to generate two layers of incentives, first for the local authorities and then for the private and voluntary agencies which actually provide the houses. This would seem to make enabling a rather unreliable strategy.

Second, fragmentation intensifies the need for inter-organizational co-operation and collaboration, which the implementation literature suggests is a recipe for slow and uncertain action. In this context it is relevant to point to the way in which provision of social rented housing is being pushed out of the control of general purpose local authorities into the hands of housing associations at a time when it is becoming clear that housing management needs to be complemented by a range of other skills and services. As the residualization of social housing gathers pace there is a tendency for the incidence of social welfare problems experienced by tenants to increase and intensify. Ownership of the stock by a multiplicity of housing associations is not necessarily the best way to ensure a co-ordinated, coherent and effective response to these problems. Fragmentation again places a premium on high quality inter-organizational collaboration.

Implementing housing policy: the way ahead

The 1992 General Election campaign was remarkable for the lack of debate about housing. Despite the electoral gains attributed by the Conservatives to their housing policies in 1979, in 1992 the Party seemed unwilling to talk about the equally radical housing policies which had been introduced in the late 1980s. One explanation for this may lie in the fact that the Conservatives were never challenged to justify their housing policies; it was as if the Labour Party was equally unwilling to discuss the issue. Given the numbers known to be sleeping on the streets and the unprecedented levels of homes being taken into possession by mortgage lenders, it is perhaps surprising that Labour did not attack on housing. However, there is a case for saying that one of the achievements of 13 years of Conservative government was to undermine both council housing and owner occupation as vote winning policies. The Thatcher governments quite deliberately set out to attack and discredit council housing, but over-enthusiasm for home ownership in the 1980s, in combination with the effects of the recession in the early 1990s meant that for many households owner occupation had acquired a distinctly tarnished image.

Thus, housing was not discussed in the 1992 General Election campaign because neither of the two main parties had anything distinctive or convincing to say to the electorate. In our context, it is relevant to refer to one key issue on which there is widespread agreement about the need for reform, but on which the main parties remain united in their opposition to action: mortgage interest relief. This is a good example of an issue where reform is blocked by fear of implementation problems, in the form of electoral retribution for any government bold enough to bring in legislation.

The return of a fourth consecutive Conservative government suggests that there will be a high degree of continuity in housing policy. Continuity in terms of basic policy objectives and implementation strategies does not of course necessarily imply that there will be any slackening in the pace of change in the housing system. Indeed, the pace may increase if the pre-Election rumours were correct about the large numbers of authorities waiting for the election result before pressing ahead with voluntary stock transfers.

The issue of voluntary stock transfers is a difficult one to interpret, and different interpretations probably apply in different places. However, it clear that for some authorities transfer is a response motivated by political ideology and/or the desire to generate a large capital receipt for the benefit of local poll tax payers. For others transfer is a defensive response, seen as the only way to escape from the implications of the 1989 Act financial regime, with the probability of relentless upward pressure on rents, and worse, very tight restrictions on capital for renovation and new building. Transfer of ownership to a housing association appears to provide some protection from centrally imposed rent increase and gives freer access to borrowing.

Stock transfer began as a bottom-up response to the perceived threat of Tenants' Choice, but, given the failure of that policy instrument, it has itself been taken over by the centre. The emergence of stock transfer highlights the extent to which local authorities find themselves working to meet housing need in an environment of artificial and unnecessary constraints. The Government's refusal to allow authorities access to capital receipts from the sale of council houses as a source of funds for the renovation and replenishment of the rented stock is compounded by the very low levels of borrowing permitted. In these circumstances authorities have been forced into creative relationships with housing associations, banks, building societies and builders. These complex partnerships are not necessarily a better, more productive or more efficient way of providing badly needed new housing, but they look increasingly like the shape of things to come.

The issues of stock transfers and partnerships are a reminder that local level implementers can come up with solutions which respond to central government constraints, but it is also important to ask why they find themselves in this situation. A focus on implementation, as was pointed out in Chapter 2, should not blind us to the need to question the initial choice of policies and ways of achieving policy goals. There are essentially three levels to consider: first, there is the political question of the choice of policy objectives; then there is the question of the choice of appropriate instruments to implement the policies; and finally, there is the issue of whether the instruments have been deployed correctly and efficiently.

Finally, what is likely to happen in the period up to the next General Election? Predicting the future is as hazardous in housing as in other areas of life (Holmans 1991), but it is reasonable to assume that the Government will press ahead with its manifesto commitment to introduce some form of compulsory competitive tendering for local authority housing management. It also seems very likely that local authorities will respond to this in a variety of more or less enthusiastic and imaginative ways. Local level agencies in general will continue to struggle with the world as they find it, and will probably develop better local and national policy networks or consortia to reduce uncertainty and destructive competition. As in the past, local level agencies can be expected to be innovative in unpredictable ways, which are likely to generate new central government responses.

Policy areas likely to 'go wrong' from the central government point of view are likely to be those where the Government is least in control of the pace and direction of events. This refers principally to policies reliant upon market-based agencies, given the chronic instability of the British housing market in the last 20 years and the importance of housing in the management of the national economy. To a considerable extent the impact and effectiveness of Conservative housing policy is dependent upon how successful the Government is in its economic policies. Thus problems in relation to housing will not necessarily produce housing policy responses; this is particularly clear in the case of home ownership where the Government's view appears to be that recovery from recession will remove most of the problems of mortgage arrears and high possession rates. However, whatever the fate of the economy over the next few years there remain important issues to be addressed by housing policy directed towards the private sector. Having pumped up home ownership in the past 13 years the challenge to the Government in the remainder of the decade is to make it a secure and satisfying tenure. Policies in the past have concentrated on getting more people into home ownership, to the neglect of the policy implications of ownership amongst a growing proportion of less well-off households. While public attention has focused on the very real problems of mortgage arrears and possessions, problems of stock condition have been given much less attention, yet, as was shown in Chapter 8, they have greater long-term significance.

Other areas where outcomes may not match government intentions are likely to be those referred to above as Mark I policies, although even Mark III policies such as the new financial regime for local authority housing can be seen to fail in certain respects. In the case of the new financial regime the key unresolved implementation problem for central government has been the uncapped Housing Benefit budget, and it seems reasonable to predict that the Treasury will continue to press for this problem to be resolved; early legislation seems likely. Despite the major reforms of the late 1980s (or perhaps partly because of them), it seems certain that the fourth-term Conservative Government will continue the tradition of frequent legislative action in the field of housing.

References

Bowley, M. (1945) *Housing and the State 1919–1944*, London, Allen and Unwin.
HMSO (1987) *Housing: the Government's Proposals*, London.
Hoggett, P. (1991) 'A new management in the public sector?', *Policy and Politics*, Vol. 19, No. 4: 243–56.
Holmans, A. (1991) 'The 1977 National Housing Policy Review in retrospect', *Housing Studies*, Vol. 6, No. 3, July: 206–19.
Lowndes, V. and Stoker, G. (1992) 'An evaluation of neighbourhood decentralisation, part one: customer and citizen perspectives', *Policy and Politics*, Vol. 20, No. 1: 47–62.
Peters, T. (1987) *Thriving on Chaos*, London, Pan Books.
Wilding, P. (1992) 'The Welfare State: Thatcher's enduring legacy', *Policy and Politics*, Vol. 20, No. 3: 201–12.

Index